THE HISTORY OF FREEMASONRY

ITS LEGENDS AND TRADITIONS

ITS CHRONOLOGICAL HISTORY

BY ALBERT GALLATIN MACKEY, M.D., 33°

VOLUME TWO

CHAPTER XXX

FREEMASONRY AND THE HOUSE OF STUART

THE theory that connects the royal house of the, Stuarts with Freemasonry, as an Institution to be cultivated, not on account of its own intrinsic merit, but that it might serve as a political engine to be wielded for the restoration of an exiled family to a throne which the follies and even the crimes of its members had forfeited, is so repugnant to all that has been supposed to be congruous with the true spirit and character of Freemasonry, that one would hardly believe that such a theory was ever seriously entertained, were it not for many too conclusive proofs of the fact.

The history of the family of Stuart, from the accession of James I. to the throne of England to the death of the last of his descendants, the young Pretender, is a narrative of follies and sometimes of crimes.

The reign of James was distinguished only by arts which could gain for him no higher title with posterity than that of a royal pedant.

His son and successor Charles I. was beheaded by an indignant people whose constitutional rights and ideals he had sought to betray.

His son Charles II., after a long exile was finally restored to the throne, only to pass a life of indolence and licentiousness.

On his death he was succeeded by his brother James II., a prince distinguished only for his bigotry.

Zealously attached to the Roman Catholic religion, he sought to restore its power and influence among his subjects, who were for the most part Protestants.

To save the Established Church and the religion of the nation, his estranged subjects called to the throne the Protestant Prince of Orange, and James, abdicating the crown, fled to France, where he was hospitably received with his followers by Louis XIV., who could, however, say nothing better of him than that he had given three crowns for a mass.

From 1688, the date of his abdication and flight, until the year 1745 the exiled family were e ngaged in repeated but unavailing attempts to recover the throne.

It is not unreasonable to suppose that in these attempts the partisans of the house of Stuart were not unwilling to accept the influence of the Masonic Institution, as one of the most powerful instruments whereby to effect their purpose.

It is true that in this, the Institution would have been diverted from its true design, but the object of the Jacobites, as they were called, or the adherents of King James was not to elevate the character of Freemasonry but only to advance the cause of the Pretender It must however be understood that this theory which connects the Stuarts with Masonry does not suppose that the third or Master's degree was invented by them or their adherents, but only that there were certain modifications in the application of its Legend.

Thus, the Temple was interpreted as alluding to the monarchy, the death of its Builder to the execution of Charles I., or to the destruction of the succession by the compulsory abdication of James II., and the dogma of the resurrection to the restoration of the Stuart family to the throne of England.

Thus, one of the earliest instances of this political interpretation of the Master's legend was that made after the expulsion of James II. from the throne and his retirement to France.

The mother of James was Henrietta Maria, queen of Charles I. The Jacobites called her "the Widow," and the exiled James became "the Widow's son," receiving thus the title applied in the Masonic Legend to Hiram Abif, whose death they said symbolized the loss of the throne and the expulsion of the Stuarts from England? They carried this idea to such an extent as to invent a name, substitute word for the Master's degree, in the place of the old one, which was known to the English Masons at the time of the Revival in 1717.

This new word was not, as the significant words of Masonry usually are, of Hebrew origin, but was derived from the Gaelic. And this seems to have been done in compliment to the Highlanders, most of whom were loyal adherents of the Stuart cause.

The word Macbenac is derived from the Gaelic Mac, a son, and benach, blessed, and literally means the "blessed son; " and this word was applied by the Jacobites to James, who was thus not only a "widow's son" but "blessed" one, too.

Masonry was here made subservient to loyalty.

They also, to mark their political antipathy to the enemies of the Stuart family, gave to the most prominent leaders of the republican cause, the names in which old Masonry had been appropriated to the assassins of the third degree. In the Stuart Masonry we find these assassins designated by names, generally unintelligible, but, when they can be explained, evidently referring to some well-known opponent of the Stuart dynasty.

Thus, Romvel is manifestly an imperfect anagram of Cromwell, and Jubelum Guibbs doubtless was intended as an infamous embalmment of the name of the Rev. Adam Gib, an antiburgher clergyman, who, when the Pretender was in Edinburgh in 1745, hurled anathemas, for five successive Sundays against him.

But it was in the fabrication of the high degrees that the partisans of the Stuarts made the most use of Freemasonry as a political instrument.

The invention of these high degrees is to be attributed in the first place to the Chevalier Ramsay.

He was connected in the most intimate relation with the exiled family, having been selected by the titular James III., or, as he was commonly known in England, the Old Pretender, as the tutor of his two sons, Charles Edward and Henry, the former of whom afterward became the Young Pretender, and the latter Cardinal York.

Ardently attached, to this relationship, by his nationality as a Scotsman, and by his religion as a Roman Catholic, to the Stuarts and their cause, he met with ready acquiescence the advances of those who had already begun to give a political aspect to the Masonic System, and also were seeking to enlist it in the Pretender's cause.

Ramsay therefore aided in the modification of the old degrees or the fabrication of new ones, so that these views might be incorporated in a peculiar system; and hence in many of the high degrees invented either by Ramsay or by others of the same school, we will find these traces of a political application to the family of Stuart, which were better understood at that time than they are now.

Thus, one of the high degrees -received the name of "Grand Scottish Mason of James VI." Of this degree Tessier says that it is the principal degree of the ancient Master's system, and was revived and esteemed by James VI., King of Scotland and of Great Britain, and that it is still preserved in Scotland more than in any other kingdom.[1] All of this is of course a mere fiction, but it shows that there has been a sort of official acknowledgment of the interference with Masonry by the Stuarts, who did not hesitate to give the name of the first founder of their house on the English throne to one of the degrees.

Another proof is found in the word Jekson, which is a significant word in one of the high Scottish or Ramsay degrees.

It is thus spelled in the Calhiers or manuscript French rituals.

There can be no doubt that it is a corruption of Jacquesson, a mongrel word compounded of the French Jacques and the English son, and denotes the son of James, that is, of James II.

This son was the Old Pretender, or the Chevalier St. George, who after the death of his father assumed the empty title of James III., and whose son, the Young Pretender, was one of the pupils of the Chevalier Ramsay.

These, with many other similar instances, are very palpable proofs that the adherents of the Stuarts sought to infuse a political element into the spirit of Masonry, so as to make it a facile instrument for the elevation of the exiled family and the restoration of their head to the throne of England.

Of the truth of this fact, it is supposed that much support is to be found in the narrative of the various efforts for restoration made by the Stuarts.

When James II. made his flight from England he repaired to France, where he was hospitably received by Louis XIV.

He took up his residence while in Paris at the Jesuitical College of Clermont.

There, it is said, he first sought, with the assistance of the Jesuits, to establish a system of Masonry which should be employed by his partisans in their schemes for his restoration to the throne, After an unsuccessful invasion of Ireland he returned to France and repaired to St. Germain-en-Laye, a city about ten miles northwest of Paris, where he lived until the time of his death in 1701. It is one of the Stuart myths that at the Chateau of St. Germain some of the high degrees were fabricated by the adherents of James II., assisted by the Jesuits.

The story is told by Robison, a professed enemy of Freemasonry, but who gives with correctness the general form of the Stuart Legend as it was taught in the last century.

---

[1] "Manuel Generale de Maconnerie," p. 148 Robison says: "The revolution had taken place, and King James, with many of his most zealous adherents, had taken refuge in France.

But they took Freemasonry with them to the Continent, where it was immediately received by the French, and cultivated with great zeal in a manner suited to the taste and habits of that highly polished people.

The Lodges in France naturally became the rendezvous of the adherents of the exiled king, and the means of carrying on a correspondence with their friends in England."[2]

But the supposed connection of the Jesuits with Freemasonry pertains to an independent proposition. to be hereafter considered.

Robison further says that "it was in the Lodge held at St. Germain that the degree of Chevalier Macon Ecossais was added to the three symbolical degrees of English Masonry.

The Constitution, as imported, appeared too coarse for the refined taste of the French, and they must make Masonry more like the occupation of a gentleman.

Therefore the English degrees of Apprentice, Fellowcraft, and Master were called symbolical, and the whole contrivance was considered either as typical of something more elegant or as a preparation for it.

The degrees afterward superadded to this leave us in doubt which of these views the French entertained of our Masonry.

But, at all events, this rank of Scotch Knight was called the first degree of the Macon Parfait.

There is a device belonging to this Lodge which deserves notice.

A lion wounded by an arrow, and escaped from the stake to which he had been bound, with the broken rope still about his neck, is represented lying at the mouth of a cave, and occupied with mathematical instruments, which are lying near him.

A broken crown lies at the foot of the stake.

There can be little doubt but that this emblem alludes to the dethronement, the captivity, the escape, and the asylum of James II, and his hopes of re-establishment by the help of the[3] loyal Brethren. This emblem is worn as the gorget of the Scotch Knight. It is not very certain, however, when this degree was added, whether immediately after King James's abdication or about the time of the attempt to set his son on the British throne.[4]

---

[2] Robison says that at this time the Jesuits took an active part in Freemasonry, and united with the English Lodges, with the view of creating an influence in favor of the re-establishment of the Roman Catholic religion in England.
[3] "Proofs of a Conspiracy," p. 27
[4] This extract from Robison presents a very fair specimen of the way in which Masonic history was universally written in the last century and is still written by a few in the present.

Although it cannot be denied that at a subsequent period the primitive degrees were modified and changed ill their application of the death of Hiram Abif to that of Charles I., or the dethronement of James II, and that higher degrees were created with still more definite allusion to the destinies of the family of Stuart, yet it is very evident that no such measures could have been taken during the lifetime of James II.

The two periods referred to by Robison, the time of the abdication of James II, which was in 1688, and the attempt of James III, as he was called, to regain the throne, which was in 1715, as being, one or the other, the date of the fabrication of the degree of Scottish Knight or Master, are both irreconcilable with the facts of history.

The symbolical degrees of Fellow Craft and Master had not been invented before 1717, or rather a few years later, and it is absurd to speak of higher degrees cumulated upon lower ones which did not at that time exist. James II. died in 1701.

At that day we have no record of any sort of Speculative Masonry except that of the one degree which was common to Masons of all ranks.

The titular King James Ill., his son, succeeded to the claims and pretensions of his father, of course, in that year, but made no attempt to enforce them until 1715, at which time he invaded England with a fleet and army supplied by Louis XIV.

But in 1715, Masonry was in the same condition that it had been in 1701.

There was no Master's degree to supply a Legend capable of alteration for a political purpose, and the high degrees were altogether unknown.

The Grand Lodge of England, the mother of all Continental as well as English Masonry, was not established, or as Anderson improperly calls it, " revived," until 1717.

The Institution was not introduced into France until 1725, and there could, therefore, have been no political Masonry practiced in a[5] country where the pure Masonry of which it must have been a corruption did not exist.

Scottish or Stuart Masonry was a superstructure built upon the foundation of the symbolic Masonry of the three degrees.

If in 1715 there was, as we know, no such foundation, it follows, of course, that there could have been no superstructure.

---

[5] "Proofs of a Conspiracy," p. 28

The theory, therefore, that Stuart Masonry, or the fabrication of degrees and the change of the primitive rituals to establish a system to be engaged in the support and the advancement of the falling cause of the Stuarts, was commenced during the lifetime of James II., and that the royal chateau of St. Germain-en-Laye was the manufactory in which, between the years 1689 and 1701, these degrees and rituals were fabricated, is a mere fable not only improbable but absolutely impossible in all its details.

Rebold, however, gives another form to the Legend and traces the rise of Stuart Masonry to a much earlier period.

In his History of the Three Grand Lodges he says that during the troubles which distracted Great Britain about the middle of the 17th century and after the decapitation of Charles I in 1649, the Masons of England, and especially those of Scotland, labored secretly for the re-establishment of the monarchy which had been overthrown by Cromwell.

For the accomplishment of this purpose they invented two higher degrees and gave to Freemasonry an entirely political character.

The dissensions to which the country was a prey had already produced a separation of the Operative and the Accepted Masons-that is to say, of the builders by profession and those honorary members who were not Masons.

These latter were men of power and high position, and it was through their influence that Charles II., having been received as a Mason during his exile, was enabled to recover the throne in 1660.

This prince gratefully gave to Masonry the title of the " Royal Art," because it was Freemasonry that had principally contributed to the restoration of royalty.[6] Ragon, in his Masonic Orthodoxy,[7] is still more explicit and presents some new details.

He says that Ashmole and other Brethren of the Rose Croix, seeing that the Speculative Masons were surpassing in numbers the Operative, had renounced the simple initiation of the latter and established new degrees founded on the Mysteries of Egypt and Greece.

The Fellow Craft degree was fabricated in 1648, and that of Master a short time afterward.

But the decapitation of King Charles I, and the part taken by Ashmole in favor of the Stuarts produced great modifications in this third and last degree, which had become of a Biblical character.

---

[6] "Histoire de Trois Grandes Loges," p. 32
[7] Ragon, "Orthodoxie Maconnique," p. 29

The same epoch gave birth to the degrees of Secret Master, Perfect Master, and Irish Master, of which Charles I was the hero, under the name of Hiram.

These degrees, he says, were, however, not then openly practiced, although they afterward became the ornament of Ecossaism.

But the non-operative or "Accepted " members of the organization secretly gave to the Institution, especially in Scotland, a political tendency.

The chiefs or protectors of the Craft in Scotland worked, in the dark, for the re-establishment of the throne.

They made use of the seclusion of the Masonic Lodges as places where they might hold their meetings and concert their plans in safety.

As the execution of Charles I. was to be avenged, his partisans fabricated a Templar degree, in which the violent death of James de Molay called for vengeance.

Ashmole, who partook of that political sentiment, then modified the degree of Master and the Egyptian doctrine of which it was composed, and made it conform to the two preceding degrees framing a Biblical allegory, incomplete and in- consistent, so that the initials of the sacred words of these three degrees should compose those of the name and title of the Grand Master of the Templars.

Northouck,[8] who should have known better, gives countenance to these supercheries of history by asserting that Charles II. was made a Mason during his exile, although he carefully omits to tell us when, where, how, or by whom the initiation was effected; but seeks, with a flippancy that ought to provoke a smile, to prove that Charles II. took a great interest in Masonry and architecture, by citing the preamble to the charter of the Royal Society, an association whose object was solely the cultivation of the philosophical and mathematical sciences, especially astronomy and chemistry, and whose members took no interest in the art of building.

Dr. Oliver, whose unfortunate failing was to accept without careful examination all the statements of preceding writers, however absurd they might be, repeats substantially these apochryphal tales about early Stuart Masonry.

He says that, about the close of the 17th century, the followers of James II. who accompanied the unfortunate monarch in his exile carried Freemasonry to France and laid the foundation of that system of innovation which subsequently threw the Order into confusion, by the

---

[8] "Constitutions," p. 141

establishment of a new degree, which they called the Chevalier Naron Ecossais, and worked the details in the Lodge at St. Germain.

Hence, he adds, other degrees were invented in the Continental Lodges which became the rendezvous of the partisans of James, and by these means they held communication with their friends in England.[9] But as the high degrees were not fabricated until more than a third of the 18th century had passed, and as James died in 1701, we are struck with the confusion that prevails in this statement as to dates and persons.

It is very painful and embarrassing to the scholar who is really in search of truth to meet with such caricatures of history, in which the boldest and broadest assumptions are offered in the place of facts, the most absurd fables are presented as narratives of actual occurrences, chronology is put at defiance, anachronisms are coolly perpetrated, the events of the 18th century are transferred to the 17th, the third degree is said to have been modified in its ritual during the Commonwealth, when we know that no third degree was in existence until after 1717; and we are told that high degrees were invented at the same time, although history records the fact that the first of them was not fabricated until about the year 1728.

Such writers, if they really believed what they had written, must have adopted the axiom of the credulous Tertullian, who said, Credo quia impossible est - "I believe because it is impossible." Better would it be to remember the saying of Polybius, that if we eliminate truth from history nothing will remain but an idea too.

We must, then, reject as altogether untenable the theory that there was any connection between the Stuart family and Freemasonry during the time of James II., for the simple reason that at that period there was no system of Speculative Masonry existing which could have been perverted by the partisans of that family into a political instrument for its advancement.

If there was any connection at all, it must be looked for as developed at a subsequent period.

The views of Findel on this subject, as given in his History of Freemasonry, are worthy of attention, because they are divested of that mystical element so conspicuous and so embarrassing in all the statements which have been heretofore cited. His language is as follows: "Ever since the banishment of the Stuarts from England in 1688, secret alliances had been kept up between Rome and Scotland; for to the

---

[9] "Historical Landmarks, " II., p. 28

former place the Pretender James Stuart had retired in 1719 and his son Charles Edward born there in 1720; and these communications became the more intimate the higher the hopes of the Pretender rose.

The Jesuits played a very important part in these conferences.

Regarding the reinstatement of the Stuarts and the extension of the power of the Roman Church as identical, they sought at that time to make the Society of Free- masons subservient to their ends.

But to make use of the Fraternity, to restore the exiled family to the throne, could not have been contemplated, as Freemasonry could hardly be said to exist in Scotland then.

Perhaps in 1724, when Ramsay was a year in Rome, or in 1728, when the Pretender in Parma kept up an intercourse with the restless Duke of Wharton, a Past Grand Master, this idea was first entertained, and then when it was apparent how difficult it would be to corrupt the loyalty and fealty of Freemasonry in the Grand Lodge of Scotland, founded in 1736, this scheme was set on foot of assembling the faithful adherents of the banished royal family in the High Degrees! The soil that was best adapted for this innovation was France, where the low ebb to which Masonry had sunk had paved the way for all kinds of new-fangled notions, and where the Lodges were composed of Scotch conspirators and accomplices of the Jesuits.

When the path had thus been smoothed by the agency of these secret propagandists, Ramsay, at that time Grand Orator (an office unknown in England), by his speech completed the preliminaries necessary for the introduction of the High Degrees; their further development was left to the instrumentality of others, whose influence produced a result somewhat different from that originally intended."[10] After the death of James II. his son, commonly called the Chevalier St. George, does not appear to have actively prosecuted his claims to the throne beyond the attempted invasion of England in 1715.

He afterward retired to Rome, where the remainder of his life was passed in the quiet observation of religious duties.

Nor is there any satisfactory evidence that he was in any way connected with Freemasonry.

In the meantime, his sons, who had been born at Rome, were intrusted to the instructions of the Chevalier Michael Andrew Ramsay, who was appointed their tutor.

Ramsay was a man of learning and genius-a Scotsman, a Jacobite, and a Roman Catholic- but he was also an ardent Freemason.

---

[10] "Geschichte der Freimaurerei" - Translation of Lyon, p. 209

As a Jacobite he was prepared to bend all his powers to accomplish the restoration of the Stuarts to what he believed to be their lawful rights.

As a Freemason he saw in that Institution a means, if properly directed, of affecting that purpose.

Intimately acquainted with the old Legends of Masonry, he resolved so to modify them as to transfer their Biblical to political allusions.

With this design he commenced the fabrication of a series of High Degrees, under whose symbolism he concealed a wholly political object.

These High Degrees had also a Scottish character, which is to be attributed partly to the nationality of Ramsay and partly to a desire to effect a political influence among the Masons of Scotland, in which country the first attempts for the restoration of the Stuarts were to be made.

Hence we have to this day in Masonry such terms as "Ecossaim," " Scottish Knights of St.Andrew," " Scottish Master," "Scottish Architect," and the " Scottish Rite," the use of which words is calculated to produce upon readers not thoroughly versed in Masonic history the impression that the High Degrees of Freemasonry originated in Scotland-an impression which it was the object of Ramsay to make.

There is another word for which the language of Masonry has been indebted to Ramsay.

This is Heredom, indifferently spelled in the old rituals, Herodem, Heroden and Heredon.

Now the etymology of this word is very obscure and various attempts have been made to trace it to some sensible signification.

One writer[11] thinks that the word is derived from the Greek Ragon,[12] however, offers a different etymology.

He thinks that it is a corrupted form of the mediaeval Latin haredum, which signifies a heritage, and that it refers to the Chateau of St. Germain, the residence for a long time of the exiled Stuarts and the only heritage which was left to them.

If we accept this etymology I should rather be inclined to think that the heritage referred to the throne of Great Britain, which they

---

[11] London Freemasons' Magazine hieros, - "holy," - and domos, "house," and that it means the holy house, that is the Temple, is ingenious and it has been adopted by some recent authorities.

[12] "Orthodoxie Maconnique," p. 91

claimed as their lawful possession, and of which, in the opinion of their partisans, they had been unrighteously despoiled.

This derivation is equally as ingenious and just as plausible as the former one, and if adopted will add another link to the chain of evidence which tends to prove that the high degrees were originally fabricated by Ramsay to advance the cause of the Stuart dynasty.

Whatever may be the derivation of the word the rituals leave us in no doubt as to what was its pretended meaning.

In one of these rituals, that of the Grand Architect, we meet with the following questions and answers: Q. Where was your first Lodge held? A. Between three mountains, inaccessible to the profane, where cock never crew, lion roared, nor woman chattered; in a profound valley. Q. What are these three mountains named? A. Mount Moriah, in the bosom of the land of Gabaon, Mount Sinai, and the Mountain of Heredon. Q. What is this Mountain of Heredon? A. A mountain situated between the West and the North of Scotland, at the end of the sun's course, where the first Lodge of Masonry was held; in that terrestrial part which has given name to Scottish Masonry. Q. What do you mean by a profound valley? A. I mean the tranquillity of our Lodges. From this catechism we learn that in inventing the word Heredon to designate a fabulous mountain, situated in some unknown part of Scotland, Ramsay meant to select that kingdom as the birthplace of those Masonic degrees by whose instrumentality he expected to raise a powerful support in the accomplishment of the designs of the Jacobite party.

The selection of this country was a tribute to his own national prejudices and to those of his countrymen.

Again: by the "profound valley," which denoted " the tranquillity of the Lodges," Ramsay meant to inculcate the doctrine that in the seclusion of these Masonic reunions, where none were to be permitted to enter except "the well-tried, true, and trusty," the plans of the conspirators to overthrow the Hanoverian usurpation and to effect the restoration of the Stuarts could be best conducted.

Fortunately for the purity of the non-political character of the Masonic Institution, this doctrine was not generally accepted by the Masons of Scotland.

But there is something else concerning this word Heredon, in its connection with Stuart Freemasonry, that is worth attention.

There is an Order of Freemasonry, at this day existing, almost exclusively in Scotland.

It is caged the Royal Order of Scotland, and consists of two degrees, entitled "Heredon of Kilwinning," and "Rosy Cross." The first is said, in the traditions of the Order, to have originated in the reign of David I., in the 12th century, and the second to have been instituted by Robert Bruce, who revived the former and incorporated the two into one Order, of which the King of Scotland was forever to be the head.

This tradition is, however, attacked by Bro. Lyon, in his History of the Lodge of Edinburgh.

He denies that the Lodge at Kilwinning ever at any period practiced or acknowledged any other than the Craft degrees, or that there exists any tradition, local or national, worthy of the name, or any authentic document yet discovered that can in the remotest degree be held to identify Robert Bruce with the holding of Masonic courts or the institution of a secret society at Kilwinning "The paternity of the Royal Order," he says, " is now pretty generally attributed to a Jacobite Knight named Andrew Ramsay, a devoted follower of the Pretender, and famous as the fabricator of certain rites, inaugurated in France about 1735-40, and through the propagator of which it must hoped the fallen fortunes of the Stuarts would be retrieved.'"[13] On September 24, 1745, soon after the commencement of his invasion of Britain, Charles Edward, the son of the Old Pretender, or Chevalier St. George, styled by his adherents James III., is said to have been admitted into the Order of Knights Templars, and to have been elected its Grand Master, a position which he held until his death.

Such is the tradition, but here again we are met by the authentic statements of Bro. Lyon that Templarism was not introduced into Scotland until the year 1798.[14] It was then impossible that Charles Edward could have been made a Templar at Edinburgh in 1745.

It is, however, probable that he was invested with official supremacy over the high degrees which had been fabricated by Ramsay in the interest of his family, and it is not unlikely, as has been affirmed, that, resting his claim on the ritual provision that the Kings of Scotland were the hereditary Grand Masters of the Royal Order, he had assumed that title.

Of this we have something like an authentic proof, something which it is refreshing to get hold of as art oasis of history in this arid desert of doubts and conjectures and assumptions.

In the year 1747, more than twelve months after his return from his disastrous invasion of Scotland and England Charles Edward

---

[13] "History of the Lodge of Edinburgh," p. 307
[14] "History of the Lodge of Edinburgh," p. 287

issued a charter for the formation at the town of Arras in France of what is called in the instrument "a Sovereign Primordial Chapter of Rose Croix under the distinctive title of Scottish Jacobite." In 1853, the Count de Hamel, Prefect of the Department in which Arrasis situated, discovered an authentic copy of the charter in the Departmental archives..

In this document, the Young Pretender gives his Masonic titles in the following words: "We, Charles Edward, King of England, France, Scotland, and Ireland, and as such Substitute Grand Master of the Chapter of H., known by the title of Knight of the Eagle and Pelican, and since our sorrows and misfortunes by that of Rose Croix," etc.

The initial letter "H." undoubtedly designates the Scottish Chapter of Heredon.

Of this body, by its ritual regulation, his father as King of Scotland, would have been the hereditary Grand Master, and he, therefore, only assumes the subordinate one of Substitute. This charter, of the authenticity of which, as well as the transaction which it records, there appears to be no doubt, settles the question that it was of the Royal Order of Scotland and not of the Knights Templars that Charles Edward was made Grand Master, or himself assumed the Grand Mastership, during his visit in 1745 to Edinburgh.

As that Order and the other High Degrees were fabricated by the Chevalier Ramsay to promote the interests of his cause, his acceptance or assumption of the rank and functions of a presiding officer was a recognition of the plan to use Masonry as a political instrument, and is, in fact, the first and fundamental point in the history of the hypothesis of Stuart Masonry.

We here for the first time get tangible evidence that there was an attempt to connect the institution of Freemasonry with the fortunes and political enterprises of the Stuarts.

The title given to this primordial charter at Arras is further evidence that its design was really political; for the words Ecosse Jacobite, or Scottish Jacobite, were at that period universally accepted as a party name to designate a partisan of the Stuart pretensions to the throne of England.

The charter also shows that the organization of this chapter was intended only as the beginning of a plan to enlist other Masons in the same political design, for the members of the chapter were authorized " not only to make knights, but even to create a chapter in whatever town they might think proper," which they actually did in a few instances, among them one at Paris in 1780, which in 1801 ,was united to the Grand Orient of France.

A year after the establishment of the Chapter at Arras, the Rite of the Veille Bru, or the Faithful Scottish Masons, was created at Toulouse in grateful remembrance of the reception given by the Masons of that place to Sir Samuel Lockhart, the aide-de-camp of the Pretender.

Ragon says that the favorites who accompanied the prince to France were accustomed to sell to certain speculators charters for mother Lodges, patents for Chapters,etc.

These titles were their property and they did not fail to use them as a means of livelihood.

It has been long held as a recognized fact in Masonic history, that the first Lodge established in France by a warrant from the Grand Lodge of England was held in the year 1725.

There is no doubt that a Lodge of Freemasons met in that year at the house of one Hure, and that it was presided over by the titular Earl of Derwentwater.

But the researches of Bro. Hughan have incontestably proved that this was what we would now call a clandestine body, and that the first French Lodge legally established by the Grand Lodge of England was in 1732.

Besides the fact that there is no record in that Grand Lodge of England of any Lodge in France at the early date of 1725, it is most improbable that a warrant would have been granted to so conspicuous a Jacobite as Derwentwater.

Political reasons of the utmost gravity at that time would have forbidden any such action.

Charles Radcliffe, with his brother the Earl of Derwentwater, had been avenged in England for the part taken by them in the rebellion of 1715 to place James III. on the throne.

They were both condemned to death and the earl was executed, but Radcliffe made his escape to France, where he assumed the title which, as he claimed, had devolved upon him by the death of his brother's son.

In the subsequent rebellion of 1745, having attempted to join the Young Pretender, the vessel in which he sailed was captured by an English cruiser, and being carried to London, he was decapitated in December, 1746.

The titular Earl of Derwentwater was therefore a zealous Jacobite, an attainted rebel who had been sentenced to death for his treason, a fugitive from the law, and a pensioner of the Old Pretend. er or Chevalier St. George, who, by the order of Louis XIV., had been proclaimed King of England under the title of James III.

It is absurd, therefore, to suppose that the Grand Lodge of England would have granted to him and to his Jacobite associates a warrant for the establishment of a Lodge.

Its statutes had declared in very unmistakable words that a rebel against the State was not to be countenanced in his rebellion.

But no greater countenance could have been given than to make him the Master of a new Lodge.

Such, however, has until very recently been universally accepted as apart of the authentic history of Masonry in France.

In the words of a modern feuilletonist, "the story was too ridiculous to be believed, and so everybody believed it." But it is an undeniable fact that in 1725 an English Lodge was really opened and held in the house of an English confectionier named Hure.

It was however without regular or legal authority and was probably organized, although we have no recorded evidence to that effect, through the advice and instructions of Ramsay - and was a Jacobite Lodge consisting solely of the adherents and partisans of the Old Pretender.

This is the most explicit instance that we have of the connection of the Stuarts with Freemasonry.

It was an effort made by the adherents of that house to enlist the Order as an instrument to restore its fallen fortunes.

The principal members of the Lodge were Derwentwater, Maskelyne, and Heguertly or Heguety.

Of Derwentwater I have already spoken; the second was evidently a Scotsman, but the name of the third has been so corrupted in its French orthography that we are unable to trace it to its source.

It has been supposed that the real name was Haggerty; if so, he was probably an Irishman.

But they were all Jacobites.

The Rite of Strict Observance, which at one time in the last century took so strong a hold upon the Masons of Germany, and whose fundamental doctrine was that of Ramsay-that Freemasonry was only a continuation of the Templar system-is said to have been originally erected in the interests of the Stuarts, and the Brotherhood was expected to contribute liberally to the enterprises in favor of the Pretender.

Upon a review of all that has been written on this very intricate subject-the theories oftentimes altogether hypothetical, assumptions in plane of facts, conjectures altogether problematical, and the grain of history in this vast amount of traditional and mythical trash so small-we may, I think, be considered safe in drawing a few conclusions.

In the first place it is not to be doubted that at one time the political efforts of the adherents of the dethroned and exiled family of the Stuarts did exercise a very considerable effect on the outward form and the internal spirit of Masonry, as it prevailed on the continent of Europe.

In the symbolic degrees of ancient Craft Masonry, the influence was but slightly felt.

It extended only to a political interpretation of the Legend of the Master's degree, in which sometimes the decapitation of Charles I., and sometimes the forced abdication and exile of James II., was substituted for the fate of Hiram, and to a change in the substitute word so as to give an application of the phrase the " Widow's son " to the child of Henrietta Maria, the consort of Charles I. The effect of these change, except that of the word which still continues in some Rites, has long since disappeared, but their memory still remains as a relict of the incidents of Stuart Masonry.

But the principal influence of this policy was shown in the fabrication of what are called the "High Degrees," the "Hautes Grades" of the French. Until the year 1728 these accumulations to the body of Masonry were unknown.

The Chevalier Ramsay, the tutor of the Pretender in his childhood, and subsequently his most earnest friend and ardent supporter, was the first to fabricate these degrees, although other inventors were not tardy in following in his footsteps.

These degrees, at first created solely to institute a form of Masonry which should be worked for the purpose of restoring the Pretender to the throne of his ancestors, have most of them become obsolete, and their names alone are preserved in the catalogues of collectors; but their effect is to this day seen in such of them as still remain and are practiced in existing Rites, which have been derived indirectly from the system invented in the Chapter of Clermont or the Chateau of St. Germain.

The particular design has paned away but the general features still remain, by which we are enabled to recognize the relicts of Stuart Masonry.

As to the time when this system first began to be developed there can be but little doubt.

We must reject the notion that James II had any connection with it.

However unfitted he may have been by his peculiar temperament from entering into any such bold conspiracy, the question is set at rest by the simple fact that up to the time of his death there was no Masonic organization upon which he or his partisans could have used His son the Chevalier St. George was almost in the same category.

He is described in history as a prince-pious, pacific and without talents, incapable of being made the prominent actor in such a drama, and besides, Speculative Masonry had not assumed the proportions necessary to make it available as a part of a conspiracy until long after he had retired from active life to the practice of religious and recluse habits in Rome.

But his son Charles Edward, the Young Pretender as he was called, was of an ardent temperament; an active genius, a fair amount of talent, and a spirit of enterprise which well fitted him to accept the place assigned him by Ramsay.

Freemasonry had then begun to excite public attention, and was already an institution that was rapidly gaining popularity.

Ramsay saw in it what he deemed a fitting lever to be used in theelevation of his patron to the throne, and Prince Charles Edward with eagerness met his propositions and united with him in the futile effort.

To the Chevalier Ramsay we must attribute the invention of Stuart Masonry, the foundations of which he began to lay early in the 18th century, perhaps with the tacit approval of the Old Pretender.

About 1725, when the first Lodge was organized in Paris, under some illegitimate authority, he made the first public exposition of his system in the Scottish High Degrees which he at that time brought to light.

And finally the workings of the system were fully developed when the Young Pretender began his unsuccessful career in search of a throne, which once lost was never to be recovered.

This conspiracy of Ramsay to connect Freemasonry with the fortunes of the Stuarts was the first attempt to introduce politics into the institution. To the credit of its character as a school of speculative philosophy, the attempt proved a signal failure.

CHAPTER XXXI

THE JESUITS IN FREEMASONRY

The opinion has been entertained by several writers of eminence that the Company of Jesus, more briefly styled the Jesuits, sought, about the end of the 17th and the beginning of the 18th century, to mingle with the Freemasons and to bend the objects of that Institution to the ambitious designs of their own Order. This view has been denied by other writers of equal eminence, though it is admitted that Roman Catholic, if not Jesuitical, features are to be found in some of the high degrees.

It is contended by one German writer that the object of the Jesuits in seeking a control of the Masonic Institution was that they might be thus assisted in their design of establishing an aristocracy within themselves, and that they sought to accomplish this object by securing not only the direction of the Masonic Lodges, but also by obtaining a monopoly of the schools and churches, and all the pursuits of science, and even of business.

But the more generally accepted reason for this attempted interference with the Lodges is that they thus sought by their influence and secret working to aid the Stuarts to regain the throne, and then, as an expected result, to re-establish the Roman Catholic religion in England.

The first of these explanations is certainly more satisfactory than the second.

While there is a great want of historical testimony to prove that the jesuits ever mingled with Freemasonry a question to be hereafter decided there is no doubt of the egotistical and ambitious designs (Of the disciples of Loyola to secure a control of the public and private affairs of every government where they could obtain a foothold.

It was a knowledge of these designs that led to the unpopularity of the Order among even Catholic sovereigns and caused its total suppression, in 1773, by Pope Clement XIV., from which it was not relieved until 1814, when their privileges were renewed by Pope Pius VII.

But I think that we must concur with Gadeike in the conclusion to which he had arrived, that it is proved by history to be a falsehood that Freemasonry was ever concealed under the mask of Jesuitism, or that it derived its existence from that source.[15] It is, however, but fair that we should collate and compare the arguments on both sides.

Robison, who, where Masonry was concerned, could find a specter in every bush, is, of course, of very little authority as to facts; but he may supply us with a record of the opinions which were prevalent at the time of his writing.

He says that when James II fled from England to France, which was in 1688, his adherents took Freemasonry with them to the continent, where it was received and cultivated by the French in a manner suited to the tastes and habits of that people.

But he adds that " at this time, also, the Jesuits took a more active hand in Freemasonry than ever.

They insinuated themselves into the English Lodges, where they were caressed by the Catholics, who panted after the re-establishment of their faith, and tolerated by the Protestant royalists, who thought no concession too great a compensation for their services.

At this time changes were made in some of the Masonic symbols, particularly in the tracing of the Lodge, which bear evident marks of Jesuitical interference.[16] Speaking of the High Degrees, the fabrication of which, however, he greatly antedates, he says that " in all this progressive mummery we see much of the hand of the Jesuits, and it would seem that it was encouraged by the church."[17] But he thinks that the Masons, protected by their secrecy, ventured further than the clergy approved in their philosophical interpretations of the symbols, opposing at last some of " the ridiculous and oppressive superstitions of the church,"[18] and thus he accounts for the persecution of Freemasonry at a later period by the priests, and their attempts to suppress the Lodges.

---

[15] "Freimaurer Lexicon," art. "Jesuiten."
[16] "Proofs of a Conspiracy," p. 27
[17] Ibid., p. 30
[18] Ibid to the Jesuits.

The story, as thus narrated by Robison, is substantially that which has been accepted by all writers who trace the origin of Freemasonry

They affirm, as we have seen, that it was instituted about the time of the expulsion of James II. from England, or that if it was not then fabricated as a secret society, it was at least modified in all its features from that form which it originally had in England, and was adapted as a political engine to aid in the restoration of the exiled monarch and in the establishment in his recovered kingdom of the Roman Catholic religion.

These theorists have evidently confounded primitive Speculative Masonry, consisting only of three degrees, with the supplementary grades invented subsequently by Ramsay and the ritualists who succeeded him.

But even if we relieve the theory of the connsbn and view it as affirming that the Jesuits at the College of Clermont modified the third degree and invented others, such as the Scottish Knight of St. Andrew, for the purpose of restoring James II. to the throne, we shall find no scintilla of evidence in history to support this view, but, on the contrary, obstacles in the way of anachronisms which it will be impossible to overcome.

James II abdicated the throne in 1688, and, after an abortive attempt to recover it by an unsuccessful invasion of Ireland, took up his residence at the Chateau of St. Germain-en-Laye, in France, where he died in 1701.

Between the two periods of 1688, when James abdicated, and 1701, when he died, no one has been enabled to find either in England or elsewhere any trace of a third degree.

Indeed, I am very sure it can be proved that this degree was not invented until 1721 or 1722.

It is, therefore, absolutely impossible that any modification could have been made in the latter part of the 17th century of that which did not exist until the beginning of the 18th.

And if there was no Speculative Masonry, as distinguished from the Operative Art practiced by the mediaeval guilds, during the lifetime of James, it is equally absurd to contend that supplementary grades were invented to illustrate and complete a superstructure whose foundations had not yet been laid.

The theory that the Jesuits in the 17th century had invented Freemasonry for the purpose of effecting one of their ambitious projects, or that they had taken it as it then existed, changed it, and added to it for the same purpose, is absolutely untenable.

Another theory has been advanced which accounts for the establishment of what has been called " Jesuitic Masonry," at about the middle of the 18th century.

This theory is certainly free from the absurd anachronisms which we encounter in the former, although the proofs that there ever was such a Masonry are still very unsatisfactory.

It has been maintained that this notion of the intrusion, as it may well be called, of the Jesuits into the Masonic Order has been attributed to the Illuminati, that secret society which was established by Adam Weishaupt in Bavaria about the year 1776.

The original object of this society was, as its founder declared, to enable its members to attain the greatest possible amount of virtue, and by the association of good men to oppose the progress of moral evil. To give it influence it was connected with Freemasonry, whose symbolic degrees formed the substratum of its esoteric instructions.

This has led it incorrectly to be deemed a Masonic Rite; it could really lay no claim to that character, except inasmuch as it required a previous initiation into the symbolic degrees to entitle its disciples to further advancement.

The charges made against it, that it was a political organization, and that one of its deigns was to undermine the Christian religion, although strenuously maintained by Barruel, Robison, and a host of other adversaries, have no foundation in truth. The principles of the order were liberal and philosophical, but neither revolutionary nor anti-Christian.

As the defender of free thought, it came of course into conflict with the Roman Catholic Church and the Company of Jesus, whose tendencies were altogether the other way.

The priests, therefore, became its most active enemies, and their opposition was so successful that it was suppressed in 1784.

There was also between Illuminism and the many Masonic Rites, which about the period of its popularity were constantly arising in Germany and in France, a species of rivalry.

With the natural egotism of reformers, the Illuminati sought to prove the superiority of their own system to that of their rivals.

With this view they proclaimed that all the Lodges of Free. masons were secretly controlled by the Jesuits; that their laws and their mysteries were the inventions of the same Order, of whom every Freemason was unconsciously the slave and the instrument.

Hence they concluded that he who desired to possess the genuine mysteries of Masonry must seek them not among the degrees of Rose Croix or the Scottish Knights, or still less among the English Masons and the disciples of the Rite of Strict Observance in Germany, but only in the Eclectic Lodges that had been instituted by the Illuminati.

Such, says Barruel, was the doctrine of the Illuminati, advanced for the purpose of elevating the character and aims of their own institution.

The French abbe is not generally trustworthy on any subject connected, with Freemasonry, of which he was the avowed and implacable foe, but we must acknowledge that he was not far from wrong in calling this story of Jesuitic Masonry " a ridiculous and contemptible fable." For once we are disposed to agree with him, when he says in his fervent declamation, "If prejudice did not sometimes destroy the faculty of reasoning, we should be astonished that the Freemasons could permit themselves to be ensnared in so clumsy a trap.

What is it, in fact, but to say to the Mother Lodge of Edinburgh, to the Grand Lodges of London and York, to their rulers, and to all their Grand Masters: You thought that you held the reins of the Masonic world, and you looked upon yourselves as the greatdepository of its secrets, the distributors of its diplomas; but you are not so, and, without even knowing it, are merely puppets of which the Jesuits hold the leading-strings, and which they move at their pleasure.'"[19] I think that with a little trouble we may be able to solve this apparently difficult problem of the Jesuitical interference with Freemasonry.

The Jesuits appear to have taken the priests of Egypt for their model.

Like them, they sought to be the conservators and the interpreters of religion.

The vows which they took attached them to their Order with bonds as indissoluble as those that united the Egyptian priests in the sacred college of Memphis.

Those who sought admission into their company were compelled to pass through trials of their fortitude and fidelity.

Their ambition was as indomitable as their cunning was astute. They strove to be the confessors and the counsellors of kings, and to control the education of youth, that by these means they might become

---

[19] "Memoires pour servir a l'Histoire du Jacobanisme," T.N., p. 291

of importance in the state, and direct the policy of every government where they were admitted.

And this policy was on all occasions to be made subservient to the interests of the church.

At one time they had not less than an hundred schools or colleges in France, the most important being that of Clermont, which, though at one time suppressed, had received renewed letters patent from Louis XIV.

It was this College of Clermont, where James II. was a frequent guest, led there by his religious feelings, that is said to have been the seat of that conspiracy of the Stuart faction which was to terminate either in the invention or the adoption of Freemasonry as a means of restoring the monarch to his throne, and of resuscitating the Roman Catholic religion in heretical England.

Now we may readily admit that the Jesuits were exceedingly anxious to accomplish both these objects, and that for that purpose they would enter into any intrigue which would probably lead to success.

With this design there can be but little doubt that they united with the adherents of the Stuarts.

But this conspiracy could not have had any reference to a Masonic organization, because Freemasonry was during the life of James II. wholly unknown in France, and known in England only as a guild of Operative Masons, into which a few non-Masons had been admitted through courtesy.

It certainly had not yet assumed the form in which we are called upon to recognize it as the political engine used by the Jesuits.

The Grand Lodge of England, the mother of all modern Speculative Masonry, had no existence until 1717, or sixteen years after the death of the king.

We are bound, therefore, if on the ground of an anachronism alone, to repudiate any theory that connects the Jesuits with Freemasonry during the life of James II., although we may be ready to admit their political conspiracy in the interests of that dethroned monarch.

During the life of his son and putative successor, the titular James III., Speculative Masonry was established in England and passed over into France.

The Lodge established in Paris in 1725 was, I have no doubt, an organization of the adherents of the Stuart family, as has already been shown.

It is probable that most of the members were Catholics and under the influence of the Jesuits.

But it is not likely that those priests took an active part in the internal organization of the Lodge. They could do their work better outside of it than within it. In the Rose Croix and some other of the High Degrees we find the influences of a Roman Catholic spirit in the original rituals, but this might naturally arise from the religious tendencies of their founders, and did not require the special aid of Jesuitism.

After the year 1738 the bull of excommunication of Pope Clement XII. must have precluded the Jesuits from all connection with Freemasonry except as its denouncers and persecutors, parts which up to the present day they have uninterruptedly played.

In conclusion we must, I think, refuse to accept the theory which makes a friendly connection between Freemasonry and Jesuitism as one of those mythical stories which, born in the imagination of its inventors, has been fostered only by the credulity of its believers.

At this day I doubt if there is a Masonic scholar who would accept it as more it as a fable not even " cunningly devised," though there was a time when it was received as a part of the authentic history of Freemasonry.

CHAPTER XXXII

OLIVER CROMWELL AND FREEMASONRY

Three fables have been invented to establish a connection between Freemasonry and the dynasty of the Stuarts one which made it the purpose of the adherents of James II. to use the Institution as a means of restoring that monarch to the throne; a second in which the Jesuits were to employ it for the same purpose, as well as for the re-establishment of the Roman Catholic religion in England; the third and most preposterous of these fables is that which attributes the invention of Freemasonry as a secret society to Oliver Cromwell, who is supposed to have employed it as a political engine to aid him in the dethronement of Charles I., in the abolition of the monarchy, and in the foundation of a republic on its ruins, with himself for its head.

The first and second of these fables have already been discussed.

The consideration of the third will be the subject of the present chapter.

The theory that Freemasonry was instituted by Oliver Cromwell was not at first received like the other two by any large portion of the fraternity.

It was the invention of a single mind and was first made public in the year 1746, by the Abbe Larudan, who presented his views in a work entitled Les Franc-Macons ecrasses, a book which Klass, the bibliographer, says is the armory from which all the enemies of Masonry have since delved their weapons of abuse.

The propositions of Larudan are distinguished for their absolute independence of all historical authority and for the bold assumptions which are presented to the reader in the place of facts.

His strongest argument for the truth of his theory is that the purposes of the Masonic Institution and of the political course of Cromwell are identical, namely, to sustain the doctrines of liberty and equality among mankind.

Rejecting all the claims to antiquity that have been urged in behalf of the Institution, he thinks that it was in England where the Order of Freemasonry first saw the light of day, and that it is to Cromwell that it owes its origin.

And this theory he claims (with what truth we know not) to have received from a certain Grand Master with whose astuteness and sincerity he was well acquainted.

But even this authority, he says, would not have been sufficient to secure his belief, had it not afterward been confirmed by his reading of the history of the English Protector and his mature reflections on the morals and the laws of the Order, where he detected at every step the presence of Cromwell.

The object of Cromwell, as it has been already said, was by the organization of a secret society, whose members would be bound by the most solemn ties of fraternity, to reconcile the various religions and political sects which prevailed in England in the reign of Charles I to the prosecution of his views, which were equally opposed to the supremacy of the king and to the power of the Parliament, and as a consequence of the destruction of both, to the elevation of himself to the headship of affairs. In the execution of this plan Cromwell proceeded with his usual caution and address.

He first submitted the outline to several of his most intimate friends such as Algernon Sidney, Harrington, Monk, and Fairfax, and he held with them several private meetings.

"But it was not until the year 1648 that he began to take the necessary steps for bringing it to maturity.

In that year, at a dinner which he gave to a large number of his friends, he opened his designs to the company.

When his guests, among whom were many members of Parliament, both Presbyterians and Independents the two rival religious sects of the day, had been well feasted, the host dexterously led the conversation to the subject of the unhappy condition of England.

He showed in a pathetic manner how the unfortunate nation had suffered distracting conflicts of politics and religion, and he declared that it was a disgrace that men so intelligent as those who then heard him did not make an exertion to put an end to these distracting contests of party. Scarcely had Cromwell ceased to speak when Ireton, his son-in-law, who had been prepared for the occasion, rose, and, seconding the sentiments of his leader, proceeded to show the absolute necessity for the public good of a conciliation and union of the many discordant parties which were then dividing the country.

He exclaimed with fervor that he would not, himself, hesitate to sacrifice his fortune and his life to remedy such calamities, and to show to the people the road they ought to take, to relieve themselves from the yoke which was oppressing them and to break the iron scepter under which they were groaning.

But to do this it was first necessary, he insisted, to destroy every power and influence which had betrayed the nation.

Then, turning to Cromwell, he conjured him to explain his views on this important matter, and to suggest the cure for these evils.

Cromwell did not hesitate to accept the task which had, apparently without his previous concurrence, been assigned to him.

Addressing his guests in that metaphorical style which he was accustomed to use, and the object of which was to confuse their intellects and make them more ready to receive his boldest propositions, he explained the obligation of a worship of God, the necessity to repel force by force, and to deliver mankind from oppression and tyranny.

He then concluded his speech, exciting the curiosity of his auditors by telling them that he knew a method by which they could succeed in this great enterprise, restore peace to England, and rescue it from the depth of misery into which it was plunged.

This method, he added, if communicated to the world, would win the gratitude of mankind and secure a glorious memory for its authors to the latest posterity.

The discourse was well managed and well received.

All of his guests earnestly besought him to make this admirable expedient known to them. But Cromwell would not yield at once to their importunities, but modestly replying that so important an enterprise was beyond the strength of any one man to accomplish, and that he would rather continue to endure the evils of a bad government than, in seeking to remove them by the efforts of his friends, to subject them to dangers which they might be unwilling to encounter.

Cromwell well understood the character of every man who sat at the table with him, and he knew that by this artful address he should still further excite their curiosity and awaken their enthusiasm.

And so it was that, after a repetition of importunities, he finally consented to develop his scheme, on the condition that all the guests should take a solemn oath to reveal the plan to no one and to consider it after it had been proposed with absolutely unprejudiced mind.

This was unanimously assented to, and, the oath of secrecy having been taken, Cromwell threw himself on his knees and, extending his hands toward heaven, called on God and all the celestial powers to witness the innocence of his heart and the purity of his intentions.

All this the Abbe Larudan relates with a minuteness of detail which we could expect only from an eye-witness of the scene.

Having thus made a deep impression on his guests, Cromwell said that the precise moment for disclosing the plan had not arrived, and that an inspiration from heaven, which he had just received, instructed him not to divulge it until four days had elapsed.

The companion though impatient to receive a knowledge of the important secret, were compelled to restrain their desires and to agree to meet again at the appointed time and at a place which was designated.

On the fourth day all the guests repaired to a house in King Street, where the meeting took place, and Cromwell proceeded to develop his plan. (And here the Abbe Larudan becomes fervid and diffuse in the minuteness with which he describes what must have been a wholly imaginary scene.) He commenced by conducting the guests into a dark room, where he prepared their minds for what was going to occur by a long prayer, in the course of which he gave them to understand that he was in communion with the spirits of the blessed.

After this he told them that his design was to found a society whose only objects would be to render due worship to God and to restore to England the peace for which it so ardently longed. But this project, he added, requited consummate prudence and infinite address to secure its success.

Then taking a censer in his bands, be filled the apartment with the most subtle fumes, so as to produce a favorable dies position in the company to hear what he had further to say.

He informed them that at the reception of a new adherent it was necessary that be should undergo a certain ceremony, to which all of them, without exception, would have to submit.

He asked them whether they were willing to pass through this ceremony, to which proposition unanimous consent was given.

He then chose from the company five assistants to occupy appropriate places and to perform prescribed functions.

These assistants were a Master, two Wardens, a Secretary, and an Orator.

Having made these preparations, the visitors were removed to another apartment, which had been prepared for the purpose, and in which was a picture representing the ruins of King Solomon's Temple.

From this apartment they were transferred to another, and, being blindfolded, werefinally invested with the secrets of initiation.

Cromwell delivered a discourse on religion and politics, the purport of which was to show to the contending sects of Presbyterians and Independents, representatives of both being present, the necessity, for the public good, of abandoning all their frivolous disputes, of becoming reconciled, and of changing the bitter hatred which then inspired them for a tender love and charity toward each other.

The eloquence of their artful leader had the desired effect, and both sects united with the army, in the establishment of a secret association founded on the professed principles of love of God and the maintenance of liberty and equality among men, but whose real design was to advance the projects of Cromwell, by the abolition of the monarchy and the establishment of a commonwealth of which he should be the head.

It is unfortunate for the completed symmetry of this rather interesting fable that the Abbe has refrained from indulging his imagination by giving us the full details of the form of initiation.

He has, however, in various parts of his book alluded to so much of it as to enable us to learn that the instructions were of a symbolic character, and that the Temple of Solomon constituted the most prominent symbol.

This Temple had been built by divine command to be the sanctuary of religion and as a place peculiarly consecrated to the performance of its august ceremonies.

After several years of glory and magnificence it had been destroyed by a formidable army, and the people who had been there accustomed to worship were loaded with chains and carried in captivity to Babylon.

After years of servitude, an idolatrous prince, chosen as the instrument of Divine clemency, had permitted the captives to return to Jerusalem and to rebuild the Temple in its primitive splendor.

It was in this allegory, says the Abbe, that the Freemasons of Cromwell found the exact analogy of their society.

The Temple in its first splendor is figurative of the primitive state of man.

The religion and the ceremonies which were there practiced are nothing else than that universal law engraved on every heart whose principles are found in the ideas of equity and charity to which all men are obliged. The destruction of this Temple, and the captivity and slavery of its worshippers, symbolized the pride and ambition which have produced political subjection among men.

The unpitying hosts of Assyrians who destroyed the Temple and led the people into captivity are the kings, princes, and magistrates whose power has overwhelmed oppressed nations with innumerable evils.

And finally, the chosen people charged with the duty of rebuilding the Temple are the Freemasons, who are to restore men to their original dignity.

Cromwell had divided the Order which he founded into three classes or degrees.

The third or Master's degree was of course not without its Hiramic legend, but the interpretation of its symbolism was very different from that which is given at the present day.

The Abbe thus explains it.

The disorder of the workmen and the confusion at the Temple were intended to make a profound impression upon the mind of the candidate and to show him that the loss of liberty and equality, represented by the death of Hiram, is the cause of all the evils which affect mankind.

While men lived in tranquillity in the asylum of the Temple of Liberty they enjoyed perpetual happiness.

But they have been surprised and attacked by tyrants who have reduced them to a state of slavery.

This is symbolized by the destruction of the Temple, which it is the duty of the Master Masons to rebuild; that is to say, to restore that liberty and equality which had been lost.

Cromwell appointed missionaries or emissaries, says Larudan, who propagated the Order, not only over all England, but even into Scotland and Ireland, where many Lodges were established.

The members of the Order or Society were first called Freemasons; afterward the name was repeatedly changed to suit the political circumstances of the times, and they were called Levelers, then Independents, afterward Fifth Monarchy Men, and finally resumed their original title, which they have retained to the present day.

Such is the fable of the Cromwellian origin of Freemasonry, which we owe entirely to the inventive genius of the Abbe Larudan.

And yet it is not wholly a story of the imagination, but is really founded on an extraordinary distortion of the facts of history.

Edmund Ludlow was an honest and honorable man who took at first a prominent part in the civil war which ended in the decapitation of Charles I., the dissolution of the monarchy, and the establishment of the Commonwealth.

He was throughout his whole life a consistent and unswerving republican, and was as much opposed to the political schemes of Cromwell for his own advancement to power as he was to the usurpation of unconstitutional power by the King.

In the language of the editor of his memoirs, " He was an enemy to all arbitrary government, though gilded over with the most specious pretences; and not only disapproved the usurpation of Cromwell, but would have opposed him with as much vigor as he had done the King, if all occasions of that nature had not been cut off by the extraordinary jealousy or vigilance of the usurpers."[20] Having unsuccessfully labored to counteract the influence of Cromwell with the army, he abandoned public affairs and retired to his home in Essex, where he remained in seclusion until the restoration of Charles II., when he fled to Switzerland, where he resided until his death.

During his exile, Ludlow occupied his leisure hours in the composition of his Memoirs, a work of great value as a faithful record of the troublous period in which he lived and of which he was himself a great part.

In these memoirs he has given a copious narrative of the intrigues by which Cromwell secured the alliance of the army and destroyed the influence of the Parliament.

The work was published at Vevay, in Switzerland, under the title of Memoirs of Edmund Ludlow, Esq.- Lieutenant-General of the Tories in Ireland, One of the Council of State, and a Member of the Parliament which began on November 3, 1640. It is in two volumes, with a supplementary one containing copies of important papers.

The edition from which I cite bears the date of 1698.

There may have been an earlier one.

With these memoirs the Abbe Larudan appears to have been well acquainted.

He had undoubtedly read them carefully, for be has made many quotations and has repeatedly referred to Ludlow as his authority.

But unfortunately for the Abbe's intelligence, or far more probably for his honesty, he has always applied that Ludlow said of the

---

[20] Ludlow's "Memoirs," Preface, p. iv.

intrigues of Cromwell for the organization of a new party as if it were meant to describe the formation of a new and secret society.

Neither Ludlow nor any other writer refers to the existence of Freemasonry as we now have it and as it is described by the Abbe Larudan in the time of the civil wars.

Even the Operative Masons were not at that period greatly encouraged, for, says Northouck," no regard to science and elegance was to be expected from the sour minds of the puritanical masters of the nation between the fall of Charles I and the restoration of his son."[21] The Guild of Freemasons, the only form in which the Order was known until the 18th century, was during the Commonwealth discouraged and architecture was neglected.

In the tumult of war the arts of peace are silent.

Cromwell was, it is true, engaged in many political intrigues, but he had other and more effective means to accomplish his ends than those cd Freemasonry of whose existence at that time, except as a guild of workmen, we have no historical evidence, but a great many historical facts to contradict its probability.

The theory, therefore, that Freemasonry owes its origin to Oliver Cromwell, who invented it as a means of forwarding his designs toward obtaining the supreme power of the state, is simply a fable, the invention of a clerical adversary of the Institution, and devised by him plainly to give to it a political character, by which, like his successors Barruel and Robison, he sought to injure it.

---

[21] Northouck's Constitutions," p. 141 P. 300

CHAPTER XXXIII

THE ROYAL SOCIETY AND FREEMASONRY

The hypothesis that Freemasonry was instituted in the 17th century and in the reign of Charles II., by a set of philosophers and scientists who organized it under the title of the " Royal Society," is the last of those theories which attempts to connect the Masonic Order with the House of Stuart that we will have to investigate.

The theory was first advanced by an anonymous writer in the German Mercury, a Masonic journal published about the close of the last century at Weimar, and edited by the celebrated Christopher Martin Wieland.

In this article the writer says that Dr. John Wilkins one of the most learned men of his time, and the brother-in-law of Oliver Cromwell, becoming discontented with the administration of Richard Cromwell, his son and successor, began to devise the means of re-establishing the royal authority.

With this view he suggested the idea of organizing a society or club, in which, under the pretence of cultivating the sciences the partisans of the king might meet together with entire freedom.

General Monk and several other military men, who had scarcely more learning than would enable them to write their names, were members of this academy.

Their meetings were always begun with a learned lecture, for the sake of form, but the conversation afterward turned upon politics and the interests of the king.

And this politico-philosophical club, which subsequently assumed, after the Restoration, the title of the "Royal Society of Sciences," he asserts to have been the origin of the fraternity of Freemasons.

We have already had abundant reason to see, in the formation of Masonic theories, what little respect has been paid by their framers to the contradictory facts of history nor does the present hypothesis afford any exception to the general rule of dogmatic assumption and unfounded assertion.

Christopher Frederick Nicolai, a learned bookseller of Berlin, wrote and published, in 1783, an Essay on the Accusations made against the Order of Knights Templar and their Mystery with an appendix on the Origin of the Fraternity of Freemasons.[22] In this work he vigorously attacks the theory of the anonymous writer in Wieland's Mercury, and the reasons on which he grounds his dissent are well chosen but they do not cover the whole ground.

Unfortunately, Nicolai had a theory of his own to foster, which also in a certain way connects Freemasonry with the real founders of the Royal Society, and the impugnment of the hypothesis of Wieland's contribution in its whole extent impugns also his own.

Two negatives in most languages are equivalent to an affirmative, but nowhere are two fictions resolvable into a truth.

The arguments of Nicolai against the Wieland theory are, however, worth citation, before we examine his own.

He says that Wilkins could scarcely have been discontented with the government of Richard Cromwell, since it was equally as advantageous to him as that of his father.

He was (and he quotes Wood in the Athena Oxonienses as his authority) much opposed to the court, and was a zealous Puritan before the rebellion.

In 1648 he was made the Master of Wadham College, in the place of a royalist who had been removed.

In 1649, after the decapitation of Charles I, he joined the republican party and took the oath of allegiance to the Commonwealth.

In 1656 he married the sister of Cromwell, and under Richard received the valuable appointment of Master of Trinity College, which, however, he lost upon the restoration of the monarchy in the following year.

"Is it credible," says Nicolai, "that this man could have instituted a society for the purpose of advancing the restoration of the king; a society all of whose members were of the opposite party? The celebrated Dr. Goddard, who was one of the most distinguished members, was the

---

[22] "Versuch uber die Besschuldigungen, welche dem Tempelherrn orden gemacht worden und uber dessen Geheimniss; nebst einem Anhange uber das Enstehen der Freimaurergesellschaft," Berlin and Stettin, 1783.

physician and favorite of Cromwell, whom, after the death of the King, he attended in his campaigns in Ireland and Scotland.

It is an extraordinary assertion that a discontent with the administration of Richard Cromwell should have given rise in 1658 to a society which was instituted in 1646.

It is not less extraordinary that this society should have held its meetings in a tavern.

It is very certain that in those days of somber Puritanism the few taverns to be found in London could not have been used as places of meeting for associations consisting of men of all conditions, as is now the custom.

There would have been much imprudence in thus exposing secret deliberations on an affair equally dangerous and important to the inspection of all the spies who might be congregated in a tavern." He asserts that the first meetings of the society were held at the house of Dr. Goddard and of another member, and afterward at Cheapside and at Gresham College.

And these facts are proved by the records of the society, as published by its annalists.

As to the statement that Monk was one of the members of the society-a fact that would be important in strengthening the theory that it was organized by the friends of the monarchy and with a design of advancing its restoration - he shows the impossibility that it could be correct, because Monk was a prisoner in the Tower from 1643 until 1647, and after his release in that year spent only a month in London, not again visiting that city till 1659, when he returned at the head of an army and was engaged in the arrangement of such delicate affairs and was so narrowly watched that it is not possible to be behaved that with his well-known caution he would have taken part in any sort of political society whatever, while the society would have acted very inconsiderately in admitting into its ranks military men who could scarcely write, and that too at a time when distrust had risen to its height.

But a better proof than any advanced by Nicolai, that Monk had nothing to do with the establishment of the Royal Society, whatever may have been its object, is that his name does not appear upon the list of original or early members, taken from the official records and published by Dr. Thompson in his history of the society.

Finally Nicolai asserts very truthfully that its subsequent history has shown that this society was really engaged in scientific pursuits, and that politics were altogether banished from its conferences.

But he also contends, but with less accuracy, that the political principles of its members were opposed to the restoration of the monarchy, for which statement there is no positive authority.

Hence Nicolai concludes that " there is no truth in the statements of the anonymous writer in Wieland's Mercury, except that the restoration was opposed in secret by a certain society." And now he advances his own theory, no less untenable than the one he is opposing, that this society "was the Freemasons, who had nothing in common with the other, except the date of foundation, and whose views in literature as well as in politics were of an entirely opposite character." This was the theory of Nicolai-not that Freemasonry originated in the Royal Society, but that it was established by certain learned men who sought to advance the experimental philosophy which had just been introduced by Bacon.

But the same idea was sought by the originators of the Royal Society, and as many of the founders of this school were also among the founders of the Royal Society, it seems difficult to separate the two theories so as to make of each a distinct and independent existence.

But it will be better to let the Berlin bookseller explain his doctrine in his own language, before an attempt is made to apply to it the canons of criticism.

He commences by asserting that one of the effects of the labors of Andrea and the other Rosicrucians was the application of a wholesome criticism to the examination of philosophical and scientific subjects.

He thinks even that the Fama Fraternitatis, the great work of Andrea, had first suggested to Bacon the notion of his immortal work on The Advancement of Learning.

At the same time in which Bacon flourished and taught his inductive philosophy, the Rosicrucians had introduced a system of philosophy which was established on the phenomena of nature.

Lord Bacon had cultivated these views in his book De Augmentis Scientiarum, except that he rejected the Rosicrucian method of esoteric instruction.

Everything that he taught was to be open and exoteric. Therefore, as he had written his great work in the Latin language, for the use of the learned, he now composed his New Atlantis in English, that all classes might be able to read it.

In this work is contained his celebrated romance of the House of Solomon, which Nicolai thinks may have had its influence in originating the society of Freemasons.

In this fictitious tale Bacon supposes that a vessel lands on an unknown island, called Bensalem, over which in days of yore a certain King Solomon reigned. This King had a large establisliment, which was called the House of Solomon or the College of the Six Days' Work, in allusion to the six days of the Mosaic account of the creation. He afterward describes the immense apparatus which was there employed in physical researches.

There were deep grottoes and tall bowers for the observation o f the phenomena of nature; artificial mineral-waters; huge buildings in which meteors, the wind, rain and thunder and lightning were imitated; extensive botanic gardens, and large fields in which all kinds of animals were collected for the study of their instinct and habits, and houses filled with all the wonders of nature and art.

There were also a great number of learned men, to whom the direction of these things was intrusted.

They made journeys into foreign countries, and observations on what they saw.

They wrote, they collected, they determined results, and deliberated together as to what was proper to be published.

This romance, says Nicolai, which was in accord with the prevailing taste of the age, contributed far more to spread the views of Bacon on the observation of nature than his more learned and profound work had been able to do.

The House of Solomon attracted the attention of everybody. King Charles I was anxious to establish something like it, but was prevented by the civil wars.

Nevertheless this great idea, associated with that of the Rosicrucians, continued to powerfully agitate the minds of the learned men of that period, who now began to be persuaded of the necessity of experimental knowledge.

Accordingly, in 1646, a society of learned men was established, all of whom were of Bacon's opinion, that philosophy and the physical sciences should be placed within the reach of all thinking minds.

They held meetings at which-believing that instruction in physics was to be sought by a mutual communication of ideas-they made many scientific experiments in common.

Among these men were John Wallis, John Wilkins, Jonathan Goddard, Samuel Foster, Francis Glisson, and many others, all of whom were, fourteen years afterward, the founders of the Royal Society.

But proceedings like these were not congenial with the intellectual condition of England at that period.

A melancholy and somber spirit had overshadowed religion, and a mystical theology, almost Gnostic in its character had infected the best minds. Devotion had passed into enthusiasm and that into fanaticism, and sanguinary wars and revolutions were the result. It was then that such skillful hypocrites as Cromwell and Breton took advantage of this weakness for the purpose of concealing and advancing their own designs.

The taint of this dark and sad character is met with in all the science, the philosophy, and even in the oratory and poetry of the period.

Astrology and Theurgy were then in all their glory.

Chemistry, which took the place of experimental science, was as obscure as every other species of learning, and its facts were enveloped in the allegories of the Alchemists and the Rosicrucians.

A few learned men, disheartened by this obscuration of intellectual light, had organized a society in 1646; but as they were still imbued with a remnant of the popular prejudice, they were the partisans of the esoteric method of instruction, and did not believe that human knowledge should be exoterically taught so as to become accessible to all. Hence their society became a secret one.

The first members of this society were, says Nicolai, Elias Ashmole, the celebrated antiquary; William Lilly, a famous astrologer; Thomas Wharton, a physician; George Wharton; William Oughtred, a mathematician; Dr. John Hewitt, and Dr. John Pearson, both clergymen, and several others.

The annual festival of the Astrologers gave rise to this association.

It had previously held one meeting at Warrington, in Lancashire, but it was first firmly established at London.

Its object was to build the House of Solomon in a literal sense but the establishment was to remain as secret as the island of Bensalem in Bacon's New Atlantis,- that is, they were to be engaged in the study of nature, but the instructions were to remain within the society in an esoteric form; in other words, it was to be a secret society. Allegories were used by these philosophers to express their ideas.

First were the ancient columns of Hermes, by which Jamblichus pretended that he had enlightened all the doubts of Porphyry.

You then mounted, by several steps, to a checkered floor divided into four regions, to denote the four superior sciences, after which came the types of the six days, which expressed the object of the society.

All of which was intended to teach the doctrines that God created the world and preserves it by fixed principles, and that he who seeks to know these principles, by an investigation of the interior of nature, approximates to God and obtains from His grace the power of commanding nature.

This, says Nicolai, was the essence of the mystical and alchemical doctrine of the age, so that we may conclude that the society which he has been describing was in reality an association of alchemists, or rather of astrologers.

In these allegories, for which Nicolai may have been indebted to the alchemical writings of that period, to which he refers, or for which he may have drawn on his own imagination-we are uncertain which, as he sees no authorities-we may plainly detect Masonic symbols, such as the pillars of the porch of the Temple, the mystical ladder of steps, and the mosaic pavement, and thus it is that he seems to find an analogy between Freemasonry and the secret society that he has been describing.

He still further pursues the hypothesis of their identity in the following remarks: "It is known," he say, " that all who have the right of citizenship in London, whatever may be their rank or condition, must be recognized as members of some company or corporation.

But it is always easy for a man of quality or of letters to gain admission into one of these companies.

Now, several members of the society that has just been described were also members of the Company of Masons.

This was the reason of their holding their meetings at Masons' Hall, in Masons' Alley, Basinghall Street.

They all entered the company and assumed the name of Free and Accepted Masons, adopting, besides, all its external marks of distinction.

Free is the title which every member of this body assumes in England; the right or franchise is called Freedom,- the brethren call themselves Freemen, Accepted means, in this place, that this private society had been accepted or incorporated into that of the Masons, and thus it was that chance gave birth to that denomination of Freemasons which afterward became so famous, although it is possible that some allusion may also have been intended to the building of the House of Solomon, an allegory with which they were also familiar." Hence, according to the theory of Nicolai, two famous associations, each of a character peculiar to itself, were at the same period indebted to the same cause for their existence.

These were the Royal Society and the Freemasony " Both," he says, " had the same object and the difference in their proceedings arose only from a difference in some of the opinions of their members.

The one society had adopted as its maxim that the knowledge of nature and of natural science should be indiscriminately communicated to all classes of men, while the other contended that the secrets of nature should be restricted to a small number of chosen recipients.

The former body, which was the Royal Society, therefore held open meetings; the latter, which was the Society of Freemasons, enveloped its transactions in mystery." "In those days," says Nicolai, "the Freemasons were altogether devoted to the King and opposed to the Parliament, and they soon occupied themselves at their meetings in devising the means of sustaining the royal cause.

After the death of Charles I., in 1649, the Royalists becoming still more closely united, and, fearing to be known as such, they joined the assemblies of the Freemasons for the purpose of concealing their own identity, and the good intentions of that society being well known many persons of rank were admitted into it.

But as the objects which occupied their attention were no other than to diminish the number of the partisans of Parliament, and to prepare the way for the restoration of Charles II. to the throne, it would have been very imprudent to communicate to all Freemasonry without exception, the measures which they deemed it expedient to take, and which required an inviolable secrecy.

Accordingly they adopted the method of selecting a certain number of their members, who met in secret, and this committee, which had nothing at all to do with the House of Solomon, selected allegories, which had no relation to the former ones, but which were very appropriate to their design.

These new Masons took Death for their symbol.

They lamented the death of their master, Charles I; they nursed the hope of vengeance on his murderers; they sought to re-establish the Word, or his son, Charles II., for they applied to him the word Logos, which, in its theological sense, means both the Word and the Son; and the queen, Henrietta Maria, the relict of Charles I., being thenceforth the head of the party, they designated themselves the Widow's Sons.

"They agreed also upon private signs and modes of recognition, by which the friends of the royal cause might be able to distinguish each other from their enemies.

This precaution was of great utility to those who traveled, and especially to those of them who retired with the court to Holland, where, being surrounded by the spies of the Commonwealth, it was necessary to be exceedingly diligent in guarding their secret." Nicolai then proceeds to show how, after the death of Oliver Cromwell and the abdication of his son Richard, the administration of affairs fell into the hands of the chiefs of various parties, whence resulted confusion and dissensions, which tended to render the cause of the monarchy still more popular.

The generals of the army were, however, still opposed to any notion of a restoration and the hopes of the royalists centered upon General Monk, who commanded the army in Scotland, and who, it was known, had begun to look favorably on propositions which he had received in 1659 from the exiled King.

It then became necessary to bind their secret committee still more closely, that they might treat of Scottish affairs in reference to the interests of the King.

They selected new allegories, which symbolized the critical state to which they were reduced, and the virtues, such as prudence, pliancy, and courage, which were necessary to success.

They selected a new device and a new sign, and in their meetings spoke allegorically of taking care, in that wavering and uncertain condition of falling, lest the arms should be broken." It is probable that, in this last and otherwise incomprehensible sentence, Nicolai refers to some of the changes made in the High Degrees, fabricated about the middle of the 18th century, but whose invention he incorrectly, but like most Masonic historians of his day, attributes to an earlier date.

As some elucidation of what he says respecting the fact of failing and the broken arm, we find Nicolai afterward quoting a small dictionary which he says appeared about the beginning of the 18th century, and in which we meet with the following definition: "Mason's Wound, An imaginary wound above the elbow, to represent a fracture of the arm occasioned by a fall from an elevated place." "This," says Nicolai, "is the authentic history of the origin of the Society of Freemasons, and of the first changes that it underwent, changes which transformed it from an esoteric society of natural philosophers into an association of good patriots and loyal subjects; and hence it was that it subsequently took the name of the Royal Art as applied to Masonry." He concludes by affirming that the Society of Freemasons continued to assemble after the Restoration, in 1660, and even made, in 1663, several regulations for its preservation, but the zeal of its members was diminished by the changes which science and manners underwent during the reign of Charles II.

Its political character ceased by the advent of the king, and its esoteric method of teaching the natural sciencess must have been greatly interrupted.

The Royal Society, whose method had been exoteric and open, and from whose conferences politics were excluded, although its members were, in principle, opposed to the Restoration, had a more successful progress, and was joined by many of the Freemasons, the most prominent of whom was Elias Ashmole, who, Nicolai says, changed his opinions and became a member of the Royal Society.

But, to prevent its dissolution, the Society of Freemasons made several changes in its constitution, so as to give it a specific design.

This was undertaken and the symbols of the Society were altered so as to substitute the Temple of Solomon in the place of Bacon's House of Solomon, as a more appropriate allegory to express the character of the new institution. Nicolai thinks that the building of St. Paul's Church and the persecutions endured by Sir Christopher Wren may have contributed to the selection of these new symbols.

But on this point he does not insist.

Such is the theory of Nicolai.

Rejecting the idea that the origin of the Order of Freemasonry is to be traced to the founders of the Royal Society, he claims to have found it in a society of contemporaneous philosophers who met at Masons' Hall, in Basinghall Street, and assumed the name of Free and Accepted Masons, and who, claiming, in opposition to the views of the members of the Royal Society, that all s6ences should be communicated esoterically, therefore held their meetings in secret, their real object therefor being to nourish a political conspiracy for the advancement of the cause of the monarchy and the restoration of the exiled King.

Nicolai does not expressly mention the Astrologers, but it is very evident that he alludes to them as the so-called philosophers who originated this secret society, and to them, therefore, he attributes the invention of the Masonic system, as it now exists, after the necessary changes which policy and the vicissitudes of the times had induced.

Nicholas de Bonneville, the author of the essay entitled The Jesuits chased out of Freemasonry, entertained a similar opinion.

He says that in 1646 a society of Rosicrucians was formed at London, modeled on the ideas of the New Atlantis of Bacon.

It assembled in Masons' Hall, where Ashmole and other Rosicrucians modified the formula of reception of the Operative

Masons, which had consisted only of a few ceremonies used by craftsmen, and substituted a mode of initiation founded in part on the mysteries of Ancient Egypt and Greece.

They then fabricated the first degree of Masonry as ive non, have it, and, to distinguish themselves from common Masons, called themselves Freemasons.

Thory cites this without comment in his Acta Latomorum, and gives it as a part of the authentic annals of the Order. But ingenious and plausible as are these views, both of Nicolai and Bonneville, they unfortunately can not withstand the touchstone of all truth, the proofs of authentic history.

It will be seen that we have two hypotheses to investigate-first that advanced by the contributor to Wieland's Mercury, that the Society of Freemasons was originated by the founders of the Royal Society, and that maintained by Nicolai and Bonneville, that it owes its invention to the Astrologers who were contemporary with these founders.

Both hypotheses place the date of the invention in the same year, 1646, and give London as the place of the invention.

We must first direct our attention to the theory which maintains that the Royal Society was the origin of Freemasonry, and that the founders of that academy were the establishers of the Society of Freemasons.

This theory, first advanced, apparently, by the anonymous contributor to Wieland's Mercury, was exploded by Nicolai, in the arguments heretofore quoted, but something may be added to increase the strength of what he has said.

We have the explicit testimony of all the historians of that institution that it was not at all connected with the political contests of the day, and that it was founded only as a means of pursuing philosophical and scientific inquiries.

Dr. Thompson, who derives his information from the early records of the society, says that " it was established for the express purpose of advancing experimental philosophy, and that its foundation was laid during the time of the civil wars and was owing to the accidental association of several learned men who took no part in the disturbances which agitated Great Britain."[23] He adds that "about the year 1645 several ingenious men who resided in London and were interested in the progress of mathematics and natural philosophy agreed to meet once a week to discourse upon subjects connected with these sciences.

---

[23] "History of the Royal Society," by Thomas Thompson, M.D., F.R.S., LL.D. London, 1812, p. 1

These meetings were suspended after the resignation of Richard Cromwell, but revived in 1660, upon the Restoration."[24] They met at first in private rooms, but afterward in Gresham College and then in Arundel House.

Their earliest code of laws shows that their conferences were not in secret, but open to properly introduced visitors, as they still continue to be.

Weld, the librarian of the society, says that to it "attaches the renown of having from its foundation applied itself with untiring zeal and energy to the great objects of its institution."[25] He states that, although the society was not chartered until 1660, " there is no doubt that a society of learned men were in the habit of assembling together to discuss scientific subjects for many years previous to that time."[26] Spratt, in his history of the society, says that in the gloomy season of the civil wars they had selected natural philosophy as their private diversion, and that at their rneetings " they chiefly attended to some particular trials in Chemistry or Mechanics." The testimony of Robert Boyle, Wallis, and Evelyn, contemporaries of the founders, is to the same effect, that the society was simply philosophical in its character and without any political design Dr. Wallis, who was one of the original founders, makes this statement concerning the origin and objects of the society in his Account of some Passages in my own Life.[27] "About the year 1645, while I lived in London (at a time when, by our civil wars, academic studies were much interrupted in both our Universities), besides the conversation of divers eminent divines, as to matters theological, I had the opportunity of being acquainted with divers worthy persons inquisitive into natural philosophy and other paths of human learning, and particularly what has been called the New Philosophy or Experimental Philosophy.

We did, by agreements, divers of us meet weekly in London on a certain day to treat and discourse of such affairs." Wallis says that the subjects pursued by them related to physics, astronomy, and natural philosophy, such as the circulation of the blood, the Copernican system, the Torricellian experiment, etc.

In all these authentic accounts of the object of the society there is not the slightest allusion to it as a secret organization, nor any

---

[24] "History of the Royal Society," by Thomas Thompson, M.D., F.R.S., LL.D., London, 1812, p.1
[25] "A History of the Royal Society," with Memoirs of its Presidents, by Charles Richard Weld, Esq., 2 vols., London, 1848, I. 27
[26] Ibid
[27] In Hearne's edition of Langsteff's chronicle.

mention of a form of initiation, but only a reception by the unanimous vote of the members, which reception, as laid down in the bylaws consisted merely in the president taking the newly elected candidate by the found and saluting him as a member or fellow of the society.

The fact is that at that period many similar societies had been instituted in different countries of Europe, such as the Academia del Corriento at Florence and the Academy of Sciences at Paris, whose members, like those of the Royal Society of London, devoted themselves to the development of science.

This encouragement of scientific pursuits may be principally attributed to many circumstances that followed the revival of learning; the advent of Greeks into Western Europe, imbued with (Grecian literature; Bacon's new system of philosophy, which alone was enough to awaken the intellects of all thinking men; and the labors of Galileo and his disciples.

All these had prepared many minds for the pursuit of philosophy by experimental and inductive methods, which took the place of the superstitious dogmas of preceding ages.

It was through such influences as these, wholly unconnected with any religious or political aspirations, that the founders of the Royal Society were induced to hold their meetings and to cultivate without the restraints of secrecy their philosophical labors, which culminated in 1660 in the incorporation of an institution of learned men which at this day holds the most honored and prominent place among the learned societies of the world.

But it is in vain to look in this society, either in the mode of its organization, in the character of its members, or in the nature of their pursuits, for any connection with Freemasonry, an institution entirely different in its construction and its objects.

The theory, therefore, that Freemasonry is indebted for is origin to the Royal Society of London must be rejected as wholly without authenticity or even plausibility. But the theory of Nicolai, which attributes its origin to another contemporaneous society, whose members were evidently Astrologers, is somewhat more plausible, although equally incorrect.

Its consideration must, however, be reserved as the subject of another chapter.

CHAPTER XXXIV

THE ASTROLOGERS AND THE FREEMASONS

We have seen, in the preceding chapter, that Nicolai had sought to trace the origin of Freemasonry to a society organized in 1646 by a sect of philosophers who were contemporary with, but entirely distinct from, those who founded the Royal Society.

Though he does not explicitly state the fact, yet, from the names of the persons to whom he refers, there can be no doubt that he alluded to the Astrologers, who at that time were very popular in England.

Judicial astrology, or the divination of the future by the stars, was, of all the delusions to which the superstition of the Middle Ages gave birth, the most popular.

It prevailed over all Europe, so that it was practiced by the most learned, and the predictions of its professors were sought with avidity and believed with confidence by the most wealthy and most powerful. Astrologers often formed a part of the household of princes, who followed their counsels in the most important matters relating to the future, while men and women of every rank sought these charlatans that they might have their nativities cast and secure the aid of their occult art in the recovery of stolen goods or the prognostications of happy marriages or of successful journeys.

Astrology was called the Daughter of Astronomy, and the scholars who devoted themselves to the study of the heavenly bodies for the purposes of pure science were often called upon to use their knowledge of the stars for the degrading purpose of astrological predictions.

Kepler, the greatest astronomer of that age, was compelled against his will to pander to the popular superstition, that he might thus gain a livelihood and be enabled to pursue his nobler studies.

In one of his works he complains that the scanty reward of an astronomer would not provide him with bread, if men did not entertain hopes of reading the future in the heavens. And so he tampered with the science that he loved and adorned, and made predictions for inquisitive consulters, although, at the same time, he declared to his friends that "they were nothing but worthless conjecture." Cornelius Agrippa, though he cultivated alchemy, a delusion but little more respectable than that of astrology, when commanded by his patroness, the Queen mother of France, to practice the latter, expressed his annoyance at the task.

Of the Astrologers he said, in his great work on the Vanity of the Arts and Sciences, "these fortune tellers do find entertainment among princes and magistrates, from whom they receive large salaries; but, indeed, there is no class of men who are more pernicious to a commonwealth.

For, as their skill lies in the adaptation of ambiguous predictions to events after they have happened, so it happens that a man who lives by falsehood shall by one accidental truth obtain more credit than he will lose by a hundred manifest errors." The 16th and 17th centuries were the golden age of astrology in England. We know all that is needed of this charlatanism and of the character of its professors from the autobiography of William Lilly, himself an English astrologer of no mean note; perhaps, indeed, the best-educated and the most honest of those who practiced this delusion in England in the 17th century, and who is one of those to whom Nicolai ascribes the formation of that secret society, in 1646, which invented Freemasonry.

It will be remembered that Nicolai says that of the society of learned men who established Freemasonry, the first members were Elias Ashmole, the skillful antiquary, who was also a student of astrology, William Lilly, a famous astrologer, George Wharton, likewise an astrologer, William Oughtred, a mathematician, and some others.

He also says that the annual festival of the Astrologers gave rise to this association. "It had previously held ," says Nicolai, "one meeting at Warrington, in Lancashire, but it was first firmly established at London." Their meetings, the same writer asserts, were held at Masons' Hall, in Masons' Alley, Basinghall Street.

Many of them were members of the Masons' Company, and they all entered it and assumed the title of Free and Accepted Masons, adopting, besides, all its external marks of distinction.

Such is the theory which makes the Astrologers, incorporating themselves with the Operative Masons, who met at their Hall in Basinghall Street, the founders of the Speculative Order of Free and Accepted Masons as they exist at the present day.

It is surprising that in a question of history a man of letters of the reputation of Nicolai should have indulged in such bold assumptions and in statements so wholly bare of authority.

But unfortunately it is thus that Masonic history has always been written.

I shall strive to eliminate the truth from the fiction in this narrative.

The task will be a laborious one, for, as Goethe has well said in one of his maxims "It is much easier to perceive error than to find truth. The former lies on the surface, so that it is easily reached; the latter lies in the depth, which it is not every man's business to search for." The Astrologers, to whose meeting in the Masons' Hall is ascribed the origin of the Freemasons, were not a class of persons who would have been likely to have united in such an attempt, which showed at least a desire for some intellectual progress.

Lilly, perhaps the best-educated and the most honest of these charlatans, has in the narrative of his life, written by himself, given us some notion of the character of many of them who lived in London when he practiced the art in that city.[28] Of Evans, who was his first teacher, he tells us that he was a clergyman - of Staffordshire, whence he "had been in a manner enforced to fly for some offences very scandalous committed by him "; of another astrologer, Alexander Hart, he says " he was but a cheat." Jeffry Neve he calls, a smatterer; William Poole was a frequenter of taverns with lewd people and fled on one occasion from London under the suspicion of complicity in theft; John Booker, though honest was ignorant of his profession; William Hodges dealt with angels, but " his life answered not in holiness and sanctity to what it should," for he was addicted to profanity; and John A Windsor was given to debauchery.

Men of such habits of life were not likely to interest themselves in the advancement of science or in the establishment of a society of speculative philosophers.

It is true that these charlatans lived at an earlier period than that ascribed by Nicolai to the organization of the society in Masons'

---

[28] "The Life of William Lilly, Student in Astology, wrote by himself in the 66th year of his Age, at Hersham, in the Parish of Walton upon Thames, in the County of Surrey, Propria Manu."

Hall, but in the few years that elapsed it is not probable that the disciples of astrology had much improved in their moral or intellectual condition.

Of certain of the men named by Nicolai as having organized the Society of Freemasons in 1646, we have some knowledge.

Elias Ashmole, the celebrated antiquary, and founder of the Ashmolean Museum in the University of Oxford, is an historical character.

He wrote his own life, in the form of a most minute diary, extending from July 2, 1633, to October 9, 1687. In this diary, in which he registers the most trivial as well as the most important events of his life-recording even the cutting of his wisdom teeth, or the taking of a sudorific-he does not make the slightest allusion to the transaction referred to by Nicolai.

The silence of so babbling a chronicler as to such an important event is itself sufficient proof that it did not occur. What Ashmole has said about Freemasonry will be presently seen.

Lilly, another supposed actor in this scene, also wrote his life with great minuteness.

His complete silence on the subject is equally suggestive. Nicolai says that the persons he cites were either already members of the Company of Masons or at once became so.

Now, Lilly was a member of the Salter's Company, one of the twelve great livery companies, and would not have left it to join a minor company, which the Masons was.

Oughtred could not have been united with Ashmole in organizing a society in 1646, for the latter, in a note to Lilly's life, traces his acquaintance with him to the residence of both as neighbors in Surrey.

Now, Ashmole did not remove to Surrey until the year 1675, twenty nine years after his supposed meeting with Oughtred at the Masons Hall.

Between Wharton and Lilly, who were rival almanac-makers, there was, in 1646, a bitter feud, which was not reconciled until years afterward.

In an almanac which Wharton published in 1645 he had called Lilly " an impudent, senseless fellow, and by name William Lilly." It is not likely that they would have been engaged in the fraternal task of organizing a great society at that very time.

Dr. Pearson, another one of the supposed founders, is celebrated in literary and theological history as the author of an Exposition of the Creed.

Of a man so prominent as to have been the Master of Jesus College, Cambridge, and afterward Bishop of Chester, Ashmole makes no mention in his diary.

If he had ever met him or been engaged with him in so important an affair, this silence in so minute a journal of the transactions of his every-day life would be inexplicable.

But enough has been said to show the improbability of any such meeting as Nicolai records. Even Ashmole and Lilly, the two leaders, were unknown to each other until the close of the year 1646.

Ashmole says in his diary of that year: Mr. Jonas Moore brought and acquainted me with Mr. William Lilly: it was on a Friday night, and I think on the 20th Nov. (1646)." That there was an association, or a club or society, of Astrologers about that time in London is very probable.

Pepys, in his memoirs, says that in October, 1660, he went to Mr. Lilly's, "there being a club that night among his friends." There he met Esquire Ashmole and went home accompanied by Mr. Booker, who, he says, " did tell me a great many fooleries, which may be done by nativities, and blaming Mr. Lilly for writing to please his friends, and not according to the rules of art, by which he could not well eue as he had done" The club, we may well suppose, was that of the Astrologers, held at the house of the chief member of the profession.

That it was not a secret society we conclude from the fact that Pepys, who was no astrologer, was permitted to be present.

We know also from Ashmole's diary that the Astrologers held an annual feast, generally in August, sometimes in March, July, or November, but never on a Masonic festival.

Ashmole regularly attended it from 1649 to 1658, when it was suspended, but afterward revived, in 1682.

In 1650 he was elected a steward for the following year he mentions the place of meeting only three times, twice at Painters' Hall, which was probably the usual place, and once at the Three Cranes, in Chancery Lane. Had the Astrologers and the Masons been connected, Masons' Hall, in Basinghall Street, would certainly have been the place for holding their feast.

Again, it is said by Nicolai that the object of this secret society which organized the Freemasons was to advance the restoration of the King.

But Lilly had made, in 1645, the year before the meeting, this declaration: "Before that time, I was more Cavalier than Roundbead, but after that I engaged body and soul the cause of Parliament." He still expressed, it is true, his attachment to monarchy; but his life during the Commonwealth showed his devotion to Cromwell, of whom he was a particular favorite.

After the Restoration he had to sue out a pardon, which was obtained by the influence of his friends, but which would hardly have been necessary if he had been engaged in a secret society the object of which was to restore Charles II to the throne.

But Charles I was not beheaded until 1649, so that a society could not have been organized in 1646 for the restoration of his son.

But it may be said that the Restoration alluded to was of the monarchy, which at that time was virtually at an end.

So this objection may pass without further comment.

But the fact is that the whole of this fiction of the organization, 1646, of a secret society by a set of philosophers or astrologers, or both, which resulted in the establishment of Freemasonry, arose out of a misconception or a misrepresentation - whether willful or not, I will not say-of two passages in the diary of Elias Ashmole.

Of these two passages, and they are the only ones in his minute diary of fifty-four years in which there is any mention of Freemasonry, the first is as follows: "1646, Octob. 16- 4 Hor. 30 minutes post merid. I was made a Free- Mason at Warrington in Lancashire, with Colonel Henry Mainwarring of Karticham in Cheshire; the names of those that were then at the lodge, Mr. Richard Penket Warden, Mr. James Collier, Mr. Richard Sankey, Henry Littler, John Ellam, and Hugh Brewer." And then, after an interval of thirty-five years, during which there is no further allusion to Masonry, we find the following memoranda: " 1682, Mar. 10. About 5 Hor. Post merid. I received a summons to appear at a lodge to be held the next day at Masons Hall, London.

II. Accordingly I went, and about noon was admitted into the fellowship of Freemasons, by Sir William Wilson Knight, Captain Richard Borthwick, Mr. William Wodman, Mr. William Grey, Mr. Samuel Taylour, and Mr. William Wise.

"I was the senior fellow among them (it being thirty-five years since I was admitted) there was present besides myself, the fellows after mentioned. Mr. Thomas Wise, Master of the Masons Company, this present year; Mr. Thomas Shorthose, Mr. Thomas Shadbolt, Wardsford, Esq; Mr. Nicholas Young, Mr. John Shorthose, Mr. William Hamon, Mr. John Thompson, and Mr. William Stanton. We all dined at the Half-Moon-Tavern, in Cheapside, at a noble dinner prepared at the charge of the new accepted Masons." Without the slightest show of reason or semblance of authority, Nicolai transmutes the Lodge at Warrington, in which Ashmole was made a Freemason, into an annual feast of the Astrologers.

The Society of Astrologers, he says, "had previously held one meeting at Warrington, in Lancashire, but it was first firmly established at London." And he cites as His authority for this statement the very passage from Ashinole's diary in which that antiquary records his reception in a Masonic Lodge.

These events in the life of Ashmole, which connect him with the Masonic fraternity, have given considerable embarrassment to Masonic scholars who have been unable to comprehend the two apparently conflicting statements that he was made a Freemason at Warrington in 1646 and afterward received into the fellowship of the Freemasons, in 1682, at London.

The embarrassment and misapprehension arose from the fact that we have unfortunately no records of the meetings of the Operative Lodges of England in the 17th century, and nothing but traditional and generally mythical accounts of their usages during that period.

The sister kingdom of Scotland has been more fortunate in this respect, and the valuable work of Brother Lyon, on the History of the Lodge of Edinborough, has supplied us with authentic records of the Scottish Lodges at a much earlier date.

These records will furnish us with some information in respect to the contemporaneous English Lodges which was have every reason to suppose were governed by usages not very different from those of the Lodges in the adjacent kingdom. Mr. Lyon has on this subject the following remarks, which may be opportunely quoted on the present occasion.

"The earliest date at which non-professionals are known to have been received into an English Lodge is 1646.

The evidence of this is derived from the diary of one of the persons so admitted; but the preceding minutes[29] afford authentic instances of Speculative Masons having been admitted to the fellowship of the Lodge of Edinburgh twelve years prior to the reception of Colonel Main warring and Elias Ashmole in the Lodge of Warrington and thirty-eight years before the date at which the presence of Gentleman Masons is first discernible in the Lodge of Kilwinning by the election of Lord Cassillis to the deaconship.

---

[29] Minutes of the Lodge of Cannongate, Kilwinning, for 1635, quoted by him in a precedding page.

It is worthy of remark that, with singularly few exceptions, the non-operatives who were admitted to Masonic fellowship in the Lodges of Edinburgh and Kilwinning, during the 17th century, were persons of quality, the most distinguished of whom, as the natural result of its metropolitan position, being made in the former Lodge.

Their admission to fellowship in an institution composed of Operative Masons associated together for purposes of their Craft would in all probability originate in a desire to elevate its position and increase its influence, and once adopted, the system would further recommend itself to the Fraternity by the opportunities which it presented for cultivating the friendship and enjoying the society of gentlemen to whom in ordinary circumstances there was little chance of their ever being personally known.

On the other hand, non-professionals connecting themselves with the Lodge by the ties of membership would, we believe, be actuated partly by a disposition to reciprocate the feelings that had prompted the bestowal of the fellowship partly by curiosity to penetrate the arcana of the Craft, and partly by the novelty of the situation as members of a secret society and participants in its ceremonies and festivities.

But whatever may have been the rnotives which animated the parties on either side, the tie which united them was a purely honorary one."[30] What is here said by Lyon of the Scottish Lodges may, I think, be with equal propriety applied to those of England at the same period.

There was in 1646 a Lodge of Operative Masons at Warrington, just as there was a similar one at Edinburgh.

Into this Lodge Colonel Mainwarring and Elias Ashmole, both non- professional gentlemen, were admitted as honorary members, or, to use the language of the latter, were " made Freemasons," a technical term that has been preserved to the present day.

But thirty-five years afterward, being then a resident of London, he was summoned to attend a meeting of the Company of Masons, to be held at their hall in Masons' Alley, Basinghall Street, and there, according to His own account, he was "admitted into the fellowship of Freemasons." How are we to explain this apparent double or renewed admission? But mark the difference of language.

In 1646 he was "made a Freemason." In 1682 he was admitted into the fellowship of Freemasons." The distinction is an important one.

---

[30] Lyon, "History of the Lodge of Edinburgh," p. 81

The Masons' Company in 1682 constituted in London one of those many city companies which embraced the various trades and handicrafts of the metropolis.

Stowe, in his Survey of London, says that " the Masons, otherwise termed Freemasons, were a society of ancient standing and good reckoning, by means of affable and kind meetings divers time, and as a loving brotherhood should use to do, did frequent their mutual assemblies in the time of King Henry IV, in the 12th year of whose most gracious reign they were incorporated." In Cheswell's New View of London, printed in 1708, it is said that the Masons' Company "were incorporated about the year 1410, having been called the Free Masons, a Fraternity of great account, who have been honored by several Kings, and very many of the Nobility and Gentry being of their Society.

They are governed by a Master, 2 Wardens, 25 Assistants, and there are 65 on the Livery." Maitland, in his London and its Environs, says, speaking of the Masons: "This company had their arms granted by Clarencieux, King-at-Arms, in the year 1477, though the members were not incorporated by letters patent till they obtained them from King Charles II. in 1677.

They have a small convenient hall in Masons' Alley, Basinghall Street." There were then, in the time of Ashmole, two distinct bodies of men practicing the Craft of Operative Masonry, namely, the Lodges which were to be found in various parts of the country, and the Company of Masons, whose seat was at London.

Into one of the Lodges, which was situated at Warrington, in Lancashire, Ashmole had in 1646 received honorary membership, which, in compliance with the technical language of that and of the present day, he called being "made a Freemason." But this did not constitute him a member of the Masons' Company of London, for this was a distinct incorporated society, with its exclusive rules and regulations, and admission into which could only be obtained by the consent of the members.

There were many Masons who were not members of the Company.

Ashmole, who had for thirty-five years been a Freemason, by virtue of his making at Warrington, was in 1682 elected a member of this Masons' Company, and this he styles being "admitted into the fellowship of Freemasons "-that is, he was admitted to the fellowship or membership of the Company and made " free " of it.

From all of which we may draw the following conclusions: First, that in 1646, at the very date assigned by Nicolai for the organization of the Freemasons as a secret political society, under the leadership of Ashmole and Lilly, the former, being as yet unacquainted with the latter, was at Warrington, in Lancashire, where he found a Lodge of Masons already organized and with its proper officers and its members, by whom he was admitted as an honorary non-professional member of the Craft.

And secondly, that while in London be was admitted, being already a Freemason, to the fellowship of the Masons' Company.

And thirdly, that he was also a member of the fraternity of Astrologers, having been admitted probably in 1649, and regularly attended their annual feast from that year to 1658, when the festival, and perhaps the fraternity, was suspended until 1682, when it was again revived.

But during all this time it is evident from the memoranda of Ashmole that the Freemasons and the Astrologers were two entirely distinct bodies.

Lilly, who was the head of the Astrologers, was, we may say almost with certainty, not a Freemason, else the spirit of minuteness with which he has written his autobiography would not have permitted him to omit what to his peculiar frame of maid would have been so important a circumstance as connecting him still more closely with his admired friend, Elias Ashmole, nor would the latter have neglected to record it in his diary, written with even still greater minuteness than Lilly's memoirs.

Notwithstanding the clear historical testimony which shows that Lodges of Freemasons had been organized long before the time of Ashmok, and that he had actually been made a Freemason in one of them, many writers, both Masonic and profane, have maintained the erroneous doctrine that Ashmole was the founder of the Masonic Society.

'Thus Chambers, in their Encyclopedia say that " Masonry was founded by Ashmole some of his literary friends," and De Quincey expressed the same opinion.

Mr. John Yarker, in his very readable Notes on the Scientific and Religious Mysteries of Antiquity, offers a modified view and a compromise of the subject.

He refers to the meeting of the chemical adepts at Masons' Hall (a fact of which we have no evidence), and then to the "Feast of the Astrologers " which Ashmole attended.

He follows Nicolai in asserting that their allegories were founded on Bacon's House of Solomon, and says that they used as emblems the sun, moon, square, triangle, etc.

And he concludes, "it is possible that Ashmole may have consolidated the customs of the two associations, but there is no evidence that any Lodge of this, his speculative rite, came under the Masonic Constitution."[31] We may also say that it is possible that Ashmole may have invented a speculative rite of some kind, but there is no evidence that he did so.

Many things are possible that are not probable, and many probable that are not actual.

History is made up of facts, and not of possibilities or probabilities.

Ashmole himself entertained a very different and much more correct notion of the origin of Masonry than any of those who have striven to claim him as its founder.[32]

Dr. Knipe, of Christ Church, Oxford, in a letter to the publisher of Ashmole's Life, says: " What from Mr. E. Ashmole's collections I could gather was, that the report of our society's taking rise from a bull granted by the Pope in the reign of Henry III, to some Italian architects to travel over all Europe, to erect chapels, was illfounded.

Such a bull there was, and these architects were Masons; but this bull, in the opinion of the learned Mr. Ashmole, was confirmative only, and did not, by any means, create our Fraternity, or even establish them in this kingdom." This settles the question.

Ashmole could not have been the founder of Freemasonry in London in 1646, since he himself expressed the belief that the Institution had existed in England before the 13th century.

There is no doubt, as I have already said, that he was very intimately connected with the Astrologers.

Dr. Krause, in his Three Oldest Documents of the Masonic Brotherhood, quotes the following passage from Lilly's History of my Life and Titles. (I can not find it in my own copy of that work, but the statements are corroborated by Ashmole's diary.) " "The King's affairs being now grown desperate, Mr. Ashmole withdrew himself, after the surrender of the Garrison of Worcester, into Cheshire, where he continued till the end of October, and then came up to London, where he became acquainted with Master, afterwords Sir Jonas Moore, Mr. William Lilly, and Mr. John Booker, esteemed the greatest astrologers iii the world, by whom he was caressed, instructed and received into their fraternity, which then made a very considerable figure, as appeared by the great resort of persons of distinction to their annual feast, of which

---

[31] "Notes on the Scientific and Religious Mysteries of Antiquity," p. 106
[32] "Die drei altesten Kunsturkunden der Freimaurerbruderschaft," IV., 286

Mr. Ashmole was afterwards elected Steward." Ashmole left Worcester for Cheshire July 24, 1646, and moved from Cheshire to London October 25, of the same year.

In that interval of three months he was made a Freemason, at Warrington.

At that time he was not acquainted with Lilly, Moore, or Booker, and knew nothing of astrology or of the great astrologers.

This destroys the accuracy of Nicolai's assertion that the meeting held at Masons' Hall, in 1682, by Ashmole, Lilly, and other astrologers, when they founded the Society of Freemasons, was preceded by a similar and initiatory one, in 1646, at Warrington.

A few words must now be said upon the subject of Bacon's House of Solomon, which Nicolai and others supposed to have first given rise to the Masonic allegory which was afterward changed to that of the Temple of Solomon.

Bacon, in his fragmentary and unfinished romance of the New Atlantis, had devised the fable of an island of Bensalem, in which was an institution or college called the House of Solomon, the fellows of which were to be students of philosophy and investigators of science.

He thus described their occupations: "We have twelve that sail into foreign countries, who bring in the books and patterns of experiments of all other parts; these we call merchants of light.

We have three that collect the experiments that are in all books; these are called depredators.

We have three that collect experiments of all mechanical arts, and also of liberal sciences, and also of practices which are not brought into the arts; these we call mystery men.

We have three that try new experiments such as themselves think good; these we call pioneers or miners. We have three that draw the experiments of the former four into titles and tablets to give the better light for the drawing of observations and axioms out of them; these we call compilers.

We have three that bind themselves looking into the experiments of their fellows and cast about how to draw out of them things of use and practice for man's life and knowledge as well for iworks as for plain demonstrations and the easy and clear discovering of the virtues and parts of bodies; these we call doing men and benefactors. Then after divers meetings and consults of our whole number to consider of the former labors and collections, we have three to take care out of them to direct new experiments of higher light, more penetrating into nature than the former; these we call lamps.

We have three others that do execute the experiments so directed and report them; these we call inoculators.

Lastly we have three that raise the former discoveries by experiments into greater observations, axioms and aphorisms; these we call interpreters of nature."[33] It is evident from this schedule of the occupations of the inmates of the House of Solomon that it could not in the remotest degree have been made the foundation of a Masonic allegory.

In fact, the suggestion of a Masonic connection could have been derived only from a confused idea of the relation of the House to the Temple of Solomon, a misapprehension which a reading of the New Atlantis would readily remove.

As Plato had written his Republic and Sir Thomas More his Utopia to give their ideas of a model commonwealth, so Lord Bacon commenced his New Atlantis to furnish his idea of a model college to be instituted for the study and interpretation of nature by experimental methods. These views were first introduced in his Advancement of Human Learning, and would have been perfected in his New Atlantis had he ever completed it.

The new philosophy of Bacon had produced a great revolution in the minds of thinking men, and that group of philosophers who in the 17th century, as Dr. Whewell says, "began to knock at the door where truth was to be found " would very wisely seek the key in the inductive and experimental method taught by Bacon.

To the learned men, therefore, who first met at the house of Dr. Goddard and the other members, and whose meetings finally ended in the formation of the Royal Society, the allegory of the House of Solomon very probably furnished valuable hints for the pursuit of their experimental studies.

To Freemasons in any age the allegory would have been useless and unprofitable, and could by no ingenious method have been twisted into a foundation for their symbolic science The hypothesis that it was adopted in 1646 by the founders of Freemasonry as a fitting allegory for their esoteric system of instruction is evidently too absurd to need further refutation.

In conclusion, we may unhesitatingly concur with Bro. W. J. Hughan in his opinion that the theory which assigns the foundation of Freemasonry to Elias Ashmole and his friends the Astrologers " is opposed to existing documents dating before and since his initiation." It

---

[33] "New Atlantis," Works, vol. ii., p. 376

is equally opposed to the whole current of authentic history, and is unsupported by the character of the Institution and true nature of its symbolism.

CHAPTER XXXV

THE ROSICRUCIANS AND THE FREEMASONS

Of all the theories which have been advanced in relation to the origin of Freemasonry from some one of the secret sects, either of antiquity or of the Middle Ages, there is none more interesting than that which seeks to connect it with the Hermetic philosophy, because there is none which presents more plausible claims to our consideration.

There can be no doubt that in some of what are called the High Degrees there is a very palpable infusion of a Hermetic element.

This can not be denied, because the evidence will be most apparent to any one who examines their rituals, and some by their very titles, in which the Hermetic language and a reference to Hermetic principles are adopted, plainly admit the connection and the influence.

There is, therefore, necessity to investigate the question whether or not some of those High or Philosophic Degrees which were fabricated about the middle of the last century are or are not of a Hermetic character, because the time of their invention, when Craft Masonry was already in a fixed condition, removes them entirely out of the problem which relates to the origin of the Masonic Institution.

No matter when Freemasonry was established, the High Degrees were an afterthought, and might very well be tinctured with the principles of any philosophy which prevailed at the period of their invention.

But it is a question of some interest to the Masonic scholar whether at the time of the so-called Revival of Freemasonry, in the early part of the 18th century, certain Hermetic degrees did not exist which sought to connect themselves with the system of Masonry.

And it is a question of still greater interest whether this attempt was successful so far, at least, as to impress upon the features of that early

Freemasonry a portion of the characteristic tints of the Hermetic philosophy, some of the marks of which may still remain in our modern system.

But as the Hermetic philosophy was that which was invented and taught by the Rosicrucians, before we can attempt to resolve these important and interesting questions, it will be necessary to take a brief glance at the history and the character of Rosicrucianism.

On the 17th of August, 1586, Johann Valentin Andred was born at Herrenberg, a small market-town of what was afterward the kingdom of Wurtemburg. After a studious youth, during which he became possessed of a more than moderate share of learning, he departed in 1610 on a pilgrimage through Germany, Austria, Italy, and France, supplied with but little money, but with an indomitable desire for the acquisition of knowledge. Returning home, in 1614, he embraced the clerical profession and was appointed a deacon in the town of Vaihingen, and by subsequent promotions reached, in 1634, the positions of Protestant prelate of the Abbey of Bebenhausen and spiritual counsellor of the Duchy of Brunswick.

He died on the 27th of June, 1654, at the ripe age of sixty-eight years.

On the moral character of Andred his biographers have lavished their encomiums.

A philanthropist from his earliest life, he carried, or sought to carry, his plans of benevolence into active operation.

Wherever, says Vaughan, the church, the school, the institute of charity have fallen into ruin or distress, there the indefatigable Andred sought to restore them.

He was, says another writer, the guardian genius and the comforter of the suffering; he was a practical helper as well as a theoretical adviser; in the times of dearth and famine, many thousand poor were fed and clothed by his exertions, and the town of Kalw, of which, in 1720, he was appointed the superintendent, long enjoyed the benefit of many charitable institutions which owed their origin to his solicitations and zeal.

It is not surprising that a man indued with such benevolent feelings and actuated by such a spirit of philanthropy should have viewed with deep regret the corruptions of the times in which he lived, and should have sought to devise some plan by which the condition of his fellow-men might be ameliorated and the dry, effete[34] theology of the church be converted into some more living, active, humanizing system.

For the accomplishment of this purpose he could see no better method than the establishment of a practical philanthropical fraternity, one that did not at that time exist, but the formation of which he resolved to suggest to such noble minds as might be stimulated to the enterprise.

With this view he invoked the assistance of fiction, and hence there appeared, in 1615, a work which he entitled the Report of the Rosicrucian Brotherhood, or, in its original Latin, Fama Fraternitatis Rose Crucis.

An edition had been published the year before with the title of Universal Reformation of the Whole World, with a Report of the Worshipful Order of the Rosicrucian Brotherhood, addressed to all the Learned Men and Nobility of Europe.[35] There was another work, published in 1616, with the title of Chemische Hochzeit, or Chemical Nuptials, by Christian Rosencreutz.

All of these books were published anonymously, but they were universally attributed to the pen of Andreá, and were all intended for one purpose, that of discovering by the character of their reception who were the true lovers of wisdom and philanthropy, and of inducing them to come forward to the perfection of the enterprise, by transforming this fabulous society into a real and active organization. The romantic story of Christian Rosencreutz, the supposed founder of the Order, is thus told by Andrea.

I have borrowed for the most part the language of Mr. Sloane,[36] who, although his views and deductions on the subject are for the most part erroneous, has yet given us the best English epitome of the myth of Andreá.

According to Andrea's tale, a certain Christian Rosencreutz, though of good birth, found himself compelled from poverty to enter the cloister at a very early period of life.

He was only sixteen years old when one of the monks purposed a pilgrimage to the Holy Sepulcher, and Rosencreutz, as a special favor, was permitted to accompany him.

---

[34] Biographical Sketch by Wm. Bell, in Freemasons' Quarterly Magazine, London, vol. ii., N.S., 1854, p. 27
[35] " Allgemeine und General Reformation der ganzen, weiten Welt. Beneben der Fama Fraternitatis des Loblichen Ordens des Rosencreutzes, an alle Gelehrte und Haupter Europae geschreiben," Cassel, 1614.
[36] "New Curiosities of Literature," vol. ii., p. 44

At Cyprus the monk is taken ill, but Rosencreutz proceeds onward to Damascus with the intention of going on to Jerusalem.

While detained in the former city by the fatigues of his journey, he hears of the wonders performed by the sages of Damascus, and, his curiosity being excited, he places himself under their direction.

Three years having been spent in the acquisition of their most hidden mysteries, he sets sail from the Gulf of Arabia for Egypt.

There he studies the nature of plants and animals and then repairs, in obedience to the instructions of his Arabian masters, to Fez, in Africa.

In this city it was the custom of the Arab and African sages to meet annually for the purpose of communicating to each other the results of their experience and inquiries, and here he passed two years in study. He then crossed over to Spain, but not meeting there with a favorable reception, he returned to his native country.

But as Germany was then filled with mystics of all kinds, his proposals for a reformation in morals and science meets with so little sympathy from the public that he resolves to establish a society of his own.

With this view he selects three of his favorite companions from his old convent.

To them, under a solemn vow of secrecy, he communicates the -knowledge which he had acquired during his travels.

He imposes on them the duty of committing it to writing and of forming a magical vocabulary for the benefit of future students.

But in addition to this task they also undertook to prescribe gratuitously for all the sick who should ask their assistance, and as in a short time the concourse of patients became so great as materially to interfere with their other duties, and as a building which Rosencreutz had been erecting, called the Temple of the Holy Ghost, was now completed, he determines to increase the number of the brotherhood, and accordingly initiates four new members.

When all is completed, and the eight brethren are instructed in the mysteries of the Order, they separate, according to agreement, two only staying with Father Christian.

The other six, after traveling for a year, are to return and communicate the results of their experience.

The two who had stayed at home are then to be relieved by two of the travelers, so that the founder may never be alone, and the six again divide and travel for a year.

The laws of the Order as they had been prescribed by Rosencreutz were as follows: 1. That they should devote themselves to no other Occupation than that of the gratuitous practice of physic. 2. That they were not to wear a particular habit, but were to conform in this respect to the customs of the country in which they might happen to be. 3. That each one was to present himself on a certain day in the year at the Temple of the Holy Ghost, or send an excuse for his absence. 4. That each one was to look out for a brother to succeed him in the event of his death. 5. That the letters R. C. were to be their seal, watchword, and title. 6. That the brotherhood was to be kept a secret for one hundred years.

When one hundred years old, Christian Rosencreutz died, but the place of his burial was unknown to any one but the two brothers who were with him at the time of his death, and they carried the secret with them to the grave.

The society, however, continued to exist unknown to the world, always consisting of eight members only, until another hundred and twenty years had elapsed, when, according to a tradition of the Order, the grave of Father Rosencreutz was to be discovered, and the brotherhood to be no longer a mystery to the world.

It was about this time that the brethren began to make some alterations in their building, and thought of removing to another and more fitting situation the memorial tablet, on which were inscribed the names of their associates.

The plate, which was of brass, was affixed to the wall by means of a nail in its center, and so firmly was it fastened that in tearing it away a portion of the plaster of the wall became detached and exposed a concealed door.

Upon this door being still further cleansed from the incrustation, there appeared above it in large letters the following words: POST CXX ANNOS PATEBO - after one hundred and twenty years I will be opened.

Although the brethren were greatly delighted at the discovery, they so far restrained their curiosity as not to open the door until the next morning, when they found themselves in a vault of seven sides each side five feet wide and eight feet high.

It was lighted by an artificial sun in the center of the arched roof, while in the middle of the floor, instead of a tomb, stood a round altar covered with a small brass plate, on which was this inscription: A. C. R. C. Hoc, universi compendium, vivus mihi sepulchrum feci- while living, I made this epitome of the universe my sepulcher.

About the outer edge was: Jesus mihi omnia -, Jesus is all things to me.

In the center were four figures, each enclosed in a circle, with these words inscribed around them: 1.Nequaquam vacuus. 2.Legis Jugum. 3.Liberias Evangelii 4.Dei gloria intacia.

That is - 1. By no means void. 2. The yoke of the Law. 3. The liberty of the Gospel. 4. The unsullied Glory of God.

On seeing all this, the brethren knelt down and returned thanks to God for having made them so much wiser than the rest of the world.

Then they divided the vault into three parts, the roof, the wall, and the pavement.

The first and the last were divided into seven triangles, corresponding to the seven sides of the wall, each of which formed the base of a triangle, while the apices met in the center of the roof and of the pavement.

Each side was divided into ten squares, containing figures and sentences which were to be explained to the new initiates.

In each side there was also a door opening upon a closet, wherein were stored up many rare articles, such as the secret books of the Order, the vocabulary of Paracelsus, and other things of. a similar nature.

In one of the closets they discovered the life of their founder; in others they found curious mirrors, burning lamps, and a variety of objects intended to aid in rebuilding the Order, which, after the lapse of many centuries, was to fall into decay.

Pushing aside the altar, they came upon a strong brass plate, which being removed, they beheld the corpse of Rosencreutz as freshly preserved as on the day when it had been deposited, and under his arm a volume of vellum with letters of gold, containing, among other things, the names of the eight brethren who had founded the Order.

Such is an outline of the story of Christian Rosencreutz and his Rosicrucian Order as it is told in the Fama Fraternitatis.

It is very evident that Andrea composed this romance - for it is nothing else not to record the existence of any actual society, but only that it might serve as a suggestion to the learned and the philanthropic to engage in the establishment of some such benevolent association.

"He hoped;" says Vaughan, " that the few nobler minds whom he desired to organize would see through the veil of fiction in which he had invested his proposal; that he might communicate personally with some such, if they should appear, or that his book might lead them to form among themselves a practical philanthropic confederacy answering to the serious purpose he had embodied in his fiction."[37] But his design was misunderstood then, as it has been since, and everywhere his fable was accepted as a fact.

Diligent search was made by the credulous for the discovery of the Temple of the Holy Ghost.

Printed letters appeared continually, addressed to the unknown brotherhood, seeking admission into the fraternity-a fraternity that existed only in the pages of the Fama.

But the irresponsive silence to so many applications awoke the suspicions of some, while the continued mystery strengthened the credulity of others.

The brotherhood, whose actual house "lay beneath the Doctor's hat of Valentin Andred," was violently attacked and as vigorously defended in numerous books and pamphlets which during that period flooded the German press.

The learned men among the Germans did not give a favoring ear to the philanthropic suggestions of Andred, but the mystical notions contained in his fabulous history were seized with avidity by the charlatans, who added to them the dreams of the alchemists and the reveries of the astrologers, so that the post-Andrean Rosicrucianism became a very different thing from that which had been devised by its original author.

It does not, however, appear that the Rosicrucians, as an organized society, made any stand in Germany.

Descartes says that after strict search he could not find a single lodge in that country.

But it extended, as we will presently see, into England, and there became identified as a mystical association.

It is strange what misapprehension, either willful or mistaken, has existed in respect to the relations of Andrea to Rosicrucianism.

We have no more right or reason to attribute the detection of such a sect to the German theologian than we have to ascribe the discovery of the republic of Utopia to Sir Thomas More, or of the island of Bensalem to Lord Bacon.

In each of these instances a fiction was invented on which the author might impose his philosophical or political thoughts, with no dream that readers would take that for fact which was merely intended for fiction.

---

[37] "Hours with the Mystics," vol. ii., p. 103

And yet Rhigellini, in his Masonry Considered as the Result of the Egyptian, Jewish, and Christian Religions, while declining to express an opinion on the allegorical question, as if there might be a doubt on the subject, respects the legend as it had been given in the Fama, and asserting that on the return of Rosencreutz to Germany " he instituted secret societies with an initiation that resembled that of the early Christians."[38] He antedates the Chemical Nuptials ials of Andred a century and a half, ascribes the authorship of that work to Christian Rosencreutz, as if he were a real personage, and thinks that he established, in 1459, the Rite of the Theosophists, the earliest branch of the Rose Croix, or the Rosicrucians; for the French make no distinction in the two words, though in history they are entirely different.

History written in this way is worse than fable-it is an ignis fatuus which can only lead astray.

And yet this is the method in which Masonic history has too often been treated.

Nicolai, although the deductions by which he connects Freemasonry with Rosicrucianism are wholly untenable, is yet, in his treatment of the latter, more honest or less ignorant. He adopts the correct view when he says that the Fama Fraternitatis only announced a general reformation and exhorted all wise men to unite in a proposed society for the purpose of removing corruption and restoring wisdom.

He commends it as a charming vision, full of poesy and imagination, but of a singular extravagance very common in the writings of that age.

And he notes the fact that while the Alchemists have sought in that work for the secrets of their mysteries, it really contains the gravest satire on their absurd pretensions.

The Fama Fraternitatis had undoubtedly excited the curiosity of the Mystics, who abounded in Germany at the time of its appear. ance, of whom not the least prominent were the Alchemists.

These, having sought in vain for the invisible society of the Rosicrucians, as it had been described in the romance of Andred, resolved to form such a society for themselves.

But, to the disappointment and the displeasure of the author of the Fama, they neglected or postponed the moral reformation which he had sought, and substituted the visionary schemes of the Alchemists, a body of quasi-philosophers who assigned their origin as students of

---

[38] "La Maconnerie consideree comme le resultant des Religions Egyptienne, Juive et Chretienne," L. iii., p. 108

nature and seekers of the philosophers stone and the elixir of immortality to a very remote period.

Thus it is that I trace the origin of the Rosicrucians, not to Valentin Andrea, nor to Christian Rosencreutz, who was only the coinage of his brain, but to the influence exerted by him upon certain Mystics and Alchemists who, whether they accepted the legend of Rosencreutz as a fiction or as a verity, at least made diligent use of it in the establishment of their new society.

I am not, therefore, disposed to doubt the statement of L. C. Orvius, as cited by Nicolai, that in 1622 there was a society of Alchemists at The Hague, who called themselves Rosicrucians and claimed Rosencreutz as their founder.

Michael Maier, the physician of the Emperor Rudolf II., devoted himself in the early part of the 17th century to the pursuits of alchemy, and, having adopted the mystical views of the Rosicrucians, is said to have introduced that society into England.

Maier was the author of many works in Latin in defense and in explanation of the Rosicrucian system.

Among them was an epistle addressed "To all lovers of true chemistry throughout Germany, and especially to that Order which has hitherto lain concealed, but is now probably made known by the Report of the Fraternity (Fama Fraternitatis) and their admirable Confession."[39] In this work he uses the following language: "What is contained in the Fama and confessio is true.

It is a very childish objection that the brotherhood have promised so much and performed so little.

The Masters of the Order hold out the Rose as a remote reward, but they impose the Cross on all who are entering.

Like the Pythagoreans and the Egyptians, the Rosicrucians extract vows of silence and secrecy.

Ignorant men have treated the whole as a fiction; but this has arisen from the probation of five years to which they subject even well qualified novices, before they are admitted to the higher mysteries, and within that period they are taught how to govern their own tongues! Although Maier died in 1622, it appears that he had lived long enough to take part in the organization of the Rosicrucian sect, which had been formed out of the suggestions of Andred.

---

[39] "Omnibus verae chymiae Amantibus per Germaniam, et precipere illi Ordini adhue delitescenti, at Fama Fraternitatis et confessione sua admiranda et probabile manifestato."

His views on this subject were, however, peculiar and different from those of most of the new disciples.

He denied that the Order had derived either its origin or its name from the person called Rosencreutz.

He says that the founder of the society, having given his disciples the letters R. C. as a sign of their fraternity, they improperly made out of them the words Rose and Cross.

But these heterodox opinions were not accepted by the Rosicrucians in general, who still adhered to Andrea's legend as the source and the signification of their Order.

At one time Maier went to England, where he became intimately acquainted with Dr. Robert Fludd, the most famous as well as the earliest of the English Rosicrucians.

Robert Fludd was a physician of London, who was born in 1574 and died in 1637.

He was a zealous student of alchemy, theosophy, and every other branch of mysticism, and wrote in defense of Rosicrucianism, of which sect he was an active member.

Among his earliest works is one published in 1616 under the title of A Compendious Apology clearing the Fraternity of the Rosy Cross from the stains of suspicion and infamy cast upon them.

There is much doubt whether Maier communicated the system of Rosicrucianism to Fludd or whether Fludd had already received it from Germany before the visit of Maier.

The only authority for the former statement is De Quincey (a most unreliable one), and the date of Fludd's Apology militates against it.[40]

Fludd's explanation of the name of the sect differs from that of both Andrea and Maier.

It is, he says, to be taken in a figurative sense, and alludes to the cross dyed with the blood of Christ.

In this explanation he approaches very nearly to the idea entertained by the members of the modern Rose Croix degree.

No matter who was the missionary that brought it over, it is very certain that Rosicrucianism was introduced from Germany, its birthplace, into England at a very early period of the 17th century, and it is equally certain that after its introduction it flourished, though an exotic, with more vigor than it ever had in its native soil.

---

[40] "Apologia Compendiaria, Fraternitatem de Rosea Cruce suspicionis et infamiae maculis aspersum abluens."

That there were in that century, and even in the beginning of the succeeding one, mystical initiations wholly unconnected with Freemasonry, but openly professing a Hermetic or Rosicrucian character and origin, may very readily be supposed from existing documents.

It is a misfortune that such authors as Buhle, Nicolai, and Rhigellini, with many others, to say nothing of such nonmasonic writers as Sloane and De Quincey, who were necessarily mere sciolists in all Masonic studies, should have confounded the two institutions, and, because both were mystical, and one appeared to follow (although it really did not) the other in point of time, should have proclaimed the theory (wholly untenable) that Freemasonry is indebted for its origin to Rosicrucianism.

The writings of Lilly and Ashmole, both learned men for the age in which they lived, prove the existance of a mystical philosophy in England in the 17th century, in which each of them was a participant. The Astrologers, who were deeply imbued with the Hermetic philosophy, held their social meetings for mutual instruction and their annual feasts, and Ashmole gives hints of his initiation into what I suppose to have been alchemical or Rosicrucian wisdom by one whom he reverently calls " Father Backhouse." But we have the clearest documentary testimony of the existence of a Hermetic degree or system at the beginning of the 18th century, and about the time of what is called the Revival of Masonry in England, by the establishment of the Grand Lodge at London, and which, from other undoubted testimony, we know were not Masonic.

This testimony is found in a rare work, some portions of whose contents, in reference to this subject, are well worthy of a careful review.

In the year 1722 there was published in London a work in small octave bearing the following title:[41] "Long Livers: A curious History of such Persons of both Sexes who have lived several Ages and grown Young again: With the rare Secret of Rejuvenescency of Arnoldus de Villa Nova.

And a great many approved and invaluable Rules to prolong Life: Also how to prepare the Universal Medicine.

Most humbly dedicated to the Grand Master, Masters, Wardens, and Brethren of the Most Ancient and Honorable Fraternity of the FREE MASONS of Great Britain and Ireland.

By Engenius Philaiethes, F. R. S., Author of the Treatise of the Plague. Viri Fratres audite me.

---

[41] A copy of this work, and, most probably, the only one in this country, is in the valuable library of Bro. Carson, of Cincinnati, and to it I am indebted for the extracts that I have made.

Act. xv. 13. Diligite Fraternitatem timete Deum honorate Regem.1. Pet. ii. 17. LONDON.

Printed for J. Holland, at the Bible and Ball, in St. Paul's Church Yard, and L. Stokoe, at Charing Cross, 1722." pp. 64-199.

Engenius Philalethes was the pseudonym of Thomas Vaughn, a celebrated Rosicrucian of the 17th century, who published, in 1659, a translation of the Fama Fraternitatis into English.

But, as he was born in 1612, it is not to be supposed that he wrote the present work.

It is, however, not very important to identify this second Philalethes.

It is sufficient for our purpose to know that it is a Hermetic treatise written by a Rosicrucian, of which the title alone-the references to the renewal of youth, one of the Rosicrucian secrets, to the recipe of the great Rosicrucian Villa Nova, or Arnold de Villaneuve, and to the Universal Medicine, the Rosicrucian Elixir Vitae-would be sufficient evidence.

But the only matter of interest in connection. with the present subject is that this Hermetic work, written, or at least printed, in 1722, one year before the publication of the first edition of Anderson's constitutions, refers explicitly to the existence of a higher initiation than that of the Craft degrees, which the author seeks to interweave in the Masonic system.

This is evidently shown in portions of the dedication, which is inscribed to - the Grand Master, Masters, Wardens, and Brethren of the Most Ancient and Most Honorable Fraternity of the Free Masons of Great Britain and Ireland"; and it is dedicated to them by their " Brother Engenius Philalethes." This fraternal subscription shows that he was a Freemason as well as a Rosicrucian, and therefore must have been acquainted with both systems.

The important fact, in this dedication, is that the writer alludes, in language that can not be mistaken, to a certain higher degree, or to a more exalted initiation, to the attainment of which the primitive degrees of Ancient Craft Masonry were preparatory.

Thus he says, addressing the Freemasons: "I present you with the following sheets, as belonging more properly to you than any else.

But what I here say, those of you who are not far illuminated, who stand in the outward place and are not worthy to look behind the veil, may find no disagreeable or unprofitable entertainment; and those who are so happy as to have greater light, will discover under these shadows, somewhat truly great and noble and worthy the serious attention of a genius the most elevated and sublime-the spiritual, celestial cube, the only true, solid, and immovable basis and foundation of all knowledge, peace, and happiness." (Page iv.) Another passage will show that the writer was not only thoroughly acquainted with the religious, philosophical, and symbolic character of the institution, but that he wrote evidently under the impression (rather I should say the knowledge) that at that day others besides himself had sought to connect Freemasonry with Rosicrucianism.

He says: "Remember that you are the salt of the earth, the light of the world, and the fire of the universe.

Ye are living stones, built up a spiritual house, who believe and rely on the chief Lapis Angularis, which the refractory and disobedient builders disallowed; you are called from darkness to light; you are a chosen generation, a royal priesthood." Here the symbolism is Masonic, but it is also Rosicrucian.

The Masons had derived their symbol of the STONE from the metaphor of the Apostle, and like him had given it a spiritual signification.

The Rosicrucians had also the Stone as their most important symbol.

"Now," says one of them, "in this discourse will I manifest to thee the natural condition of the Stone of the Philosophers, apparelled with a triple garment, even this Stone of Riches and Charity, the Stone of Relief from Languishment - in which is contained every secret; being a Divine Mystery and Gift of God, than which there is nothing more sublime."[42] It was natural that a Rosicrucian, iii addressing Freemasons, should refer to a symbol common to both, though each derived its interpretation through a different channel.

In another passage he refers to the seven liberal arts, of which he calls Astronomy "the grandest and most sublime."

Quoted by Hitchcock in his "Alchemy and the Alchemists," p. 39 This was the Rosicrucian doctrine.

In that of the Freemasons the precedency is given to Geometry.

Here we find a difference between the two institutions which proves their separate and independent existence.

Still more important differences will be found in the following passages, which, while they intimate a higher degree, show that it was a Hermetic one, which, however, the Rosicrucian writer was willing to ingraft on Freemasonry.

---

[42] Dialogue of Arislaus in the Alchemist's Enchiridion, 1672.

He says: "And now, my Brethren, you of the higher class (note that he does not call it a degree) permit me a few words, since you are but few; and these few words I shall speak to you in riddles, because to you it is given to know those mysteries which are hidden from the unworthy.

"Have you not seen then, my dearest Brethren, that stupendous bath, filled with the most limpid water, than which no pure can be purer, of such admirable mechanism, that makes even the greatest philosopher gaze with wonder and astonishment, and is the subject of the contemplation of the wisest men.

Its form is a quadrate sublimely placed on six others, blazing all with celestial jewels, each angularly supported with four lions.

Here repose our mighty King and Queen, (I speak foolishly, I am not worthy to be of you), the King shining in his glorious apparel of transparent, incorruptible gold, beset with living sapphires; he is fair and ruddy, and feeds among the lilies; his eyes, two carbuncles, the most brilliant, darting prolific never-dying fires; and his large, flowing hair, blacker than the deepest black or plumage of the long-lived crow; his royal consort vested in tissue of immortal silver, watered with emeralds, pearl and coral. O mystical union! O admirable commerce! "Cast now your eyes to the basis of this celestial structure, and you will discover just before it a large basin of porphyrian marble, receiving from the mouth of a large lion's head, to which two bodies displayed on each side of it are conjoined, a greenish fountain of liquid jasper.

Ponder this well and consider.

Haunt no more the woods and forests; (I speak as a fool) haunt no more the fleet; let the flying eagle fly unobserved; busy yourselves no longer with the dancing idiot, swollen toads, and his own tail- devouring dragon; leave these as elements to your Tyrones.

" The object of your wishes and desires (some of you may, perhaps have attained it, I speak as a fool), is that admirable thing which has a substance, neither too fiery nor altogether earthy, nor simply watery; neither a quality the most acute or most obtuse, but of a middle nature, and light to the touch, and in some manner soft, at least not hard, not having asperity, but even in some sort sweet to the taste, odorous to the smell, grateful to the sight, agreeable and delectable to the hearing, and pleasant to the thought; in short, that one only thing besides which there is no other, and yet everywhere possible to be found, the blessed and most sacred subject of the square of wise men, that is....... I had almost blabbed it out and been sacrilegiously perjured.

I shall therefore speak of it with a circumlocution yet more dark and obscure, that none but the Sons of Science and those who are illuminated with the sublimest mysteries and profoundest secrets of MASONRY may understand.

. . It is then what brings you, my dearest Brethren, to that pellucid, diaphanous palace of the true disinterested lovers of wisdom, that triumphant pyramid of purple salt, more sparkling and radiant than the finest Orient ruby, in the center of which reposes inaccessible light epitomized, that incorruptible celestial fire, blazing like burning crystal, and brighter than the sun in his full meridian glories, which is that immortal, eternal, never-dying PYROPUS; the King of genius, whence proceeds everything that is great and wise and happy.

"These things are deeply hidden from common view, and covered with pavilions of thickest darkness, that what is sacred may not be given to dogs or your pearls cast before swine, lest they trample them under foot, and turn again and rend you." All this is Rosicrucian thought and phraseology.

Its counterpart may be found in the writings of any of the Hermetic philosophers.

But it is not Freemasonry and could be understood by no Freemason relying for his comprehension only on the teaching he had received in his own Order.

It is the language of a Rosicrucian adept addressed to other adepts, who like himself had united with the Fraternity of Freemasons, that they might out of its select coterie choose the most mystical and therefore the most suitable candidates to elevate them to the higher mysteries of their own brotherhood.

That Philalethes and his brother Rosicrucians entertained an opinion of the true character of Speculative Masonry very different from that taught by its founders is evident from other passages of this Dedication.

Unlike Anderson, Desaguliers, and the writers purely Masonic who succeeded them, the author of the Dedication establishes no connection between Architecture and Freemasonry.

Indeed it is somewhat singular that although he names both David and Solomon in the course of his narrative, it is with little respect, especially for the latter, and he does not refer, even by a single word, to the Temple of Jerusalem.

The Freemasonry of this writer is not architectural, but altogether theosophic.

It is evident that as a Hermetic philosopher he sought to identify the Freemasons with the disciples of the Rosicrucian sect rather than with the Operative Masons of the Middle Ages.

This is a point of much interest in the discussion of the question of a connection between the two associa- tions, considering that this work was published only five years after the revival.

It tends to show not that Freemasonry was established by the Rosicrucians, but, on the contrary, that at that early period the latter were seeking to ingraft themselves upon the former, and that while they were willing to use the simple degrees of Craft Masonry as a nucleus for the growth of their own fraternity, they looked upon them only as the medium of securing a higher initiation, altogether unmasonic in its character and to which but few Masons ever attained.

Neither Anderson nor Desaguliers, our best because contemporary authority for the state of Masonry in the beginning of the 18th century, give the slightest indication that there was in their day a higher Masonry than that described in the Book of Constitutions of 1723.

The Hermetic clement was evidently not introduced into Speculative Masonry until the middle of the 18th century, when it was infused in a fragmentary form into some of the High Degrees which were at that time fabricated by certain of the Continental manufacturers of Rites.

But if, as Engenius Philalethes plainly indicates, there were in the year 1723 higher degrees, or at least a higher degree, attached to the Masonic system and claimed to be a part of it, which possessed mystical knowledge that was concealed from the great body of the Craft, " who were not far illuminated, who stood in the outward place and were not worthy to look behind the veil "-by which it is clearly implied that there was another class of initiates who were far illuminated, who stood within the inner place and looked behind the veil-then the question forces itself upon us, why is it that neither Anderson nor Desaguliers nor any of the writers of that period, nor any of the rituals, make any allusion to this higher and more illuminated system? The answer is readily at hand.

It is because no such system of initiation, so far as Freemasonry was concerned, existed.

The Master's degree was at that day the consummation and perfection of Speculative Masonry There was nothing above or beyond it.

The Rosicrucians, who, especially in their astrological branch, were then in full force in England, had, as we see from this book, their own initiation into their Hermetic and theosophic system.

Freemasonry then beginning to become popular and being also a mystical society, these mystical brethren of the Rosy Cross were ready to enter within its portals and to take advantage of its organization.

But they soon sought to discriminate between their own perfect wisdom and the imperfect knowledge of their brother Masons, and, Rosicrucian-like, spoke of an arcana which they only possessed.

There were some Rosicrucians who, like Philalethes, became Freemasons, and some Freemasons, like Elias Ashmole, who became Rosicrucians.

But there was no legitimate derivation of one from the other.

There is no similarity between the two systems-their origin is different; their symbols, though sometimes identical, have always a different interpretation; and it would be an impossible task to deduce the one historically from the other.

Yet there are not wanting scholars whose judgment on other matters has not been deficient, who have not hesitated to trace Freemasonry to a Rosicrucian source.

Some of these, as Buhle, De Quincey, and Sloane, were not Freemasons, and we can easily ascribe their historical errors to their want of knowledge, but such writers as Nicolai and Reghellini have no such excuse for the fallacy of which they have been guilty.

Johann Gottlieb Buhle was among the first to advance the hypothesis that Freemasonry was an off shoot of Rosicrucianism.

This he did in a work entitled On the Origin and the Principal a Events ,of the Orders of Rosicrucianism and Freemasonry [43] published in 1804.

His theory was that Freemasonry was invented in the year 1629, by John Valentin Andrea, and hence that it sprang out of the Rosicrucian system or fiction which was the fabrication of that writer.

His fallacious views and numerous inaccuracies met with many refutations at the time, besides those of Nicolai, produced in the work which has been heretofore cited.

Even De Quincey himself, a bitter but flippant adversary of Freemasonry, and who translated, or rather paraphrased, the views of Buhle, does not hesitate to brand him as illogical in his reasoning and confused in his arrangement.

---

[43] "Uber den Ursprung und die vornehmstem Schicksale des Ordens der Rosenkreutzen und Freimauer."

Yet both Nicolai and De Quincey have advanced almost the same hypothesis, though that of the former is considerably modified in its conclusions.

The flippancy and egotism of De Quincey, with his complete ignorance as a profane, of the true elements of the Masonic institution, hardly entitle his arguments to a serious criticism.

His theory and his self-styled facts may be epitomized as follows: He thinks that the Rosicrucians where attracted to the Operative Masons by the incidents, attributes and legends of the latter, and that thus the two Orders were brought into some connection with each other.

The same building that was used by the guild of Masons offered a desirable means for the secret assemblies of the early Freemasons, who, of course, were Rosicrucians.

An apparatus of implements and utensils, such as was presented in the fabulous sepulcher of Father Rosencreutz, was introduced, and the first formal and solemn Lodge of Freemasons on which occasion the name of Freemasons was publicly made known, was held in Masons' Hall, Masons' Alley, Basinghall Street, London, in the year 1646.

Into this Lodge he tells us that Elias Ashmole was admitted.

Private meetings he says may have been held, and one at Warrington in Lancashire, which is mentioned in Ashmole's Life, but the name of a Freemasons' Lodge, with the insignia, attributes, and circumstances of a Lodge, first, he assures us, came forward at the date above mentioned.

All of this he tells us, is upon record, and thus refers to historical testimony, though he does not tell us where it is to be found.

Now, all these statements we know, from authentic records, to be false.

Ashmole is our authority, and he is the very best authority, because he was an eye-witness and a personal actor in the occurrences which he records.

It has already been seen, by the extracts heretofore given from Ashmole's diary, that there is no record of a Lodge held in 1646 at Masons' Hall; that the Lodge was held, with all ,the attributes and circumstances of a Lodge," at Warrington; that Ashmole was then and there initiated as a Freemason, and not at London; and finally, that the record of the Lodge held at Masons' Hall, London, which is made by the same Ashmole, was in 1683 and not in 1646, or thirty- five years afterward.

An historian who thus falsifies records to sustain a theory is not entitled to the respectful attention of a serious argument.

And so De Quincey may be dismissed for what he is worth.

I do not concede to him the excuse of ignorance for he evidently must have had Ashmole's diary under his eyes, and his misquotations could only have been made in bad faith.

Nicolai is more honorable in his mode of treating the question.

He does not attribute the use of Freemasonry directly and immediately from the Rosicrucian brotherhood.

But he thinks that its mystical theosophy was the cause of the outspring of many other mystical associations, such as the Theosophists, and that, passing over into England, it met with the experimental philosophy of Bacon, as developed especially in his New Atlantis, and that the combined influence of the two, the esoteric principles of the one and the experimental doctrines of the other, together with the existence of certain political motives, led to a meeting of philosophers who established the system of Freemasonry at Masons' Hall in 1646.

He does not explicitly say so, -but it is evident from the names that he gives that these philosophers were Astrologers, who were only a sect of the Rosicrucians devoted to a specialty.

The theory and the arguments of Nicolai have already been considered in the preceding chapter of this work, and need no further discussion here.

The views of Rhigellini are based on the book of Nicolai, and differ from them only in being, from his Gallic ignorance of English history, a little more inaccurate.

The views of Rhigellini have already been referred to on a preceding page.

And now, we meet with another theorist, who is scarcely more respectful or less flippant than De Quincey, and who, not being a Freemason, labors under the disadvantage of an incorrect knowledge of the principles of the Order.

Besides we can expect but little accuracy from one who quotes as authentic history the spurious Leland Manuscript.

Mr. George Sloane, in a very readable book published in London in 1849, under the title of New Curiosities of Literature, has a very long article in his second volume on The Rosicrucians and Freemasons.

Adopting the theory that the latter are derived from the former, he contends, from what he calls proofs, but which are no proofs at all, that " the Freemasons are not anterior to the Rosicrucians; and their principles, so far as they were avowed about the middle of the 17th century, being identical, it is fair to presume that the Freemasons were, in reality, the first incorporated body of Rosicrucians or Sapientes." As he admits that this is but a presumption, and as presumptions are not facts, it is hardly necessary to occupy any time in its discussion.

But he proceeds to confirm his presumption, in the following way.

"In the Fama of Andrea," he says, " we have the first sketch of a constitution which bound by oath the members to mutual secrecy, which proposed higher and lower grades, yet leveled all worldly distinctions in the common bonds of brotherhood, and which opened its privileges to all classes, making only purity of mind and purpose the condition of reception." This is not correct.

Long before the publication of the Fama Fraternitatis there were many secret associations in the Middle Ages, to say nothing of the Mysteries of antiquity, in which such constitutions prevailed, enjoining secrecy under the severest penalties, dividing their system of esoteric instruction into different grades, establishing a bond of brotherhood, and always making purity of life and rectitude of conduct the indispensable qualifications for admission.

Freemasonry needed not to seek the model of such a constitution from the Rosicrucians.

Another argument advanced by Mr. Sloane is this: "The emblems of the two brotherhoods are the same in every respect- the plummet, the level, the compasses, the cross, the rose, and all the symbolic trumpery which the Rosicrucians named in their writings as the insignia of their imaginary associations, and which they also would have persuaded a credulous,,, world concealed truths ineffable by mere language; both, too, derived their wisdom from Adam, adopted the same myth of building, connected themselves in the same unintelligible way with Solomon's Temple, affected to be seeking light from the East-in other words, the Cabala-and accepted the heathen Pythagoras among their adepts." In this long passage there are almost as many errors and mis- statements as there are lines.

The emblems of the two Orders were not the same in any respect.

The square and compasses were not ordinary nor usual Rosicrucian emblems.

In one instance, in a plate in the Azoth Philosophorum of Basil Valentine, published in the 17th century, we will, it is true, find these implements forming part of a Rosicrucian figure but they are there evidently used as phallic symbols, a meaning never attached to them in Freemasonry, whose interpretation of them is derived from their operative use.

Besides, we know, from a relic discovered near Limerick, in Ireland, that the square and the level were used by the Operative Masons as emblems in the 16th or, perhaps, the 15th century, with the same signification that is given to them by the Freemasons of the present day.

The Speculative Masons delved nearly all of their symbols from the implements and the language of the Operative art; the Rosicrucians took theirs from astronomical and geometrical problems, and were connected in their interpretations with a system of theosophy and not with the art of building.

The cross and the rose, referred to by Mr. Sloane, never were at any time, not even at the present day, emblems recognized in Craft Masonry, and were introduced into such of the High Degrees fabricated about the middle of the 18th century as had in them a Rosicrucian element.

Again, the Rosicrucians had nothing to do with the Temple of Solomon.

Their "invisible house," or their Temple, or "House of the Holy Ghost," was a religious and philosophic idea, much more intimately connected with Lord Bacon's House of Solomon in the Island of Bensalem than it was with the Temple of Jerusalem. And, finally, the early Freemasons, like their successors of the present day, in "seeking light from the East," intended no reference to the Cabala, which is never mentioned in any of their primitive rituals, but alluded to the East as the source of physical light - the place of sunrising, which they adopted as a symbol of intellectual and moral light.

It would, indeed, be easier to prove from their symbols that the first Speculative Masons were sun-worshippers than that they were Rosicrucians, though neither hypothesis would be correct.

If any one will take the trouble of toiling through the three books of Cornelius Agrippa's Occult Philosophy, which may be considered as the text-book of the old Rosicrucian philosophy, he will see how little there is in common between Rosicrucianism and Freemasonry.

The one is a mystical system founded on the Cabala; the other the outgrowth of a very natural interpretation of symbols derived from the usages and the implements of an operative art.

The Rosicrucians were theosophists, whose doctrines were of angels and demons of the elements, of the heavenly bodies and their influence on the affairs of men, and of the magical powers of numbers, of suffumigations, and other sorceries.

The Alchemists, who have been called "physical Rosicrucians," adopted the metals and their transmutation, the elixir of life, and their universal solvent, as symbols, if we may believe Hitchcock[44] by which they concealed the purest dogmas of a religious life.

But Freemasonry has not and never had anything of this kind in its system.

Its founders were, as we will see when we come to the historical part of this work, builders, whose symbols, applied in their architecture, were of a religious and Christian character; and when their successors made this building fraternity a speculative association, they borrowed the symbols by which they sought to teach their philosophy, not from Rosicrucianism, not from magic, nor from the Cabala, but from the art to which they owed their origin.

Every part of Speculative Masonry proves that it could not have been derived from Rosicrucianism.

The two Orders had in common but one thing-they both had secrets which they scrupulously preserved from the unhallowed gaze of the profane.

Andrea sought, it is true, in his Fama Fraternitatis, to elevate Rosicrucianism to a more practical and useful character, and to make it a vehicle for moral and intellectual reform.

But even his system, which was the only one that could have exerted any influence on the English philosophers, is so thoroughly at variance in its principles from that of the Freemasonry of the 17th century, that a union of the two, or the derivation of one from the other, must have been utterly impracticable.

It has been said that when Henry Cornelius Agrippa was in London, in the year 1510, he founded a secret society of Rosicrucians.

This is possible although, during; his brief visit to London, Agrippa was the guest of the learned Dean Colet, and spent his time with his host in the study of the works of the Apostle to the Gentiles.

"I labored hard," he says himself, "at the Epistles of St. Paul." Still he may have found time to organize a society of Rosicrucians.

In the beginning of the 16th century secret societies "chiefly composed" says Mr. Morley, " of curious and learned youths had become numerous, especially among the Germans, and towards the close of that century these secret societies were developed into the form of

---

[44] "Remarks upon Alchemy and the Alchemists," passim.

brotherhoods of Rosicrucians, each member of which gloried in styling himself Physician, Theosophist, Chemist, and now, by the mercy of God, Rosicrucian."[45] But to say of this society, established by Agrippa in England in 1510 (if one was actually established), as has been said by a writer of the last century that " the practice of initiation, or secret incorporation, thus and then first introduced has been handed down to our own times, and hence, apparently, the mysterious Eleusinian confederacies now known as the Lodges of Freemasonry,"[46] is to make an assertion that is neither sustained by historical testimony nor supported by any chain of reasoning or probability.

I have said that while the hypothesis that Freemasonry was originally derived from Rosicrucianism, and that its founders were the English Rosicrucians in the 17th century, is wholly untenable, there is no doubt that at a later period, a century after this, its supposed origin, a Rosicrucian clement, was very largely diffused in the Hautes Grades or High Degrees which were invented on the continent of Europe about the middle of the 18th century.

This subject belongs more appropriately to the domain of history than to that of legend, but its consideration will bring us so closely into connection with the Rosicrucian or Hermetic philosophy that I have thought that it would be more convenient not to dissever the two topics, but to make it the subject of the next chapter.

---

[45] "The Life of Henry Cornelius Agrippa von Netteshuri," by Henry Morley, vol. i., p. 58
[46] Monthly Review, London, 1798 vol. xxv., p. 30 P. 351

CHAPTER XXXVI

THE ROSICRUCIANISM OF THE HIGH DEGREES

The history of the High Degrees of Masonry begins with the inventions of the Chevalier Michael Ramsay, who about the year 1728 fabricated three which he called Ecossais, Novice, and Knight Templar.

But the inventions of Ramsay had nothing in them of a Rosicrucian character.

They were intended by him to support his hypothesis that Freemasonry originated in the Crusades, and that the first Freemasons were Templars.

His degrees were therefore not philosophic but chivalric.

The rite-manufacturers who succeeded him, followed for the most part in his footsteps, and the degrees that were subsequently invented partook of the chivalric and military character, so that the title of " Chevalier " or " Knight," unknown to the early Freemasons, became in time so common as to form the designation in connection with another noun of most of the new degrees.

Thus we find in old and disused Rites, as well as in those still existing, such titles as " Knight of the Sword," " Knight of the Eagle," " Knight of the Brazen Serpent," and so many more that Ragon, in his Nomenclature, furnishes us with no less than two hundred and ninety-two degrees of Masonic Knighthood, without having exhausted the catalogue.

But it was not until long after the Masonic labors of Ramsay had ceased that the element of Hermetic philosophy began to intrude itself into still newer degrees.

Among the first to whom we are to ascribe the responsibility of this novel infusion is a Frenchman named Antoine Joseph Pernelty, who was born in 1716 and died in 1800, having passed, therefore, the most active and rigorous portion of his life in the midst of that flood of Masonic novelties which about the middle quarters of the 18th century inundated the continent of Europe and more especially the kingdom of France.

Pernelty was at first a Benedictine monk, but, having at the age of forty-nine obtained a dispensation from his vows, he removed from Paris to Berlin, where for a short time he served Frederick the Great as his librarian.

Returning to Paris, he studied and became infected with the mystical doctrines of Swedenborg, and published a translation of one of the most important of his works. He then repaired to Avignon, where he established a new Rite, which, on its transference to Montpellier, received the name of the " Academy of True Masons." Into this Rite it may well be supposed that he introduced much of the theosophic mysticism of the Swedish sage, in parts of which there is a very strong analogy to Rosicrucianism, or at least to the Hermetic Doctrines of the Rosicrucians. It will be remembered that the late General Hitchcock, who was learned on mystical topics, wrote a book to prove that Swedenborg was a Hermetic philosopher; and the arguments that he advances are not easily to be confuted.

But Pernelty was not a Swedenborgian only.

He was a man of multifarious reading and had devoted his studies, among other branches of learning, to theology, philosophy, and the mathematical sciences.

The appetite for a mystical theology, which had led him to the study and the adoption of the views of Swedenborg, would scarcely permit him to escape the still more appetizing study of the Hermetic philosophers.

Accordingly we find him inventing other degrees, and among them one, the " Knight of the Sun," which is in its original ritual a mere condensation of Rosicrucian doctrines, especially as developed in the alchemical branch of Rosicrucianism.

There is not in the wide compass of Masonic degrees, one more emphatically Rosicrucian than this.

The reference in its ritual to Sylphs, one of the four elementary spirits of the Rosicrucians; to the seven angels which formed a part of the Rosicrucian hierarchy; the dialogue between Father Adam and Truth in which the doctrines of Alchemy and the Cabala are discussed in the search of man for theosophic truth, and the adoption as its principal word of recognition of that which in the Rosicrucian system was deemed the primal matter of all things, are all sufficient to prove the Hermetic spirit which governed the founder of the degree in its fabrication.

There have been many other degrees, most of which are now obsolete, whose very names openly indicate their Hermetic origin. Such are the "Hermetic Knight," the "Adept of the Eagle" (the word adept being technically used to designate an expert Rosicrucian), the "Grand Hermetic Chancellor," and the " Philosophic Cabalist." The list might be increased by fifty more, at least, were time and space convenient.

There have been whole rites fabricated on the basis of the Rosicrucian or Hermetic philosophy, such as the "Rite of Philalethes" the "Hermetic Rite," and the "Rite of Illuminated Theosophists," invented in 1767 by Benedict Chartanier, who united in it the notions of the Hermetic philosophy and the reveries of Swedenborg.

Gadicke tells us also, in his Freimaurer-Lexicon, of a so-called Masonic system which was introduced by the Marquis of Lernais into Berlin in 1758, the objects of which were the Hermetic arcana and the philosopher's stone.

But the Hermetic degree which to the present day has exercised the greatest influence upon the higher grades of Masonry is that of the Rose Croix.

This name was given to it by the French, and it must be noticed that in the French language no distinction has ever been made between the Rosenkreutzer and Rose Croix; or, rather, the French writers have always translated the Rosenkreutzer of the German and the Rosacrucian of the English by their own words, Rose Croix, and to this philological inaccuracy is to be traced an historical error of some importance, to be soon adverted to.

The first that we hear in history of a Rosicrucian Masonry, under that distinctive name, is about the middle of the 18th century.

The society to which I allude was known as the "Gold-und-Rosenkreutzer," or the "Golden Rosicrucians." We first find this title in a book published at Berlin, in 1714, by one Samuel Richter, under the assumed name of Sincerus Renatus, and with the title of A True and Complete Preparation of the Philosopher's Stone by the Order of the Golden Rosicrucians.

In it is contained the laws of the brotherhood, which Findel thinks bear unmistakable evidence of Jesuitical intervention.

The book of Richter describes a society which, if founded on the old Rosicrucians, differed essentially from them in its principles.

Findel speaks of these "Golden Rosicrucians" as if originally formed on this work of Richter, and in the spirit of the Jesuits, to repress liberty of thought and the healthy development of the intellect.

If formed at that early period, in the beginning of the 18th century, it could not possibly have had a connection with Freemasonry.

But the Order, as an appendant to Masonry, was not really perfected until about the middle of the 18th century.

Findel says after 1756.

The Order consisted of nine degrees, all having Latin names, viz.: 1, Junior; 2, Theoreticus; 3, Practicus; 4, Philosophus; 5, Minor; 6, Major; 7, Adeptus; 8, Magister; 9, Magus.

It based itself on the three primitive degrees of Freemasonry only as giving a right to entrance; it boasted of being descended from the ancient Rosicrucians, and of possessing all their secrets, and of being the only body that could give a true interpretation of the Masonic symbols, and it claimed, therefore, to be the head of the Order.

There is no doubt that this brotherhood was a perfect instance of the influence sought to be cast, about the middle of the 18th century, upon Freemasonry by the doctrines of Rosicrucianism.

The effort, however, to make it a Hermetic system failed.

The Order of the Golden Rosicrucians, although for nearly half a century popular in Germany, and calling into its ranks many persons of high standing, at length began to decay, and finally died out, about the end of the last century.

Since that period we hear no more of Rosicrucian Masonry, except what is preserved in degrees like that of the Knight of the Sun and a few others, which are still retained in the catalogue of the Ancient and Accepted Scottish Rite.

I have said that the translation of the word Rosicrucian by Rose Croix has been the source of an important historical error.

This is the confounding of the French degree of "Rose Croix," or "Knight of the Eagle and Pelican," with Rosicrucianism, to which it has not the slightest affinity.

Thus Dr. Oliver, when speaking of this degree, says that the earliest notice that he finds of it is in the Fama Fraternitatis, evidently showing that he deemed it to be of Rosicrucian origin.

The modern Rose Croix, which constitutes the summit of the French Rite, and is the eighteenth of the Ancient and Accepted Scottish Rite, besides being incorporated into several other Masonic systems, has not in its construction the slightest tinge of Rosicrucianism, nor is there in any part of its ritual, rightly interpreted, the faintest allusion to the Hermetic philosophy.

I speak of it, of course, as it appears in its original form.

This has been somewhat changed in later days.

The French Masons, objecting to its sectarian character, substituted for it a modification which they have called the "Philosophic Rose Croix." In this they have given a Hermetic interpretation to the letters on the cross, an example that has elsewhere been more recently followed.

But the original Rose Croix, most probably first introduced to notice by Prince (Charles Edward, the "young pretender," in the Primordial chapter which he established in 1747, at Arras, in France, was a purely Christian, if not a Catholic degree.

Its most prominent symbols, the rose, the cross, the eagle, and the pelican, its ceremonies, and even its words and signs of recognition, bore allusion to Jesus Christ, the expounder of the new law, which was to take the place of the old law that had ceased to operate when " the veil of the temple was rent." The Rose Croix, as we find it in its pure and uncorrupted ritual, was an attempt to apply the rites, symbols, and legends of the primitive degrees of Ancient Craft Masonry to the last and greatest dispensation; to add to the first temple of Solomon, and the second of Zerubbabel, a third, which is the one to which Christ alluded when he said, " Destroy this temple, and in three days will I raise it up "an expression wholly incomprehensible by the ignorant populace who stood around him at the time, but the meaning of which is perfectly intelligible to the Rose Croix Mason who consults the original ritual of his degree.

In all this there is nothing alchemical, Hermetic, or Rosicrucian and it is a great error to suppose that there is anything but Christian philosophy in the degree as originally invented.

The name of the degree has undoubtedly led to the confusion in its history.

But, in fact, the words "Rosa Crucis," common both to the ancient Rosicrucian philosophers and to the modern Rose Croix Masons, had in each a different meaning, and some have supposed a different derivation.

In the latter the title has by many writers been thought to allude to the ros, or dew, which was deemed by the alchemists to be a powerful solvent of gold, and to crux, the cross, which was the chemical hieroglyphic of light.

Mosheim says: "The title of Rosicrucians evidently denotes the chemical philosophers and those who blended the doctrines of religion with the secrets of chemistry.

The denomination itself is drawn from the science of chemistry; and they only who are acquainted with the peculiar language of the chemists can understand its true signification and energy.

It is not compounded, as many imagine, of the two words rosa and crux, which signify rose and cross, but of the latter of these words and the Latin word ros, which signifies dew.

Of all natural bodies dew is the most powerful solvent of gold.

The cross, in the chemical style, is equivalent to light, because the figure of the cross exhibits at the same time the three letters of which the word lux, i.e., light, is compounded.

Now, lux is called by this sect the seed or menstrum of the red dragon,- or, in other words, that gross and corporeal, when properly digested and modified, produces gold."[47] Notwithstanding that this learned historian has declared that it all other explications of this term are false and chimerical," others more learned perhaps than he, in this especial subject, have differed from him in opinion, and trace the title to rosa, not to ros.

There is certainly a controversy about the derivation of Rosicrucian as applied to the Hermetic philosophers, but there is none whatever in reference to that of the Masonic.Rose Croix.

Everyone admits, because the admission is forced upon him by the ritual and the spirit of the degree, that the title comes from rose and cross, and that rose signifies Christ, and cross the instrument of his passion.

In the Masonic degree, Rose Croix signifies Christ on the cross, a meaning that is carried out by the jewel, but one which is never attached to the rose and now of the Rosicrucians, where rose most probably was the symbol of silence and secrecy, and the cross may have had either a Christian or a chemical application, most probably the latter.

Again, we see in the four most important symbols of the Rose Croix degree, as interpreted in the early rituals (at least in their spirit), the same Christian interpretation, entirely free from all taint of Rosicrucianism.

---

[47] Mosheim "Ecclesiastical History," Maclane's Translation, cent. xvii., sec. i., vol. iii., p. 436, note

These symbols are the eagle, thelelican, the rose, and the cross, all of which are combined to form the beautiful and expressive jewel of the degree.

Thus the writer of the book of Exodus, in allusion to the belief that the eagle assists its feeble younglings in their first flights by bearing them on its pinions, represents Jehovah as saying, "Ye have seen what I did to the Egyptians, and how I bore you on eagle's wings and brought you unto myself." Hence, appropriating this idea, the Rose Croix Masons selected the eagle as a symbol of Christ in his divine character, bearing the children of his adoption in their upward course, and teaching them with unequaled love and tenderness to poise their fledgling wings, and soar from the dull corruptions of earth to a higher and holier sphere.

And hence the eagle in the jewel is represented with expanded wings, as if ready for flight.

The pelican, "vulning herself and in her piety," as the heralds call it, is, says Mr. Sloane Evans, " a sacred emblem of great beauty and striking import, and the representation of it occurs not unfrequently among the ornaments of churches.[48] The allusion to Christ as a Saviour, shedding his blood for the sins of the world, is too evident to need explanation.

Of the rose and the cross I have already spoken.

The rose is applied as a figurative appellation of Christ in only one passage of Scripture, where he is prophetically called the " rose of Sharon," but the flower was always accepted in the iconography of the church as one of his symbols. But the fact that in the jewel of the Rose Croix the blood-red rose appears attached to the center of the cross, as though crucified upon it, requires no profound knowledge of the science of symbolism to discover its meaning.

The cross was, it is true, a very ancient symbol of eternal life, especially among the "Egyptian, but since the crucifixion it has been adopted by Christians as an emblem of him who suffered upon it.

"The cross," says Didron, "is more than a mere figure of Christ; it is, in iconography, either Christ himself or his symbol." As such, it is used in the Masonry of the Rose Croix.

It is evident, from these explanations, that the Rose Croix was, in its original conception, a purely Christian degree.

There was no intention of its founders to borrow for its construction anything from occult philosophy, but simply to express in its symbolization a purely Christian sentiment.

---

[48] "The Art of Blazon," p. 130

I have, in what I have said, endeavored to show that while Rosicrucianism had no concern, as has been alleged, with the origination of Freemasonry in the 17th century, yet that in the succeeding century, under various influenced especially, perhaps, the diffusion of the mystical doctrines of Swedenborg, a Hermetic or Rosicrucian element was infused into some of the High Degrees then newly fabricated.

But the diffusion of that element went no farther; it never affected the pure Masonic system; and, with the few exceptions which I have mentioned, even these degrees have ceased to exist.

Especially was it not connected with one of the most important and most popular of those degrees.

From the beginning of the 19th century Rosicrucianism has been dead to Masonry, as its exponent the Hermetic philosophy, has been to literature.

It has no life now, and we preserve its relics only as memorials of a past obscuration which the sunbeams of modern learning have dispersed.

CHAPTER XXXVII

THE PYTHAGOREANS AND FREEMASONRY

The theory which ascribes, if not the actual origin of Freemasonry to Pythagoras, at least its introduction into Europe by him, through the school which he established at Crotona, in Italy, which ,was a favorite one among our early writers, may very properly be placed among the legends of the Order, since it wants all the requisites of historical authority for its support.

The notion was most probably derived from what has been called the Leland Manuscript, because it is said to have been found in the Bodleian Library, in the handwriting of that celebrated antiquary.

The author of the Life of Leland gives this account of the manuscript: "The original is said to be the handwriting of King Henry VI. and copied by Leland by order of his highness, King Henry VIII.

If the authenticity of this ancient monument of literature remains unquestioned, it demands particular notice in the present publication, on account of the singularity of the subject, and no less from a due regard to the royal writer and our author, his transcriber, indefatigable in every part of literature.

It will also be admitted, acknowledgment is due to the learned Mr. Locke, who, amidst the closest studies and the most strict attention to human understanding, could unbend his mind in search of this ancient treatise, which he first brought from obscurity in the year 1796.'"[49] This production was first brought to the attention of scholars by being published in the Gentlemen's Magazine for September, 1753, where it is stated to have been previously printed at Frankfort, in Germany, in 1748, from a copy found in " the writing-desk of a deceased

---

[49] "Life of John Leland," p. 67

brother." The title of it, as given in the magazine, is in the following words: Certeyne Questyons wyth Answeres to the same, concerynge the Mystery of Maconrye; wrytenne by the hande of Kynge Henrye the Sixthe of the Name, and faythefullye copyed by me Johan Leylande, Antiquarius, by the commaunde of His Highnesse." The opinion of Masonic critics of the present day is that the document is a forgery.

It was most probably written about the time and in the spirit in which Chatterton composed his imitations of the Monk Rowley, and of Ireland with his impositions of Shakespeare, and was fabricated as an unsuccessful attempt to imitate the archaic language of the 15th century, and as a pious fraud intended to elevate the character and sustain the pretensions of the Masonic Fraternity by furnishing the evidence of its very ancient origin.

Such were not, however, the views of the Masonic writers of the last and beginning of the present century.

They accepted the manuscript, or rather the printed copy of it - for the original codex has never been seen--with unhesitating, faith as an authentic document.

Hutchinson gave it as an appendix to his Spirit of Masonry, Preston published in the second and enlarged edition of his Illustrations, Calcott in his Candid Disquisition , Dermott in his Ahiman Rezon, and Krause in his Drei Altesten Kunslurkunden.

In none of these is there the faintest hint of its being anything but an authentic document.

Oliver said: "I entertain no doubt of the genuineness and authenticity of this valuable Manuscript." The same view has been entertained by Reghellini among the French, and by Krause, Fessler, and Lenning among the Germans.

Mr. Halliwell was perhaps the first of English scholars to express a doubt of its genuineness.

After a long and unsuccessful search in the Bodleian Library for the original, he came, very naturally, to the conclusion that it is a forgery.

Hughan and Woodford, both excellent judges, have arrived at the same conclusion, and it is now a settled question that the Leland or Locke Manuscript (for it is known by both titles) is a document of no historic character.

It is not, however, without its value.

To its appearance about the middle of the last century, and the unhesitating acceptance of its truth by the Craft at the time, we can, in all probability, assign the establishment of the doctrine that Freemasonry was of a Pythagorean origin, though it had been long before adverted to by Dr. Anderson.

Before proceeding to an examination of the rise and progress of this opinion, it will be proper to cite so much of the manuscript as connects Pythagoras with Masonry.

I do not quote the whole document, though it is short, because it has so repeatedly been printed, in even elementary Masonic works, as to be readily accessible to the reader.

In making my quotations I shall so far defer to the artifice of the fabricator as to preserve unchanged his poor attempt to imitate the orthography and style of the 15th century, and interpolate in brackets, when necessary, an explanation of the most unintelligible words.

The document purports to be answers by some Mason to questions proposed by King Henry VI., who, it would seem, must have taken some interest in the "Mystery of Masonry," and had sought to obtain from competent authority a knowledge of its true character.

The following are among the questions and answers: Q. Where dyd ytt [Masonry] begynne? A. Ytt dyd begynne with the fyrst menne, yn the Este, which were before the fyrste Manne of the Weste, and comyngc westlye, ytt hathe broughte herwyth alle comfortes to the wylde and comfortlesse. Q. Who dyd brynge ytt Westye? A. The Venetians [Phoenicians] who beynge grate Merchandes comed ffyrst ffrome the Este yn Venctia [Phoenicia] for the commodyte of Merchaundysinge beithe [both] Este and Weste bey the redde and Myddlelonde [Mediterranean] Sees. Q. Howe comede ytt yn Englonde? A. Peter Gower [Pythagoras] a Grecian journeyedde tor kunnynge yn Egypt and in Syria and in everyche Londe whereat the Venetians [Phoenicians] hadde plauntedde Maconrye and wynnynge Entraunce yn all Lodges of Maconnes, he lerned muche, and retournedde and woned [dwelt] yn Cirecia Magna wachsynge [growing] and becommynge a myghtye wyseacre [philosopher] and gratelyche renouned and here he framed a grate Lodge at Groton [Crotona] and maked many Maconnes, some whereoffe dyd journeye yn Fraunce, and maked manye Maconnes wherefromme, yn processe of Tyme, the Arte passed yn Engelonde." I am convinced that there was a French original of this document, from which language the fabricator translated it into archaic English. The internal proofs of this are to be found in the numerous preservations of French idioms.

Thus we meet with Peter Gower, evidently derived from Pythagore, pronounced Petagore, the French for Pythagoras; Maconrye and Maconnes, for Masonry and Masons, the French c in the word being used instead of the English s,- the phrase wynnynge the Facultye of

Abrac, which is a pure Gallic idiom, instead of acquiring the faculty, the word gayner being indifferently used in French as signifying to win or to acquire,- the word Freres for Brethren,- and the statement, in the spirit of French nationality, that Masonry was brought into England out of France.

None of these idiomatic phrases or national peculiarities would have been likely to occur if the manuscript had been originally written by an Englishman and in the English language.

But be this as it may, the document bad no sooner appeared than it seemed to inspire contemporary Masonic writers with the idea that Masonry and the school of Pythagoras, which he established at Crotona, in Italy, about five centuries before Christ, were closely connected-an idea which was very generally adopted by their successors, so that it came at last to be a point of the orthodox Masonic creed.

Thus Preston, in his Illustrations of Masonry, when commenting on the dialogue contained in this document, says that , the records of the fraternity inform us that Pythagoras was regularly initiated into Masonry; and being properly instructed in the mysteries of the Art, he was much improved, and propagated the principles of the Order in other countries into which he afterwards travelled." Calcott, in his Candid Disquisition, speaks of the Leland Manuscript as " an antique relation, from whence may be gathered many of the original principles of the ancient society, on which the institution of Freemasonry was ingrafted "-by the " ancient society meaning the school of Pythagoras.

Hutchinson, in his Spirit of Masonry, quotes this "ancient Masonic record," as he calls it, and says that " it brings us positive evidence of the Pythagorean doctrine and Basilidian principles making the foundation of our religious and moral duties." Two of the lectures in his work are appropriated to a (discussion of the doctrines of Pythagoras in connection with the Masonic system.

But this theory of the Pythagorean origin of Freemasonry does not owe its existence to the writers of the middle of the 18th century.

It had been advanced at an early period, and soon after the Revival in 1717 by Dr. Anderson.

In the first edition of the Constitutions, published in 1723, he alludes to Pythagoras as having borrowed great knowledge from the Chaldean Magi and the Babylonish Jews, but he is more explicit in his Defense of Masonry, published in 1730, wherein he says: "I am fully convinced that Freemasonry is very nearly allied to the old Pythagorean Discipline, from whence, I am persuaded, it may in some circumstances very justly claim a descent." Now, how are we to explain the way in which this tradition of the connection of the Philosopher of Samos first acquired a place among the legends of the Craft? The solution of the problem does not appear to be very difficult.

In none of the old manuscript constitutions which contain what has been called the Legend of the Guild, or the Legend of the Craft, is there, with a single exception, any allusion to the name of Pythagoras.

That exception is found in the Cooke MS., where the legendist, after relating the story of the two pillars inscribed with all the sciences, which had been erected by Jabal before the Flood, adds, in lines 318-326, this statement: "And after this flode many yeres as the cronyclc tellcth these ii were founde and as the polycronicon seyeth that a grete clerke that called putogaras [Pythagoras] fonde that one and hermes the philisophre fonde that other, and thei tought forthe the sciens that thei fonde therein ywritten." Now, although the Cooke MS. is the earliest of the old records, after the Halliwell poem, none of the subsequent constitutions have followed it in this allusion to Pythagoras.

This was because the writer of the Cooke MS., being in possession of the Polychronicon of the monk Ranulph Higden, an edition of which had been printed during his time by William Caxton, he had liberally borrowed from that historical work and incorporated parts of it into his Legend.

Of these interpolations, the story of the finding of one of the pillars by Pythagoras is one.

The writer acknowledges his indebtedness for the statement to Higden's Polychronicon. But it formed no part of the Legend of the Craft, and hence no notice is taken of it in the subsequent manuscript copies of the Legend, In none of them is Pythagoras even named.

It is evident, then, that in the 14th and following centuries, to the beginning of the 18th, the theory of the Pythagorean origin of Freemasonry, or of the connection of the Grecian philosopher with it, was not recognized by the Craft as any part of the traditional history of the Fraternity.

There is no safer rule than that of the old schoolmen, which teaches us that we must reason alike concerning that which does not appear and that which does not exist-" de non apparentibus et de non existentibus, eadem est ratio." The old craftsmen who fabricated the Legend were workmen and not scholars; they were neither acquainted with the scholastic nor the ancient philosophy; they said nothing about Pythagoras because they knew nothing about him.

But about the beginning of the 18th century a change took place, not only in the organization of the Masonic institution, but also in the character and qualifications of the men who were engaged in producing the modification, or we might more properly call it the revolution.

Although in the 17th, and perhaps in the 16th century, many persons were admitted into the Lodges of Operative Masons who were not professional builders, it is, I think, evident that the society did not assume a purely speculative form until the year 1717. The Revival in that year, by the election of Anthony Sayer, "Gentleman," as Grand Master; Jacob Lamball, a "Carpenter," and Joseph Elliott, a "Captain," as Grand Wardens, proves that the control of the society was to be taken out of the hands of the Operative Masons.

Among those who were at about that time engaged in the recon- struction of the Institution were James Anderson and Theophilus Desaguliers.

Anderson was a Master of Arts, and afterward a Doctor of Divinity, the minister of a church in London, and an author; Desaguliers was a Doctor of Laws, a fellow of the Royal Society, and a teacher of Experimental Philosophy of no little reputation.

Both of these men, as scholars, were thoroughly conversant with the system of Pythagoras, and they were not unwilling to take advantage of his symbolic method of inculcating his doctrine, and to introduce some of his symbols into the symbolism of the Order which they were renovating.

Jamblichus, the biographer of Pythagoras, tells us that while the sage was on his travels he caused himself to be initiated into all the mysteries of Byblos and Tyre and those which were practiced in many parts of Syria.

But as these mysteries were originally received by the Phoenicians from Egypt, he passed over into that country, where he remained twenty-two years, occupying himself in the study of geometry, astronomy, and all the initiations of the gods, until he was carried a captive into Babylon by the soldiers of Cambyses.

There he freely associated with the Magi in their religion;and their studies, and, having obtained a thorough knowledge of music, the science of numbers, and other arts, he finally returned to Greece.[50] The school of philosophy which Pythagoras afterward estalablished at the city of Crotona, in Italy, differed from those of all the other philosophers of

---

[50] "Jamblichus de Pythagorica Vita," c. iii., iv.

Greece, in the austerities of initiation to which his disciples were subject in the degrees of probation into which they were divided, and in the method which lie adopted of veiling his instructions under symbolic forms.

In his various travels he had imbibed the mystical notions prevalent among the Egyptians and the Chaldeans, and had borrowed some of their modes of initiation into their religious mysteries, which he adopted in the method by which he communicated his own principles.

Grote, in his History of Greece, has very justly said that "Pythagoras represents in part the scientific tendencies of his age, in part also the spirit of mysticism and of special fraternities for religious and ascetic observance which became diffused throughout Greece in the 6th century before the Christian era." Of the character of the philosophy of Pythagoras and of his method of instruction, which certainly bore a very close resemblance to that adopted by the founders of the speculative system, such cultivated scholars as Anderson and Desaguliers certainly were not ignorant.

And if, among those who were engaged with them in the construction of this new and improved school of speculative Masonry, there were any whose limited scholastic attainments would not enable them to consult the Greek biographics of Pythagoras by Jamblichus and by Porphyry, they had at hand and readily accessible an English translation of M. Dacier's life of the philosopher, containing also an elaborate explication of his symbols, together with a translation of the Commentaries of Hierodes on the Golden Verses of Pythagoras, all embraced in one volume and published in London in the year 1707, by the celebrated bibliopole Jacob Tonson.

There was abundant material and ready opportunity for the partially unlearned as well as for the more erudite to obtain a familiarity with the philosophy of Pythagoras, his method of initiation, and his system of symbols.

It is not, therefore, surprising that these " Revivalists," as they have been called, should have delighted, as Anderson has done in his Defense of Masonry, to compare the two schools of the Pythagoreans and the Freemasons; that they should have dwelt on their great similarity; and in the development of their speculative system should have adopted many symbols from the former which do not appear to have been known to or used by the old Operative Masons whom they succeeded.

Among the first Pythagorean symbols which were adopted by the Speculative Masons was the symbolism of the science of numbers, which appears in the earliest rituals extant, and of which Dr.Oliver has justly said, in his posthumous work entitled The Pythagorean Triangle, that "the Pythagoreans had so high an opinion of it that they considered it to be the origin of all things, and thought a knowledge of it to be equivalent to a knowledge of God." This symbolism of numbers, which was adopted into Speculative Masonry at a very early period after the Revival, has been developed and enlarged in successive revisions of the lectures, until at the present day it constitutes one of the most important and curious parts of the system of Freemasonry.

But we have no evidence that the same system of numerical symbolism, having the Pythagorean and modern Masonic interpretation, prevailed among the Craft anterior to the beginning of the 18th century.

It was the work of the Revivalists, who, as scholars familiar with the mystical philosophy of Pythagoras, deemed it expedient to introduce it into the equally mystical philosophy of Speculative Masonry In fact, the Traveling Freemasons, Builders, or Operative Masons of the Middle Ages, who were the real predecessors of the Speculative Masons of the 18th century, did not, so far as we can learn from their remains, practice any of the symbolism of Pythagoras.

Their symbol, such as the vesica piscis, the cross, the rose, or certain mathematical figures, were derived either from the legends of the church or from the principles of geometry applied to the art of building.

These skillful architects who, in the dark ages, when few men could read or write, erected edifices surpassing the works of ancient Greece or Rome, and which have never been equalled by modern builders, were wonderful in their peculiar skill, but were wholly ignorant of metaphysics or philosophy, and borrowed nothing from Pythagoras.

Between the period of the Revival and the adoption of the Prestonian system, in 1772, the lectures of Freemasonry underwent at least seven revisions.

In each of these, the fabricators of which were such cultivated scholars as Dr. Desaguliers, Martin Clare, a President of the Royal Society, Thomas Dunckerley, a man of considerable literary attainments, and others of like character, there was a gradual increment of Pythagorean symbols.

Among these, one of the most noted is the forty-seventh proposition of Euclid, which is said to have been discovered by Pythagoras, and which the introducer of it into the Masonic system, in his explanation of the symbol, claims the sage to have been " an ancient brother." For some time after the Revival, the symbols of Pythagoras, growing into gradual use among the Craft, were referred to simply as an evidence of the great similarity which existed between the two systems-a theory which, so far as it respects modern Speculative Masonry, may be accepted with but little hesitation.

The most liberal belief on this subject was that the two systems were nearly allied, but, except in the modified statement of Anderson, already quoted from his Defense ofmasonry, there was no claim in the years immediately succeeding the Revival that the one was in direct descent from the other.

In none of the speeches, lectures, or essays of the early part of the last century, which have been preserved, is there any allusion to this as a received theory of the Craft.

Drake, in his speech before the Grand Lodge of York, delivered in 1726 does indeed, speak of Pythagoras, not as the founder of Masonry, but only in connection with Euclid and Archimedes as great proficients in Geometry, whose works have been the basis " on which the learned have built at different times so many noble superstructures." And of Geometry, he calls it "that noble and useful science which must have begun and goes hand in hand with Masonry," an assertion which, to use the old chorus of the Masons, nobody will deny." But to say that Geometry is closely connected with Operative Masonry, and that Pythagoras was a great geometrician, is very different from saying that he was a Mason and propagated Masonry in Europe.

Martin Clare, in his lecture on the Advantages Enjoyed by the Fraternity, whose date is 1735, does not even mention the name of Pythagoras, although, in one passage at least, when referring to "those great and worthy spirits with whom we are intimately related," he had a fair opportunity to refer to that illustrious sage.

In a Discourse Upon Masonry, delivered before a Lodge of England in 1742, now lying before me, in which the origin of the Order is fully discussed, there is not one word of reference to Pythagoras.

The same silence is preserved in a Lecture on the Connection Between Freemasonry and Religion, by the Rev. C. Brockwell, published in 1747.

But after the middle of the century the frequent references in the lectures to the Pythagorean symbols, and especially to that important one, in its Masonic as well as its geometrical value, the forty-seventh proposition, began to lead the members of tile society to give to Pythagoras the credit of a relationship to the order to which historically he had no claim.

Thus, in A Search After Truth, delivered in the Lodge in 1752, the author says that "Solon, Plato, and Pythagoras, and from them the

Grecian literati in general in a great measure, were obliged for their learning to Masonry and the labors of some of our ancient brethren." And then, when this notion of the Pythagorean origin of Freemasonry began to take root in the minds of the Craft, it was more firmly established by the appearance in 1753, in the Gentleman's Magazine, of that spurious document already quoted, in which, by a " pious fraud," the fabricator of it sought to give the form of an historical record to the statement that Pythagoras, learning his Masonry of the Eastern Magi had brought it to Italy and established a Lodge at Crotona, whence the institution was propagated throughout Europe, and from France into England.

As to this statement in the Leland MS., it may be sufficient to say that the sect of Pythagoras did not subsist longer than to the end of the reign of Alexander the Great.

So far from disseminating its Lodges or schools after the Christian era, we may cite the authority of the learned Dacier, who says that " in after ages there were here and there some disciples of Pythagoras, but these were only private persons who never established any society, nor had the Pythagoreans any longer a public school." And so the result of this investigation into the theory of the Pythagorean origin of Freemasonry may be briefly epitomized thus: The mediaeval Freemasons never entertained any such theory, nor in their architectural labors did they adopt any of his symbols.

The writer of the Cooke MS., in 1490, having at hand Higden's Polychronicon, in Trevisa's translation, a new edition of which had just been printed by Caxton, incorporated into the Legend of the Craft some of the historical statements (such as they were) of the Monk of (Chester, but they were extraneous to and formed no part of the original Legend.

Therefore, in all the subsequent Old Records these interpolations were rejected and the Legend of the Craft, as accepted by the writers of the manuscripts which succeeded that of the Cooke codex, from 1550 to 1701, contained no mention of Pythagoras.

Upon the Revival, in 1717, which was really the beginning of genuine Speculative Masonry, the scholars who fabricated the scheme, finding the symbolic teaching of Pythagoras very apposite, adopted some of its symbols, especially those relating to numbers in the new Speculative system which they were forming.

By the continued additions of subsequent ritualists these symbols were greatly increased, so that the name and the philosophy of Pythagoras became familiar to the Craft, and finally, in 1753, a forged document was published which claimed him as the founder and propagator of Masonry.

In later days this theory has continued to be maintained by a few writers, and the received rituals of the Order require it as a part of the orthodox Masonic creed, that Pythagoras was a Mason and an ancient brother and patron of the Order.

Neither early Masonic tradition nor any historical records exist which support such a belief.

CHAPTER XXXVIII

FREEMASONRY AND THE GNOSTICS

The hypothesis which seeks to trace a connection between Gnosticism and Freemasonry, and perhaps even an origin of the latter from the former, has been repeatedly advanced, and is therefore worthy of consideration.

The latest instance is in a work of Mr. C. W. King, published in 1864 under the title The Gnostics and their.Remains, Ancient and Medieval.

Mr. King is not a Freemason, and, like all the writers non-Masonic, such as Barnell, Robison, De Quincey, and a host of others, who have attempted to discuss the history and character of Freemasonry, he has shown a vast amount of ignorance.

In fact, these self-constituted critics, when treating of subjects with which they are not and can not be familiar, remind one of the busybodies of Plautus, of whom he has said that, while pretending to know everything, they in fact know nothing-" Qui omnia se simulant scise nec quicquam sciunt." Very justly has Mr. Hughan called this work of King's, so far as its Masonic theories are concerned, one of an "unmasonic and unhistoric character." But King, it must be admitted, was not the first writer who sought to trace Freemasonry to a Gnostic origin.

In a pamphlet published in 1725, a copy of which has been preserved in the Bodleian Library, among the manuscripts of Dn Rawlinson, and which bears the title of Two Letters to a Friend.

The First concerning the Society of Free-masons. The second giving an Account of the Most Ancient Order of Gormogons, etc., we find, in the first letter, on the Freemasons, the following passage: "But now, Sir, to draw towards a conclusion; and to give my opinion seriously, concerning these prodigious Virtuosi; - My belief is, that if they fall under any denomination at all, or belong to any sect of men, which has hitherto appeared in the world, they may be ranked among the Gnostics, who took their original from Simon Magus; these were a set of men, which ridiculed not only Christianity, but even rational morality; teaching that they should be saved by their capacious knowledge and understanding of no mortal man could tell what.

They babbled of an amazing intelligence they had, from nobody knows whence.

They amused and puzzled the hair-brained, unwary crowd with superstitious interpretations of extravagant talismanic characters and abstruse significations of uncommon Cabalistic words; which exactly agrees with the proceedings of our modern Freemasons." Although the intrinsic value of this pamphlet was not such as to have preserved it from the literary tomb which would have consigned it to oblivion, had not the zeal of an antiquary preserved a single copy as a relic, yet the notion of some relation of Freemasonry to Gnosticism was not in later years altogether abandoned.

Hutchinson says that "under our present profession of Masonry, we allege our morality was originally deduced from the school of Pythagoras, and that the Basilidian system of religion furnished us with some tenets, principles, and hieroglyphics."[51] Basilides, the founder of the sect which bears his name, was the most eminent of the Egyptian Gnostics.

About the time of the fabrication of the High Degrees on the continent of Europe, a variety of opinions of the origin of Masonry - many of them absurd-sprang up among Masonic scholars.

Among these theorists, there were not a few who traced the Order to the early Christians, because they found it, as they supposed, among the Gnostics, and especially its most important sect, the Basilidians.

Some German and French writers have also maintained the hypothesis of a connection, more or less intimate, between the Gnostics and the Masons.

I do not know that any German writer has positively asserted the existence of this connection.

But the doctrine has, at times, been alluded to without any absolute disclaimer of a belief in its truth.

---

[51] "Spirit of Masonry," lect. x., p. 106

Thus Carl Michaeler, the author of a Treatise on the Pheonician Mysteries, has written some observations on the subject in an article published by him in 1784, in the Vienna Journale fur Freimaurer, on the analogy between the Christianity of the early times and Freemasonry.

In this essay he adverts to the theory of the Gnostic origin of Freemasonry.

He is, however, very guarded in his deductions, and says conditionally that, if there is any connection between the two, it must be traced to the Gnosticism of Clement of Alexandria, and on which simply as a school of philosophy and history it may have been founded, while the differences between the two now existing must be attributed to changes of human conception in the intervening centuries.

But, in fact, the Gnosticism of Clement was something entirely different from that of Basilides, to whom Hutchinson and King attribute the origin of our symbols, and whom Clement vigorously opposed in his works.

It was what he himself calls it, "a true Gnostic or Christian philosophy on the bads of faith." It was that higher knowledge, or more perfect state of Christian faith, to which St. Paul is supposed to allude when he says, in his First Epistle to the Corinthians, that he made known to those who were perfect a higher wisdom.

Reghellini speaks more positively, and says that the symbols and doctrines of the Ophites, who were a Gnostic sect, passed over into Europe, having been adapted by the Crusaders, the Rosicrucians, and the Templars, and finally reached the Masons.' [52] Finally, I may refer to the Leland MS., the author of which distinctly brought this doctrine to the public view, by asserting that the Masons were acquainted with the " facultys of Abrac," by which expression he alludes to the most prominent and distinctive of the Gnostic symbols.

That the fabricator of this spurious document should thus have intimated the existence of a connection between Gnosticism and Freemasonry would lead us to infer that the idea of such a connection was not wholly unfamiliar to the Masonic mind at that period-an inference which will be strengthened by the passage already quoted from the pamphlet in the Rawlinson collection, which was published about a quarter of a century before.

But before we can enter into a proper discussion of this important question, it will be expedient for the sake of the general

---

[52] "Maconnerie consideréis comme re Resultat des Relig. Egypt. Juive et Chretienne," tom., p. 291.

reader that something should be said of the Gnostics and of the philosophical and religious system which they professed.

I propose, therefore, very briefly to reply to the questions, What is Gnosticism, and Who were the Gnostics? Scarcely had the light of Christianity dawned upon the world before a multitude of heresies sprang up to disturb the new religion.

Among these Gnosticism holds the most important position. the title of the sect is derived from the Greek word gnosis, "wisdom or knowledge," and was adopted in a spirit of ostentation, to intimate that the disciples of the sect were in possession of a higher degree of spiritual wisdom than was attainable by those who had not been initiated into their mysteries.

At so early a period did the heresy of Gnosticism arise in the Christian Church, that we find the Apostle Paul warning the converts to the new faith of the innovations on the pure doctrine of Christ, and telling his disciple Timothy to avoid "profane and vain babblings, and oppositions of science, falsely so called." The translators of the authorized version have so rendered the passage.

But, in view of the greater light that has since their day been thrown upon the religious history and spirit of the apostolic age, and the real nature of the Gnostic element which disturbed it, we may better preserve the true sense of the original Greek by rendering it "oppositions of the false gnosis." There were then two kinds of Gnosis, or Gnosticism-the true and the false, a distinction which St. Paul himself makes in a passage in his Epistle to the Corinthians, in which he speaks of the wisdom which he communicated to the perfect, in contradistinction to the wisdom of the world.

Of this true Gnosticism, Clement declared himself to be a follower.

With it and Freemasonry there can be no connection, except that rnodified one admitted by Michaeler, which relates only to the investigation of philosophical and historical truth.

The false Gnosis to which the Apostle refers is the Gnosticism which is the subject of our present inquiry.

When John the Baptist was preaching in the Wilderness, and for some time before, there were many old philosophical and religious systems which, emanating from the East, all partook of the mystical character peculiar to the Oriental mind.

These various systems were, then, in consequence of the increased communication of different nations which followed the conquests of Alexander of Macedon, beginning to approximate each other.

The disciples of Plato were acquiring some of the doctrines of the Eastern Magi, and these in turn were becoming more or less imbued with the philosophy of Greece.

The traditions of India, Persia, Egypt, Chaldea, Judea, Greece, and Rome were commingling in one mass, and forming out of the conglomeration a mystical philosophy and religion which partook of the elements of all the ingredients out of which it was composed and yet contained within its bosom a mysticism which was peculiar to itself.

This new system was Gnosticism, which derived its leading doctrines from Plato, from the Zend-Avesta, the Cabala, the Vedas, and the hieroglyphs of Egypt.

It taught as articles of fakth the existence of a Supreme Being, invisible, inaccessible, and incomprehensible, who was the creator of a spiritual world consisting of divine intelligences called aeons, emanating from him, and of matter which was eternal, the source of evil and the antagonist of the Supreme Being.

One of these aeons, the lowest of all called the Demiurge, created the world out of matter, which, though eternal, was inert and formless.

The Supreme Father, or First Principle of all things, had dwelt from all eternity in a pleroma or fullness of inaccessible light, and hence he was called Bythos, or the Abyss, to denote the unfathomable nature of his perfections.

"This Being," says Dr. Burton, in his able exposition of the Gnostic system, in the Bam o Lectures ures, by an operation purely mental, or by acting upon himself, produced two other beings of different sexes, from whom by a series of descents, more or less numerous according to different schemes, several pairs of beings were formed, who were called aeons, from the periods of their existance before time was, or emanations from the mode of their production.

These successive aeons or emanations appear to have been inferior each to the preceding; and their existence was indispensable to the Gnostic scheme, that they might account for the creation of the world, without making God the author of evil.

These aeons lived through countless ages with their first Father.

But the system of emanations seems to have resembled that of concentric circles, and they gradually deteriorated as they approached nearer and nearer to the extremity of the pleroma. Beyond this pleroma was matter, inert and powerless, though co-eternal with the Supreme God, and like him without beginning.

At length one of the aeons (the Demiurge) passed the limits of the pleroma, and, meeting with matter, created the world after the form and model of an ideal world, which existed in the plemora or the mind of the Supreme God." It is not necessary to enter into a minute recapitulation of the other points of doctrine which were evolved out of these three.

It is sufficient to say that the old Gnosticism was not an original system, but was really a cosmogony, a religion and a philosophy which was made up of portions of the older Grecian and Oriental systems, including the Platonism of the Greeks, the Parsism of the Persians, and the Cabala of the Jews.

The advent of Christianity found this old Gnosticism prevailing in Asia and in Egypt.

Some of its disciples became converts to the new religion, but brought with them into its fold many of the mystical views of their Gnostic philosophy and sought to apply them to the pure and simple doctrines of the Gospel.

Thus it happened that the name of Gnosticism was applied to a great variety of schools, differing from each other in their interpretations of the Christian faith, and yet having one common principle of unity-that they placed themselves in opposition to the conceptions of Christianity as it was generally received by its disciples.

And this was because they deemed it insufficient to afford any germs of absolute truth, and therefore they claimed for themselves the possession of an amount of knowledge higher than that of ordinary believers.

"They seldom pretended," says the Rev. Dr. Wing, "to demonstrate the principles on which their systems were founded by historical evidence or logical reasonings, since they rather boasted that these were discovered by the intuitional powers of more highly endowed minds, and that the materials thus obtained, whether through faith or divine revelation, were then worked up into a scientific form, according to each one's natural power and culture.

Their aim was to construct, not merely a theory of redemption, but of the universe-a cosmogony.

No subject was beyond their investigations.

Whatever God could reveal to the finite intellect they looked upon as within their range.

What to others seemed only speculative ideas, were by. them hypostatized or personified into real beings or historical facts.

It was in this way that they constructed systems of speculation on subjects entirely beyond the range of human knowledge, which startle us by their boldness and their apparent consciousness of reality."[53] Such was the Gnosticism whose various sects intruded with their mystical notions and their allegorical interpretations into the Church, before Christianity had been well established.

Although denounced by St. Paul as "vain babblers," they increased in strength and gave rise to many heresies which lasted until the 4th century.

The most important of these sects, and the one from which the moderns have derived most of their views of what Christian Gnosticism is, was established in the 2d century by Basilides, the chief of the Egyptian Gnostics.

The doctrine of Basilides and the Basilidians was a further development of the original Gnostic system.

It was more particularly distinguished by its adoption from Pythagoras of the doctrine of numbers and its use and interpretation of the word Abraxas - that word the meaning of which, according to the Leland MS., so greatly puzzled the learned Mr. Locke.

In the system of Basilides the Supreme God was incomprehensible, non-existent, and ineffable.

Unfolded from his perfection were seven attributes or personified powers, namely, Mind, Reason, Thought, Wisdom, Power, Holiness, and Peace.

Seven was a sacred number, and these seven powers referred to the seven days of the week.

Basilides also supposed that there were seven similar beings in every stage or region of the spiritual world, and that these regions were three hundred and sixty-five in number, thus corresponding to the days in the solar year.

These three hundred and sixty-five regions were so many heavenly mansions between the earth and the empyrean, and be supposed the existence of an equal number of angels.

The number three hundred and sixty-five was in the Basilidian system one of sacred import.

---

[53] Strong and McClintock's "Cyclopaedia of Biblical, Theological, and Ecclesiastical Literature."

Hence he fabricated the word A B R A X A S, because the Greek letters of which it is composed have the numerical value, when added together, of exactly three hundred and sixty-five.

The learned German theologian, Bellerman thinks that he has found the derivation in the Captu, or old Egyptian language, where the words abrah, signifying "word," and sadsch, signifying "blessed," "holy," or "adorable," and therefore abrahsadsch Hellenized into Abraxas, would denote "the holy, blessed, or adorable Word," thus approximating to the spirit of the Jewish Cabalists in their similar use of a Holy Name.

Whether the word was thus derived or was invented by Basilides on account of the numerical value of its letters, is uncertain. lie, however, applied it in his system as the name of the Supreme God.

This word Abraxas, like the Tetragrammaton of the Jews, became one of great importance to the sect of Basilidians.

Their reverence for it gave origin to what are called "abraxas gems." These are gems, plates, or tablets of metal, which have been discovered principally in Egypt, but have also been found in France and Spain.

They are inscribed with the word Abraxas and an image supposed to designate the Basilidian god.

Some of them have on them Jewish words, such as Jehovah or Adonai, and others contain Persian, Egyptian, or Grecian symbols.

Montfaucon, who has treated the subject of "abraxas gems " elaborately, divides them into seven classes. 1. Those inscribed with the head of a cock as a symbol of the sun. 2. Those having the head of a lion, to denote the heat of the sun, and the word Mithras. 3. Those having the image of the Egyptian god Sera is. 4. Those having the images of sphinxes, apes, and other animals. 5. Those having human figures with the words Iao, Sabaoth, Adonai, etc. 6. Those having inscriptions without figures. 7. Those having monstrous forms.

From these gems we have derived our knowledge of the Gnostic or Basilidian symbols, which are said to have furnished ideas to the builders of the Middle Ages in their decorative art, and which Mr.

King and some other writers have supposed to have been transmitted to the Freemasons.

The principal of these Gnostic symbols is that of the Supreme God, Abraxas.

This is represented as a human figure with the head of a cock, the legs being two serpents.

He brandishes a sword in one hand (sometimes a whip) and a shield in the other.

The serpent is also a very common symbol, having sometimes the head of a cock and sometimes that of a lion or of a hawk.

Other symbols, known to be of a purely Gnostic or rather Basilidian origin, from the accompanying inscription, Abraxas, or Iao, or both, are Horus, or the Sun, seated on a lotus flower, which is supported by a double lamp, composed of two phallic images conjoined at their bases; the dog; the raven; the tancross surmounted by a human head; the Egyptian god, Anubis, and Father Nilus, in a bending posture and holding in his hand the double, phallic lamp of Horus.

This last symbol is curious because the word Heilos, like Mithras, which is also a Gnostic symbol, and Abraxas, expresses, in the value of the Greek letters of which it is composed, the number three hundred and sixty-five.

All these symbols, it will be seen, make some reference to the sun, ether as the representative of the Supreme God or as the source of light, and it might lead to the supposition that in the later Gnosticism, as in the Mithraic Mysteries, there was an allusion to sunworship, which was one of the earliest and most extensively dill used of the primitive religions.

Evidently in both the Gnostic and the Mithraic symbolism the sun plays a very important part.

While the architects or builders of the Middle Ages may have borrowed and probably did borrow, some suggestions from the Gnostics in carrying out the symbolism of their art, it is not probable, from their ecclesiastical organization and their religious character, that they would be more than mere suggestions.

Certainly they would not have been accepted by these orthodox Christians with anything of their real Gnostic interpretation.

We may apply to the use of Gnostic symbols by the mediaeval architects the remarks made by Mr. Paley on the subject of the adoption of certain Pagan symbols by the same builders.

Their Gnostic origin was a mere accident.

They were employed not as the symbolism of any Gnostic doctrine, but in the spirit of Christianity, and "the Church, in perfecting their development, stamped them with a purer and sublimer character."[54] On a comparison of these Gnostic symbols with those of Ancient Craft or Speculative Masonry, I fail to find any reason to subscribe to the opinion of Hutchinson, that " the Basilidian system of religion furnished Freemasonry with some tenets, principles, and

---

[54] "Manual of Gothic Architecture," p.4

hieroglyphics." As Freemasons we will have to repudiate the tenets and principles" of the sect which was condemned by Clement and by Irenaeus; and as to its " hieroglyphics," by which is meant its symbols, we will look in vain for their counterpart or any approximation to them in the system of Speculative Masonry.

That the Masons at a very early period exhibited a tendency to the doctrine of sacred numbers, which has since been largely developed in the Masonry of the modern High Degrees, is true, but this symbolism was derived directly from the teachings of Pythagoras, with which the founders of the primitive rituals were familiar.

That the sun and the moon are briefly referred to in our rituals and may be deemed in some sort Masonic symbols, is also true, but the use made of this symbolism, and the interpretation of it, very clearly prove that it has not been derived from a Gnostic source.

The doctrine of the metempsychosis, which was. taught by the Basilidians, is another marked point which would widely separate Freemasonry from Gnosticism, the dogma of the resurrection being almost the foundation-stone on which the whole religious philosophy of the former is erected.

Mr. King, in his work on the Gnostics, to which allusion has already been made, seeks to trace the connection between Freemasonry and Gnosticism through a line of argument which only goes to prove his absolute and perhaps his pardonable ignorance of Masonic history.

It requires a careful research, which must be stimulated by a connection with the Order, to enable a scholar to avoid the errors into which he has fallen.

"The foregoing considerations," he says, " seem to afford a rational explanation of the manner in which the genuine Gnostic symbols (whether still retaining any mystic meaning or kept as mere lifeless forms, let the Order declare) have come down to these times, still paraded as things holy and of deep significance.

Treasured up amongst the dark sectaries of the Lebanon and the Sofis of Persia, communicated to the Templars, and transmitted to their heirs, the Brethren of the Rosy Cross, they have kept up an unbroken existence."[55] In the line of history which Mr. King has here pursued, he has presented a mere jumble of non-consecutive events which it would be impossible to disentangle.

---

[55] "The Gnostics and their Remains," p. 191.

He has evidently confounded the old Rosicrucians with the more modern Rose Croix, while the only connection between the two is to be found in the apparent similarity of name.

If he meant the former, he has failed to show a relation between them and the Freemasons; if the latter, he was wholly ignorant that there is not a Gnostic symbol in their system, which is .wholly constructed out of an ecclesiastical symbolism.

Such inconsequential assertions need no refutation.

Finally he says that " Thus those symbols, in their origin, embodying the highest mysteries of Indian theosophy, afterward eagerly embraced by the subtle genius of the Alexandrian Greeks, and combined by them with the hidden wisdom of Egypt, in whose captivating and profound doctrines the few bright spirits of the Middle Ages sought a refuge from the childish fables then constituting orthodoxy, engendered by monkery upon the primal Buddhistic stock; these sacred symbols exist even now, but serve merely for the insignia of what at best is but a charitable, probably nothing more in its present form than a convivial institution." These last lines indicate the precise amount of knowledge that he possesses of the character and the design of Freemasonry.

It is to be regretted that he had not sought to explain the singular anomaly that "what at best is but a charitable, and probably nothing more than a convivial institution " has been made the depository of the symbols of an abstruse theosophy.

Benevolent societies and convivial clubs do not, as a rule, meddle with matters of such high import.

But to this uncritical essay there need be no reply.

When anyone shall distinctly point out and enumerate the Gnostic symbols that made a part of the pure and simple symbolism of the primitive Speculative Masons, it will be time enough to seek the way in which they came there.

For the present we need not undergo the needless labor of searching for that which we are sure can not be found.

CHAPTER XXXIX

THE SOCINIANS AND FREEMASONRY

While some of the adversaries of Freemasonry have pretended that its origin is to be found in the efforts of the Jesuit who sought to effect certain religious and political objects through the influence of such a society, one, at least, has endeavored to trace its first rise to the Socinians, who sprang up as a religious sect in Italy about the middle of the 16th century.

This hypothesis is of so unhistorical a character that it merits a passing notice in the legendary history of the Institution.

It was first promulgated (and I do not know that it has ever since been repeated) by the Abbe Le Franc, the Superior of the House of the Eudists, at Caen, in a book published by him in the year 1791, under the title of Le Voile leve pour les curieux, ou le secret des Revolutions, revele a l'aide de la Franc-Maconnerie, or "The Veil lifted for the Inquisitive, or the Secret of Revolutions revealed by the assistance of Freemasonry." This work was deemed of so much importance that it was translated in the following year into Italian.

In this essay Le Franc, as a loyal Catholic ecclesiastic, hating both the Freemasons and the Socinians, readily seized the idea, or at all events advanced it, that the former was derived from the latter, whose origin he assigns to the year 1546.

He recapitulates, only to deny, all the other theories that have been advanced on the subject, such as that the origin of the Institution is to be sought in the fraternities of Operative Masons of the Middle Ages, or in the assembly held at York underthe auspices of King Athelstane, or in the builders of King Solomon's Temple, or in the Ancient Mysteries of Egypt.

Each of these hypotheses he refuses to admit as true.

On the contrary, he says the order can not be traced beyond the famous meeting of Socinians, which was held at the City of Vicenza, in Italy, in the year 1546, by Loclius Socinus, Ochirius, Gentilis, and others, who there and then established the sect which repudiated the doctrine of the Trinity, and whose successors, with some modification of tenets, still exist under the name of Unitarians, or Liberal Christians.

But it is to Faustus Socinus, the nephew of Loclius, he asserts, that the real foundation of Freemasonry as a secret and symbolical society is to be ascribed.

This " artful and indefatigable sectary," as he calls him, having beheld the burning of Servetus at Geneva by Calvin, for maintaining only a part of the system that he advocated, and finding that both Catholics and Protestants were equally hostile to his views, is said to have concealed it under symbols and mysterious ceremonies, accompanied by oaths of secrecy, in order that, while it was publicly taught to the people in countries where it was tolerated, it might be gradually and safely insinuated into other states, where an open confession of it would probably lead its preachers to the stake.

The propagation of this system, he further says, was veiled under the enigmatical allegory of building a temple whose extent, in the very words of Freemasonry, was to be " in length from the east to the west, and in breadth from north to south." The professors of it were therefore furnished, so as to carry out the allegory, with the various implements used in building, such as the square, the compasses, the level, and the plumb.

And here it is that the Abbe Le Franc has found the first form and beginning of the Masonic Institution as it existed at the time of his writing.

I have said that, so far as I have been able to learn, Le Franc is the sole author or inventor of this hypothesis.

Reghellini attributes it to three distinct writers, the author of the Voile leve, Le Franc, and the Abbe Barruel.

But in fact the first and second of these are identical, and Barruel has not made any allusion to it in his History of Jacobinism. He attributes the origin of Freemasonry to the Manicheans, and makes a very elaborate and learned collation of the usages and ceremonies of the two, to show how much the one has taken from the other.

Reghellini, in commenting on this theory of the Abbe Le Franc, says that all that is true in it is that there was at the same period, about the middle of the 16th century, a learned society of philosophers and literary men at Vicenza, who held conferences on the theological questions which at that time divided Europe, and particularly Germany.

The members of this celebrated academy, he says, looked upon all these questions and difficulties concerning the mysteries of the Christian religion as points of doctrine which pertained simply to the philosophy of the ancient Egyptians, Greeks and Christians and had no relation whatever to the dogmas of faith.[56] Considering that out of these meetings of the philosophers at Vicenza issued a religious sect, whose views present a very important modification of the orthodox creeds, we may well suppose that Reghellini is as much in error in his commentary as Le Franc has been in his text.

The society which met at Vicenza and at Venice, though it sought to conceal its new and heterodox doctrines under a veil of secrecy, soon became exposed to the observation of the Papal court, through whose influence the members were expelled from the Venetian republic, some of them seeking safety in Germany, but most of them in Poland, where their doctrines were not only tolerated, but in time became popular.

In consequence, flourishing congregations were established at Cracow, Lublin, and various other places in Poland and in Lithuania.

Loelius Socinus had, soon after the immigration of his followers into Poland, retired to Zurich, in Switzerland, where he died.

He was succeeded by his nephew, Faustus Socinus, who greatly modified the doctrines of his uncle, and may be considered as the real founder of the Socinian sect of Christians.

Now, authentic history furnishes us with these few simple facts.

In the 16th century secret societies were by no means uncommon in various countries of Europe In Italy especially many were to be found.

Some of these coteries were established for the cultivation of philosophical studies, some for the pursuit of alchemy, some for theological discussions, and many were of a mere social character.

In all of them, however, there was an exclusiveness which shut out the vulgar, the illiterate, or the profane.

Thus there was founded at Florence a club which called itself the Societa della Cucchiara, or the Society of the Trowel.

The name and the symbols it used, which were the trowel, the hammer, the square, and the level, have led both Lenning and Reghellini to suppose that it was a Masonic association.

---

[56] Reghellini, "La Maconnerie," tom., p. 60

But the account given of it by Vasari, in his Lives of the Painters and Sculptors, shows that it was merely a social club of Florentine artists, and that it derived its existence and its name from the accidental circumstance that certain painters and sculptors dining together once upon a time, in a certain garden, discovered, not far from their table, a heap of mortar in which a trowel was sticking.

In an exuberance of spirits they began to throw the mortar on each other, and to call for the trowel to scrape it off.

In the same sportive humor they then and there resolved to form an association which should annually thereafter dine together, and to commemorate the ludicrous event which had given rise to their association, they called it the Society of the Trowel, and adopted as emblems certain tools connected with the mystery of bricklaying.

Every city in Italy in which science was cultivated had its academy, many of which, like the Platonic Academy, established at Florence in 1540 held their sessions in secret, and admitted none but members to participate in their mystical studies.

In Germany the secret societies of the Alchemists were abundant.

These spread also into France and England.

To borrow the language of a modern writer, mystical interpretation ran riot, everything was symbolized, and metaphors were elaborated into allegories.[57] It is a matter of historical record that in 1546 there was a society of this kind, consisting of about forty persons, eminent for their learning, who, in the words of Mosheim[58] "held secret assemblies, at different times, in the territory of Venice, and particularly at Vicenza, in which they deliberated concerning a general reformation of the received systems of religion, and, in a more especial manner, undertook to refute the peculiar doctrines that were afterwards publicly rejected by the Socinians." Mosheim, who was rigorous in the application of the canons of criticism to all historical questions that came under his review, says, in a note appended to this passage: "Many circumstances and relations sufficiently prove that immediately after the reformation had taken place in Germany, secret assemblies were held and measures proposed in several provinces that were still under the jurisdiction of Rome, with a view to combat the errors and superstitions of the times." Such was the character of the secret society at Vicenza to which Le Franc attributes the origin of Freemasonry.

---

[57] Vaughan. "Hours with the Mystics," I., p. 119
[58] "Ecclesiast. Hist. XVI.," Part III., chap. iv.

It was an assembly of men of advanced thought, who were compelled to hold their meetings in secret, because the intolerance of the church and the jealous caution of the state forbade the free and open discussion of opinions which militated against the common sentiments of the period.

The further attempt to connect the doctrines of Socinus with those of Freemasonry, because, when speaking of the new religion which he was laboring to establish, he compared it to the building of a new temple- in which his disciples were to be diligent workers, is futile.

The use of such expressions is to be attributed merely to a metaphorical and allegorical spirit by no means uncommon in writers of every ago The same metaphor is repeatedly employed by St. Paul in his various Epistles, and it is not improbable that from him Socinus borrowed the idea.

There is, therefore, as I conceive, no historical evidence whatever to support the theory that Faustus Socinus and the Socinians were the founders of Freemasonry.

At the very time when he was establishing the sect whose distinctive feature was its denial of the dogma of the Trinity, the manuscript constitutions of the Masons were beginning their Legend of the Craft, with an in,vocation to " the Might of the Father, the Wisdom of the Glorious Son, and the Goodness of the Holy Ghost, three Persons and one God." The idea of any such connection between two institutions whose doctrines were so antagonistic was the dream-or rather the malicious invention-of Le Franc, and has in subsequent times received the amount of credit to which it is entitled.

CHAPTER XL

FREEMASONRY AND THE ESSENES

Lawrie, or I should rather say Brewster, was the first to discover a connection between the Freemasons and the Jewish sect of the Essenes, a doctrine which is announced in his History of Freemsonry.

He does not indeed trace the origin of the Masonic Institution to the Essenes, but only makes them the successors of the Masons of the Temple, whose forms and tenets they transmitted to Pythagoras and his school at Crotona, by whom the art was disseminated throughout Europe.

Believing as he did in the theory that Freemasonry was first organized at the Temple of Solomon by a union of the Jewish workmen with the association of Dionysian Artificers-a theory which has already been discussed in a preceding chapter - the editor of Lawrie's History meets with a hiatus in the regular and uninterrupted progress of the Order which requires to be filled up.

The ingenious mode in which he accomplishes this task may be best explained in his own words: "To these opinions it may be objected, that if the Fraternity of Freemasons flourished during the reign of Solomon, it would have existed in Judea in after ages, and attracted the notice of sacred or profane historians.

Whether or not this objection is well founded, we shall not pretend to determine; but if it can be shown That there did exist, after the building of the temple, an association of men resembling Freemasons, in the nature, ceremonies, and object of their institution, the force of the objection will not only be taken away, but additional strength will be communicated to the opinion which we have been supporting.

The association here alluded to is that of the Essenes, whose origin and sentiments have occasioned much discussion among ecclesiastical historians.

They are all, however, of one mind concerning the constitution and observances of this religious order.'"[59] The peace making quality of "if" is here very apparent.

"If it can be shown " that there is a chronological sequence from the builders of the Temple to the Essenes, and that there is a resemblance of both to the Freemasons in " the nature, ceremonies, and object of their institution," the conclusion to which Brewster has arrived will be better sustained than it would be if these premises are denied or not proved.

The course of argument must therefore be directed to these points.

In the first place we must inquire, who were the Essenes and what was their history? This subject has already been treated to some extent in a previous portion of this work.

But the integrity of the present argument will require, and I trust excuse, the necessity of a repetition.

The three sects into which the Jews were divided in the time of Christ were the Pharisees, the Sadducees, and the Essenes.

Of these, while the Saviour makes repeated mention of the first two, he never alludes in the remotest manner to the third.

This singular silence of Jesus has been explained by some imaginative Masonic writers, such, for instance, as Clavel, by asserting that he was probably an initiate of the sect.

But scholars have been divided on this subject, some supposing that it is to be attributed to the fact (which, however, has not been established) that the Essenes originated in Egypt at a later period; others that they were not an independent sect, but only an order or subdivision of Pharisaism.

However, in connection with the present argument, the settlement of this question is of no material importance.

The Essenes were an association of ascetic celibates whose numbers were therefore recruited from the children of the Jewish community in which they lived.

These were carefully trained by proper instructions for admission into the society.

---

[59] Lawrie's "History of Freemasonry," p. 33

The admission into the interior body of the society and to the possession of its mystical doctrine was only attained after a long probation through three stages or degrees, the last of which made the aspirant a participant in the full fellowship of the community. The history of the Essenes has been so often written by ancient and modern authors, from Philo and Josephus to Ginsburg, that an inquirer can be at no loss for a knowledge of the sect.

The Masonic student will find the subject discussed in the author's Encyclopedia of Freemasonry, and the ordinary reader may be referred to the able article in McClintock and Strong's Cyclopedia of Biblical, Theological, and Ecclesiastical Literature.

I shall content myself, in fairness to the theory, with quoting the brief but compendious description given by the editor of Lawrie's History.

It is in the main correct and sustained by other authorities, except a few deductions which must be attributed to the natural inclination of every theorist to adapt facts to his hypothesis.

A few interpolations will be necessary to correct manifest errors.

"When a candidate was proposed for admission, the strictest scrutiny was made into his character.

If his life had been hitherto exemplary, and he appeared capable of curbing his passions and regulating his conduct according to the virtuous though austere maxims of their order, he was presented, at the expiration of his novitiate, with a white garment, as an emblem of the regularity of his conduct and the purity of his heart." It was not at the termination, but at the beginning of the novitiate, that the white garment or robe was presented, and it was accompanied by the presentation of an apron and a spade.

"A solemn oath was then administered to him that he would never divulge the mysteries of the Order that he would make no innovations on the doctrines of the society and that he would continue in that honorable course of piety and virtue which he had begun to pursue." This is a mere abstract of the oath, which is given at length by Josephus. It was not, however, administered until the candidate had passed through all the degrees or stages, and was ready to be admitted into full fellowship.

"Like Freemasons, they instructed the young member in the knowledge which they derived from their ancestors." He might have said, like all other sects, in which the instruction of the young member is an imperative duty.

"They admitted no women into their Order." Though this is intended by the editor to show a point of identity with Freemasonry, it does no such thing. It is the common rule of all masculine associations. It distinguishes the Essenes from other religious sects, but it by no means essentially likens them to the Freemasons.

"They had particular signs for recognizing each other, which have a strong resemblance to those of Freemasons." This is a mere assumption.

That they had signs for mutual recognition is probable, because such has been in all ages the custom of secret societies.

We have classical authority that they were employed in the ancient Pagan Mysteries.

But there is no authority for saying that these signs of the Essenes bore any resemblance to those of the Freemasons.

The only allusion to this subject is in the treatise of Philo Judaeus, De Vita Contemplativa, where that author says that - the Essenes meet together in an assembly and the right hand is laid upon the part between the chin and the breast, while the left hand hangs straight by the side." But Philo does not say that it was used as a sign of recognition, but rather speaks of it as an attitude or posture assumed in their assemblies.

Of the resemblance every Mason can judge for himself: "They had colleges, or places of retirement, where they resorted to practice their rites, and settle the affairs of the society; and after the performance of these duties, they assembled in a large hall, where an entertainment was provided for them by the president, or master, of the college, who allotted a certain quantity of provisions to every individual." This was the common meal, not partaken on set occasions and in a particular place, as the writer intimates, but every day, in their usual habitation and at the close of daily labor.

"They abolished all distinctions of rank and if preference was ever given, it was given to piety, liberality, and virtue.

Treasurers were appointed in every town to supply the wants of indigent strangers.

The Essenes pretended to higher degrees of piety and knowledge than the uneducated vulgar, and though their pretensions were high, they were never questioned by their enemies.

Austerity of manners was one of the chief characteristics of the Essenian Fraternity.

They frequently assembled, however, in convivial parties, and relieved for awhile the severity of those duties which they were accustomed to perform." In concluding this description of an ascetic religious sect, the writer of Lawrie's History says that "this remarkable coincidence between the chief features of the Masonic and Essenian Fraternities can be accounted for only by referring them to the same origin." Another, and, perhaps, a better reason to account for these coincidences will be hereafter presented.

While admitting that there is a resemblance in some points of the two institutions to each other, such as their secrecy, their classification into different degrees, although there is no evidence that the Essenian initiation had any form except that of a mere passage from a lower to a higher grade and their cultivation of fraternal love, which resemblances may be found in many other secret associations, I fail to see the identity " in the nature, the object, and the external forms of the two institutions " which Brewster claims.

On the contrary, there is a total dissimilarity in each of these points.

The nature of the Essenian institution was that of an ascetic and a bigoted religious sect, and in so far has certainly no resemblance to Freemasonry.

The object of the Essenes was to preserve in its most rigid requirements the observance of the Mosaic law; that of Freemasonry is to diffuse the tolerant principles of a universal religion, which men of every sect and creed may approve.

As to the external form of the two institutions, what little we know of those of the Essenes certainly does not exhibit any other resemblance than that which is common to all secret associations, whatever may be their nature and objects.

But the most fatal objection to the theory of a connection between them, which is maintained by the author of Lawrie's History, has been admitted with some candor by himself.

"There is one point, however," he says, "which may, at first sight, seem to militate against this supposition.

The Essenes appear in no respects connected with architecture; nor addicted to those sciences and pursuits which are subsidiary to the art of building." This objection, I say, is fatal to the theory which makes the Essenes the successors of the builders of Solomon's Temple and the forerunners of the Operative Masons of the Middle Ages, out of whom sprang the Speculative Masons of the 18th century.

Admitting for a moment the reality of the organization of Masonry at the building of the Temple in Jerusalem, any chain which unites that body of builders with the Freemasonry of the present day must show, in every link, the presence and the continuance of pursuits and ideas connected with the operative art of building.

Even the Speculative Masons of the present day have not disturbed that chain, because, though the fraternity is not now composed, necessarily, of architects and builders, yet the ideas and pursuits of those professions are retained in the Speculative science, all of whose symbolism founded on the operative art.

The Essenes were not even Speculative Masons.

Their symbolism, if they had any, was not founded on nor had any reference to the art of building.

The apron which they presented to their novice was intended to be used, according to their practice, in baptism and in bathing; and the spade had no symbolic meaning, but was simply intended for practical purposes.

The defense made by the author of the History, that in modern times there are " many associations of Freemasons where no architects are members, and which have no connection with the art of building," hardly needs a reply.

There never has been an association of Freemasons, either Operative or Speculative, which did not have a connection with the art of building, in the former case practically, in the latter symbolically.

It is absurd to suppose the interpolation between these two classes of an institution which neither practically nor symbolically cultivated the art on which the very existence of Freemasonry in either condition is based.

But another objection, equally as fatal to the theory which makes the Essenes the uninterrupted successors of the Temple builders, is to be found in the chronological sequence of the facts of history.

If this succession is interrupted by any interval, the chain which connects the two institutions is broken, and the theory falls to the ground.

The Temple of Solomon was finished about a thousand years before the Christian era, and, according to the Masonic legendary account, the builders who were engaged in its construction immediately dispersed and traveled into foreign countries to propagate the art which they had there acquired. This, though merely a legend, is not at all improbable.

It is very likely that the Tyrian workmen, at least (and they constituted the larger number of those employed in the building), returned to their homes after the tasks for which they had been sent to Solomon, by the King of Tyre, had been accomplished.

If there were any Jewish Masons at all, who were not mere laborers, it is not unreasonable to suppose that they would seek employment elsewhere, in the art of building which they had acquired from their Tyrian masters.

This is a proper deduction from the tradition, considered as such.

Who, then, were left to continue the due succession of the fraternity? Brewster, in Lawrie's History, and Oliver, in his Antiquities, affirm that it was the Essenes.

But we do not hear of this sect as an organized body until eight centuries afterward.

The apocryphal statement of Pliny, that they had been in being for thousands of years - "pler seculorum millia "has met with no reception from scholars.

It is something which, as he himself admits, is incredible; and Pliny is no authority in Jewish affairs.

Josephus speaks of them, as existing in the days of Jonathan the Maccabaean; but this was only 143 years before Christ.

They are never mentioned in any of the books of the Old Testament, written subsequently to the building of the Temple, and the silence of the Saviour and the Apostles concerning them has been attributed to the fact that they were not even at that time an organized body, but merely an order of the Pharisees.

The Rabbi Nathan distinctly says that "those Pharisees who live in a state of celibacy are Essenes;" and McClintock collates from various authorities fourteen points of resemblance, which are enumerated to show the identity in the most important usages of the two institutions.

At all events, we have no historic evidence of the existence of the Essenes as a distinct organization before the war of the Maccabees, and this would separate them by eight centuries from the builders of Solomon's Temple, of whom the theory under review erroneously supposes them to be the direct descendants.

But Brewster[60] seeks to connect the Essenes and the builders of Solomon through the Assideans, whom he also calls "an order of the Knights of the Temple of Jerusalem who bound themselves to adorn the porches of that magnificent structure and to preserve it from injury and decay." He adds that "this association was composed of the greatest men

---

[60] The unfairness of the author of Lawrie's History "History" is apparent when he quotes the "Histoire des Juifs," by Basnage, as authority for the existence of the Essenes three hundred years before the Christian era. Basnage actually says that they existed in the reign of Antigonus, but this was only 105 B.C.

of Israel, who were distinguished for their charitable and peaceful dispositions; and always signalized themselves by their ardent zeal for the purity and preservation of the temple." Hence he argues that "the Essenes were not only an ancient fraternity, but that they originated from an association of architects who were connected with the building of Solomon's temple." All this is very ingenious, but it is very untrue.

It is, however, the style, now nearly obsolete, it is to be hoped, in which Masonic history has been written.

The fact is that the Assideans were not of older date than the Essenes.

They are not mentioned by the canonical writers of the Scriptures, nor by Josephus, but the word first occurs in the book of Maccabees, where it is applied, not, as Brewster calls them, to men of " peaceful dispositions," but to a body of devoted and warlike heroes and patriots who, as Kitto says, rose at the signal for armed resistance given by Mattathias, the father of the Maccabees, and who, under him and his successors, upheld with the sword the great doctrine of the unity of God, and stemming the advancing tide of Grecian manners and idolatries.

Hence the era of the Assideans, like that of the Essenes, is removed eight centuries from the time of the building of the Solomonic Temple.

Scaliger, who is cited in Lawrie's History as authority, only says that the Assideans were a confraternity of Jews whose principal devotion consisted in keeping up the edifices belonging to the Temple; and who, not content with paying the common tribute of half a shekel a head, appointed for Temple repairs, voluntarily imposed upon themselves an additional tax.

But as they are not known to have come into existence until the wars of the Maccabees, it is evident that the Temple to which they devoted their care must have been the second one, which had been built after the return of the Jews from their Babylonian captivity.

With the Temple of Solomon and with its builders the Assideans could not have had any connection.

Prideaux says that the Jews were divided, after the captivity, into two classes-the Zadikim or righteous, who observed only the written law of Moses, and the Chasidim or pious, who superadded the traditions of the elders.

These latter, he says, were the Assideans, the change of name resulting from a common alteration of the sounds of the original Hebrew letters.

But if this division took place after the captivity, a period of nearly five centuries had then elapsed since the building of Solomon's Temple, and an uninterrupted chain of sequences between that monarch's builders and the Essenes is not preserved.

After the establishment of the Christian religion we lose sight of the Essenes.

Some of them are said to have gone to Egypt, and there to have founded the ascetic sect of Therapeutists.

Others are believed to have been among the first converts to Christianity, but in a short time they faded out of all notice.

I think, from what has been said, that there can be no hesitation in pronouncing the theory of the descent of Freemasonry to modern times through the Assideans and the Essenes to be wholly untenable and unsupported by historical testimony.

In relation to what has been called the "remarkable coincidences " to be met with in the doctrines and usages of this Jewish sect and the Freemasons, giving to them all the weight demanded, the rational explanation appears to be such as I have elsewhere given, and which I may repeat here.

The truth is that the Essenes and the Freemasons derive whatever similarity or resemblance they may have from that spirit of brotherhood which has prevailed in all ages of the civilized world, the inherent principles of which, as the natural results of any fraternization, where all the members are engaged in the same pursuit and governed by one common bond of unity, are brotherly love, charity, and generally that secrecy and exclusiveness which secures to them an isolation, in the practice of their rites, from the rest of the world. And hence, between all fraternities, ancient and modern, these "remarkable coincidences" will be apt to be found.

CHAPTER XLI

THE LEGEND OF ENOCH

Before concluding this series of essays, as they night be called, on the legendary history of Freemasonry, it will be necessary, so that a completion may be given to the subject, to refer to a few Legends of a peculiar character, which have not yet been noticed.

These Legends form no part of the original Legend of the Craft.

There are, however, brief allusions in that document to them; so brief as almost to attract no especial observation, but which might possibly indicate that some form, perhaps a very mutilated one, of these Legends was familiar to the Mediaeval Masons, or, perhaps, which is more probable, that they have suggested a foundation for the fabrication of these legendary narratives at a later period by the Speculative Freemasons of the 18th century.

Or it may be supposed that both those views are correct, and that while the imperfect and fragmentary Legend was known to the Freemasons of the Middle Ages, its completed form was thereby suggested to the Fraternity at a later period, and after the era of the revival.

Whichever of these views we may accept, it is at least certain that at the present day, and in the present condition of the Order, these Legends form an important part of the ritualism of the Order.

They can not be rejected in their symbolic interpretation, unless we are willing with them to reject the whole fabric of Freemasonry, into which they have been closely interwoven.

Of these Legends and of some minor ones of the same class, Dr. Oliver has spoken with great fairness in his Historical Landmarks, in the following words: "It is admitted that we are in possession of numerous legends which are not found in holy writ, but being of very ancient date, are entitled to consideration, although their authenticity may be questioned and their aid rejected.

I shall not, however, in any case, use their evidence as a prima facie means of proving any doubtful proposition, but merely in corroboration of an argument which might probably be complete without their aid.

Our system of typical or legendary tradition adds to the dignity of the institution by its general reference to sublime truths, which were considered necessary to its existence or its consistency, although some of the facts, how pure soever at their first promulgation, may have been distorted and perverted by passing through a multitude of hands in their transmission down the stream of time, amidst the fluctuation of the earth and the downfall of mighty states and empires." Without discussing the question of their great antiquity, or of their original purity and subsequent distortion and perversion, I propose to present these Legends to the Masonic reader, because they are really not so much traditional narratives of events that are supposed to have at some time occurred, but because they are to be 'considered really as allegorical attempts to symbolize certain ethical or religious ideas, the expression of which lies at the very foundation of the Masonic system.

So considered, they must be deemed of great value.

Their interest will also be much enhanced by a comparison of the facts of history that are interwoven with them, and to certain traditions of the ancient Oriental nations which show the existence of the same Legends among them.

These may, indeed, have been the foundation on which the Masonic ones have been built, the "distortion or perversion " being simply those variations which were necessary to connect the legendary statements more intimately and consistently with the Masonic symbolic ideas.

The first of these to which our attention will be directed is the Legend of Enoch, the seventh of the Patriarchs, of whom Milton has said: "him the Most High, (Rapt in a balmy cloud with winged steeds) Did, as thou seest, receive to walk with God High in salvation and the claims of bliss, Exempt from death." I shall first present the reader with the Masonic Legend, and then endeavor to trace out the idea which it was intended to convey. by a comparison of it with historical occurrences, with Oriental traditions of a similar nature, and with the Masonic symbolism which it seems to embody. The legend as accepted by the Craft, from a time hereafter to be referred to, runs to the following effect.

Enoch, being inspired by the Most High, and in obedience to a vision, constructed underground, in the bosom of Mount Moriah, an edifice consisting of nine brick vaults situated perpendicularly beneath each other and communicating by apertures left in the arch of each vault.

He then caused a triangular plate of gold to be made, each side of which was a cubit long; he enriched it with the most precious stones and engraved upon it the ineffable name of God.

He then encrusted the plate upon a stone of agate of the same form, which he placed upon a cubical stone of marble, and deposited the whole within the ninth or innermost vault.

When this subterranean building was completed, Enoch made a slab or door of stone, and, attaching to it a ring of iron, by which it might, if necessary, be raised, he placed it over the aperture of the uppermost arch, and so covered it overwith soil that the opening could not easily be discovered.

Enoch himself was not permitted to enter it more than once a year, and on his death or translation all knowledge of this building and of the sacred treasure which it contained was lost until in succeeding ages it was accidentally discovered while Solomon was engaged in building, a temple above the spot, on the same mountain.

The Legend proceeds to inform us that after Enoch had finished the construction of the nine vaults, fearing that the principles of the arts and sciences which he had assiduously cultivated would be lost in that universal deluge of which he bad received a prophetic vision, he erected above-ground two pillars, one of marble, to withstand the destructive influences of foe, and one of brass, to resist the ac6on of water on the pillar of brass he engraved the history of the creation, the principles of the arts and sciences, and the doctrines of Speculative Masonry as they were then practiced; and on the pillar of marble he inscribed in hieroglyphic characters the information that near the spot where they stood a precious treasure was deposited in a subterranean vault.

Such is the Legend of Enoch, which forms a very important part of the legendary history of the High Degrees.

As a traditional narrative it has not the slightest support of authentic history, and the events that it relates do not recommend themselves by an air of probability.

But, accepted as the expression of a symbolic idea, it undoubtedly possesses some value.

That part of the Legend which refers to the two pillars is undoubtedly a perversion of the old Craft Legend of Lamech's sons, which has already been treated in this work.

It will need no further consideration.

The germ of the Legend is the preservation through the efforts of the Patriarch of the Ineffable Name.

This is in fact the true symbolism of the Legend, and it is thus connected with the whole system of Freemasonry in its Speculative form.

There is no allusion to this story in the Legend of the Craft.

None of the old manuscript Constitutions contain the name of Enoch, nor does he appear to have been deemed by the Mediaeval Masons to be one of the worthies of the Craft.

The Enoch spoken of in the Cooke MS. is the son of Cain, and not the seventh Patriarch.

We must conclude, therefore, that the Legend was a fabrication of a later day, and in no way suggested by anything contained in the original Craft Legend.

But that there were traditions outside of Masonry, which prevailed in the Middle Age, in reference to subterranean caves in Mount Moriah is evident from the writings of the old historians.

Thus there was a tradition of the Talmudists that when King Solomon was building the Temple, foreseeing that at some future time the edifice would be destroyed, he caused a dark and intricate vault to be constructed underground, in which the ark might be concealed whenever such a time of danger should arrive; and that Josiah, being warned by Huldah, the prophetess, of the approaching peril, caused the ark to be hidden in the crypt which had been built by Solomon.

There was also in this vault, as in that of Enoch, a cubical stone, on which the ark was placed.[61] There is a tradition also, among the Arabians, of a sacred stone found by Abraham beneath the earth, and made by him the stone of foundation of the temple which Jehovah ordered him to erect a temple the tradition of which is confined to the Mohammedans.

But the most curious story is one told by Nicephorus Callistus, a Greek historian of the 14th century, in his Ecclesiastical Histories.

When detailing the events that occurred while Julian the Apostate was making his attempt to rebuild the Temple of Jerusalem, he narrates the following fable, but of whose fabulous character the too credulous monk has not the slightest notion.

---

[61] Lightfoot, "Prospect of the Temple," ch. xv.

"When the foundations were being laid, as has been said, one of the stones attached to the lowest part of the foundation was removed from its place and showed the mouth of a cavern which had been cut out of the rock.

But as the cave could not be distinctly seen, those who had charge of the work, wishing to explore it, that they might be better acquainted with the place, sent one of the workmen down tied to a long rope.

When he got to the bottom he found water up to his legs.

Searching the cavern on every side, he found by touching with his hands that it was of a quadrangular form.

When he was returning to the mouth, he discovered a certain pillar standing up scarcely above the water.

Feeling with his hand, he found a little book placed upon it, and wrapped up in very fine and clan linen Taking possession of it, he gave the signal with the rope that those who had sent him down, should draw him up. Being received above, as soon as the book was shown all were struck with astonishment, especially as it appeared untouched and fresh notwithstanding that it had been found in so dismal and dark a place.

But when the book was unfolded, not only the Jews but the Greeks were astounded.

For even at the beginning it declared in large letters: IN THE BEGINNING WAS THE WORD WITH GOD, AND THE WORD WAS GOD.

To speak plainly, the writing embraced the whole Gospel which was announced in the Divine tongue of the Virgin disciple." [62] It is true that Enoch has been supposed to have been identical with Hermes, and Keriher says, in the OEdipus Egyptiacus, Idris among the Hebrews, has been called Enoch, among the Egyptians Osiris and Hermes, and he was the first who before the Flood had any knowledge of astronomy and geometry.

But the authors of the Legend of the Craft were hardly likely to be acquainted with this piece of archeology, and the Hermes to whom, with a very corrupt spelling, they refer as the son of Cush, was the Hermes Trismegistus, popularly known as the " Father of Wisdom." Enoch is first introduced to the Craft as one of the founders of Geometry and Masonry, by Anderson, in the year 1723, who, in the Constitutions printed in that year, has the following passage: "By some

---

[62] Nicephori Callisti "Ecclesiasticae Historiae," tom. ii., lib. x., cap. Xxxiii

vestiges of antiquity we find one of them (the offspring of Seth) prophesying of the final conflagration at the day of Judgment, as St Jude tells and likewise of the general deluge for the punishment of the world.

Upon which he erected his two large pillars (though some ascribe them to Seth), the one of stone and the other of brick, whereon were engraven the liberal sciences, etc.

And that the stone pillar remained in Syria until the days of Vespasian, the Emperor."[63] Fifteen years afterward, when he published the second edition of the Constitutions, he repeated the Legend, with the additional statement that Enoch was " expert and bright both in the science and the art " of Geometry and Masonry, an abridgment of which he placed on the pillars which he had erected.

He adds that " the old Masons firmly believed this tradition," but as there is no appearance of any such tradition in the old records, of which since his date a large number have been recovered (for in them the building of the pillars is ascribed to the sons of Lamech), we shall have to accept this assertion with many grains of allowance, and attribute it to the general inaccuracy of Anderson when citing legendary authority.

But as the first mention of Enoch as a Freemason is made by Anderson, and as we not long afterward find him incorporated into the legendary history of the Order, we may, I think, attribute to him the suggestion of the Legend, which was, however, afterward greatly developed.

It was not, however, adopted into the English system, since neither Entick nor Northouck, who subsequently edited the Book of Constitutions, say anything more of Enoch than had already been said by Anderson.

They, indeed, correct to some extent his statement, by ascribing the pillars either to Seth or to Enoch, leaning, therefore, to the authority of Josephus, but, equally with Anderson, abandoning the real tradition of the old Legend, which gave them to the children of Lamech.

It is, I think, very evident that the Legend of Enoch was of Continental origin, and I am inclined conjecturally to assign its invention to the fertile genius of the Chevalier Ramsay, the first fabricator of high degrees, or to some of his immediate successors in the manufactory of Masonic Rites. Of this we have evidence in a very

---

[63] "Constitutions," 1723, p. 3, notes Ramsay was too learned a man to be ignorant of the numerous Oriental traditions, Arabic, Egyptian, and Rabbinical, concerning Enoch, that had been long in existence.

learned work on The Philosophical Principles of Natural and Revealed Religion, published by him in 1749.

In this work[64] he refers to the tradition extant in all nations, of a great man or legislator who was the first author of sacred symbols and hieroglyphics, and who taught the people their sacred mysteries and religious rites.

This man, he says, was, among the Phoenicians, Thaut; the Greeks, Hermes; the Arabians, Edris.

But he must have known that Thaut, Hermes, and Edris were all synonymous of Enoch, for he admits that " all these lived some time before the universal deluge, and they were all the same man, and consequently some antediluvian patriarch." And, finally, he adds that "some think that this antediluvian patriarch was Enoch himself" And then he presents, in the following language, those views which most probably supplied the suggestions that were afterward developed by himself, or some of his followers, in the full form of the Masonic legend of Enoch.

"Whatever be in these conjectures," says Ramsay, " it is certain, from the principles laid down, that the antediluvian or Noevian patriarches ought to have taken some surer measures for transmitting the knowledge of divine truths to their posterity, than by oral tradition, and, consequently, that they either invented or made use of hieroglyphics or symbols to preserve the memory of these sacred truths." And these he calls the Enochian symbols.

He does not, indeed, make any allusion to a secret depository of these symbols of Enoch, and supposes that they must have been communicated to the sons of Noah and their descendants, though in time they lost their true meaning.

But the change made in the Masonic Legend was necessary to adapt it to a peculiar system of ritualism.

It is singular how Enoch ever became among the ancients a type of the mysteries of religion.

The book of Genesis devotes only three short verses to an account of him, and nothing is there said of him, his deeds, or his character, except an allusion to his piety.

The Oriental writers, however, abound in traditionary tales of the learning of the Patriarch.

---

[64] Vol. ii., p. 12 et seq.

One tradition states that God bestowed upon him the gift of knowledge, and that he received thirty volumes from Heaven, filled with all the secrets of the most mysterious sciences.

The Babylonians supposed him to have been intimately acquainted with the nature of the stars, and they attribute to him the invention of astrology.

The Jewish Rabbis maintained that he was taught by Adam how to sacrifice and to worship the Deity aright.

The Cabalistic book of Raziel says that he received the divine mysteries through the direct line of the preceding Patriarchs.

Bar Hebraeus, a Jewish writer, asserts that Enoch was the first who invented books and writing; that he taught men the art of building cities-thus evidently confounding him with another Enoch, the son of Cain that he discovered the knowledge of the Zodiac and the course of the stars; and that he inculcated the worship of God by religious rites.

There is a coincidence in the sacred character thus bestowed upon Enoch with his name and the age at which he died, and this may have had something to do with the mystical attributes bestowed upon him by the Orientalists.

The word Enoch signifies, in the Hebrew, initiated or consecrated, and would seem, as all Hebrew names are significant, to have authorized, or, perhaps, rather suggested the idea of his connection with a system of initiation into sacred rites.

He lived, the Scriptures say, three hundred and sixty-five years.

This, too, would readily be received as having a mystical meaning, for 365 is the number of the days in a solar year and was, therefore, deemed a sacred number.

Thus we have seen that the letters of the mystical word Abraxas, which was the Gnostic name of the Supreme Deity, amounted, according to their numerical value in the Greek alphabet, to 365, which was also the case with Mithras, the god to whom the Mithraic mysteries were dedicated.

And this may account for the statement of Bar Hebraeus that Enoch appointed festivals and sacrifices to the sun at the periods when that luminary entered each of the zodiacal signs.

Goldziher, one of the latest of the German ethnologists, has advanced a similar idea in his work on Mythology Among the Hebrews.

He says: "The solar character of Enoch admits of no doubt.

He is brought into connection with the buildingof towns-a solar feature.

He lives exactly three hundred and sixty-five years, the number of days of the solar year; which can not be accidental.

And even then he did not die, but Enoch walked with Elohim, and was no more (to be seen), for Elohim took him away.' In the old times when the figure of Enoch was imagined, this was doubtless called Enoch's Ascension to heaven, as in the late traditional legends Ascensions to heaven are generally acknowledged to be solar features.'"[65] These statements and speculations have been objected to, because they would tend to make Enoch an idolater and a sun-worshipper.

This is a consequence by no means absolutely necessary, but, as the whole is merely traditionary, we need waste no time in defending the orthodox character of the Patriarch's religious views.

After all, it would appear that the Legend of Enoch, being wholly unknown to the Fraternity in the Middle Ages, unrecognized in the Legend of the Craft, and the name even, not mentioned in any of the old records, was first introduced into the rituals of some of the higher degrees which began to be fabricated toward the middle of the 18th century; that it was invented by the Chevalier Ramsay, or by some of those ritual-mongers who immediately succeeded him, and that in its fabrication very copious suggestions were borrowed from the Rabbinical and Oriental traditions on the same subject.

It is impossible then to assign to this Legend the slightest historical character.

It is made up altogether out of traditions which were the inventions of Eastern imagination.

We must view it, therefore, as an allegory; but as one which has a profound symbolic character.

It was intended to teach the doctrine of Divine Truth by the symbol of the Holy Name-the Tetragrammaton-the Name most reverently consecrated iii the Jewish system as well as in others, and which has always constituted one of the most important and prominent symbols of Speculative Masonry.

In the Continental system of the High Degrees, this symbol is presented in the form of the Legend of Enoch.

From the English system of Ancient Craft Masonry, that Legend is rejected, or rather it never has been admitted into it.

In its place, there is another esoteric Legend, which, differing altogether in details, is identical in result and effects the same symbolism.

---

[65] Chap v., sect. viii., p. 127, Martineau's Translation.

But this will be more appropriately discussed when the symbolism of Freemasonry is treated. in a future part of this work.

CHAPTER XLII

NOAH AND THE NOACHITES

In reality, there is no Legend of Noah to be found in any of the Masonic Rituals.

There is no myth, like that of Enoch or Euclid, which intimately connects him with the legendary history of the institution.

And yet the story of his life has exercised a very important influence in the origin and the development of the principles of Speculative Masonry.

Dr. Oliver has related a few traditions of Noah which, he says, are Masonic, but they never had any general acceptance among the Craft, as they are referred to by no other writer, and, if they ever existed, are now happily obsolete.

The influence of Noah upon Masonic doctrine is to be traced to the almost universal belief of men in the events of the deluge, and the consequent establishment in many nations of a system of religion known to ethnologists as the "Arkite worship." Of this a brief notice must be taken before we can proceed to investigate the connection of the name of Noah with Speculative Masonry.

The character and the actions of Noah are to be looked upon from a twofold stand-point, the historic and the legendary.

The historic account of Noah is contained in portions of the sixth and seventh chapters in the Book of Genesis, and are readily accessible to every reader, with which, however, they must already be very familiar.

The legendary account is to be found in the almost inexhaustible store of traditions which are scattered among almost all the nations of the world where some more or less dim memory of a cataclysm has been preserved.

If we examine the ancient writers, we shall find ample evidence that among all the pagan peoples there was a tradition of a deluge which, at sonic remote period, had overwhelmed the earth.

This tradition was greatly distorted from the biblical source, and the very name of the Patriarch who was saved was forgotten and replaced by some other, which varied in different countries.

Thus, in different places, he had received the names of Xisuthrus, Prometheus, Deucalion, Ogyges, and many others, where the name has been rendered very unlike itself by terminations and other idiomatic changes.

But everywhere the name was accompanied by a tradition, which also varied in its details, of a deluge by which mankind had been destroyed, and the race had, through the instrumentality of this personage, been renewed.

It is to be supposed that so important an event as the deluge would have been transmitted by the Patriarch to His posterity, and that in after times, when, by reason of the oral transmission of the history, the particular details of the event would be greatly distorted from the truth, a veneration for this new founder of the race of men would be retained.

At length, when various systems of idolatry began to be established, Noah, under whatever name he may have been known, would have been among the first to whom divine honors would be paid.

Hence arose that system known to modern? scholars as the "Arkite worship," in whose rites and mysteries, which were eventually communicated to the other ancient religions, there were always some allusions to the events of the Noachic flood to the ark, as the womb of Nature, to the eight persons saved in it, as the ogdoad or sacred number- and to the renovation of the world, as symbolizing the passage from death to immortal life.

It is not, therefore, surprising that Noah should have become a mystical personage, and that the modern Speculative Masons should have sought to incorporate some reference to him in their symbolic system, though no such idea appears to have been entertained by the Operative Masons who preceded them.

On examining the old records of the Operative Masons it will be found that no place is assigned to Noah, either as a Mason or as one of the founders of the " science." He receives only the briefest mention In the Halliwell Poem his name and the flood are merely referred to as denoting an era of time in the world's history.

It is only a statement that the tower of Babel was begun many years after " Noees fled." In the Cooke MS. the record is a little more extended, but still is but an historical narrative of the flood, in accordance with the biblical details.

In the Dowland MS. and in all the other manuscripts of the Legend of the Craft that succeeded it, the reference to Noah is exceedingly meager, his name only being mentioned, and that of his sons, from whom descended Hermes, who found one of the pillars and taught the science thereon described to other men.

So far, Noah has had no part in Masonry.

Anderson, who, in the Book of Constitutions modified and enlarged the old Craft Legends at his pleasure, calls Noah and his three sons "all Masons true," and says that they brought over from the flood the traditions and arts of the antediluvians and communicated them to their growing offspring.

And this was perhaps the first time that the Patriarch was presented to the attention of the Fraternity in a Masonic character.

Anderson semms to have cherished this idea, for in the second edition of the Constitutions he still further develops it by saying that the offspring of Noah, " as they journeyed from the East (the plains of Mount Ararat, where the ark rested) towards the West, they found a plain in the land of Shinar, and dwelt there together as NOACHIDAE, or sons of Noah." And, he adds, without the slightest historical authority, that this word " Noachidae " was" the first name of Masons, according to some old traditions." It would have puzzled him to specify any such tradition.

Having thus invented and adopted the name as the distinctive designation of a Mason, he repeats it in his second edition or revision of the "Old Charges" appended to the Book of Constitutions.

The first of these charges, in the Constitutions of 1723, contained this passage: "A Mason is obliged by his tenure to obey the moral law." In the edition of 1738, Dr. Anderson has, without authority, completed the sentence by adding the words "as a true Noachida." This interpolation was reached by Entick, who edited the third and fourth editions in 1756 and 1767, and by Northouck, who published the fifth in 1784, both of whom restored the old reading, which has ever since been preserved in all the Constitutions of the Grand Lodge of England.

Dermott, however, who closely followed the second edition of Anderson, in the composition of his Ahiman Rezon of course adopted the new term.

About that time, or a little later, a degree was fabricated on the continent of Europe, bearing the name of "Patriarch Noachite," one peculiar feature of which was that it represented the existence of two classes or lines of Masons, the one descending from the Temple of Solomon, and who were called Hiramites, and the other tracing their origin to Noah, who were styled Noachites.

Neither Preston nor Hutchison, nor any other writer of the 18th century, appear to have accepted the term.

But it was a favorite with Dr. Oliver, and under his example it has become of so common use that - Noachida and Freemason have come to be considered as synonymous terms.

What does this word really signify, and how came Anderson to adopt it as a Masonic term? The answers to these questions are by no means difficult.

Noachida, or Noachides, from which we get the English Noachite, is a gentilitial name, or a name designating the member of a family or race, and is legitimately formed according to Greek usage, where Atrides means a descendant of Atreus, or Heraclides a descendant of Heracles.

And so Noachides, or its synonyms Noachida or Noachites, means a descendant of Noah.

But why, it may be asked, are the Freemasons called the descendants of Noah? Why has he been selected alone to represent the headship of the Fraternity? I have no doubt that Dr. Anderson was led to the adoption of the word by the following reason.

After Noah's emergence from the ark, he is said to have promulgated seven precepts for the government of the new race of men of whom he was to be the progenitor.

These seven precepts are: 1, to do justice; 2, worship God; 3, abstain from idolatry; 4, preserve chastity; 5, do not commit murder; 6, do not steal; 7, do not eat the blood.

These seven obligations, says the Rev. Dr. Raphall[66] are held binding on all men, inasmuch as all are descendants of Noah, and the Rabbis maintain that he who observes them, though he be not an Israelite, has a share in the future life, and it is the duty of every Jew to enforce their due observance whenever he has the power to do so.

In consequence of this the Jewish religion was not confined during its existence in Palestine to the Jewish nation only, but proselytes of three kinds were freely admitted.

---

[66] "Genesis, with Translation and Notes," by Rev. Morris J. Raphall, p. 52

One of these classes was the "proselytes of the gate." These were persons who, without undergoimg the rite of circumcision or observing the ritual prescribed by the law of Moses, engaged to worship the true God and to observe the seven precepts of Noah, and these things they were to do whether they resided in Judea or in foreign lands.

They were not, however, admitted to all the privileges of the Jewish religion; marriage with Israelites was forbidden, and they were not permitted to enter within the sacred inclosure of the temple.

So that, although they were Noachidoe, they were not considered equal to the true children of Abraham.

Anderson, who was a theologian, was, of course, acquainted with these facts, but, with a more tolerant spirit than the Jewish law, which gave the converted Gentiles only a qualified reception, he was disposed to admit into the full fellowship of Freemasonry all the descendants of Noah who would observe the precepts of the Patriarch; these being the only moral laws inculcated by Masonry.

In giving the history of the introduction of the word into Masonry, I have not cited among the authorities the document known as the Stonehouse MS., because it was verified by a person of that name, but more usually the Krause MS., because it was first published in a German translation by Dr. Krause in his Three Oldest Documents.

It is alleged to be a copy of the York Constitutions, enacted in 926, but is generally admitted by scholars to be spurious.

Yet, as it is probable that it was originally written by a contemporary of Anderson, and about the time of the publishing of the Constitutions Of 1738, it may be accepted, so far as it supplies us with a suggestion of the motive that induced Anderson to interpolate the word "Noachida " into the "Old Charges." In the Krause MS., under the head of "The Laws or Obligations laid before his Brother Masons by Prince Edwin," we find the following article. (I translate from the German of Krause, because the original English document is nowhere to be found.) "The first obligation is that you shall sincerely honor God and obey the laws of the Noachites, because they are divine laws, which should be obeyed by all the world. Therefore, you must avoid all heresies and not thereby sin against God." The language of this document is more precise than that of Anderson, though both have the same purpose.

The meaning is that the only religious laws which a Freemason is required to obey are those which are contained in the code that has been attributed to Noah.

This sentiment is still further expressed toward the close of the " Old Charges," where it is said that the Mason is obliged only " to that religion in which all men agree," excluding, therefore, atheism, and requiring the observance of such simple laws of morality as are enjoined in the precepts of Noah.

Anderson had, however, a particular object in the use of the word "Noachida." The Krause MS. says that the Mason "must obey the laws of the Noachites; " that is, that he is to observe the seven precepts of Noah, without being required to observe any other religious dogmas outside of these-a matter which is left to himself.

But Anderson says he "must obey the moral law as a true Noachida," by which he intimates that that title is the proper designation of a Mason.

And he has shown that this was his meaning by telling us, in a preceding part of his book, that , Noachidae was the first name of Masons, according to some old traditions." Now the object of Anderson in introducing this word into the second edition of the Constitutions was to sustain his theory that Noah was the founder of the science of Freemasonry after the flood.

This was the theory taught by Dr. Oliver a century afterward, who followed Anderson in the use of the word, with the same meaning and the same object, and his example has been imitated by many recent writers.

But when Anderson speaks of a Noachida or a Noachite as a word synonymous with Freemason, he is in error; for although all Freemasons are necessarily the descendants of Noah, all the descendants of Noah are not Freemasons.

And if by the use of the word he means to indicate that Noah was the founder of post-diluvian Freemasonry, he is equally in error; for that theory, it has heretofore been shown, can not be sustained, and his statement that Noah and his three sons were " all Masons true " is one for which there is no historical support, and which greatly lacks an clement of probability.

It is better, therefore, when we speak or write historically of Freemasonry, that this word Noachida, or Noachite, should be avoided, since its use leads to a confusion of ideas, and possibly to the promulgation of error.

CHAPTER XLIII

THE LEGEND OF HIRAM ABIF

This is the most important of all the legends of Freemasonry.

It will therefore be considered in respect to its origin, its history, and its meaning; Before, however, proceeding to the discussion of these important subjects, and the investigation of the truly mythical character of Hiram Abif, it will be proper to inquire into the meaning of his name, or rather the meaning of the epithet that accompanies it.

In the places in Scripture in which he is mentioned he is called at one time (in 2 Chronicles ii., 13), by the King of Tyre, in the letter written by him to King Solomon, Churam Abi; in another place (in 2 Chronicles iv., 16), where the writer of the narrative is recording the work done by him for Solomon, Churam Abiv, or, as it might be pronounced according to the sound of the Hebrew letters, Abiu.

But Luther, in his German translation of the Bible, adopted the pronunciation Abif, exchanging the flat v for the sharp f. In this he was followed by Anderson, who was the first to present the full name of Hiram Abif to the Craft.

This he did in the first edition of the English book of Constitutions.

And since his time at least the appellation of Hiram Abif has been adopted by and become familiar to the Craft as the name of the cunning or skillful artist who was sent by Hiram, King of Tyre, to assist King Solomon in the construction of the Temple.

In Chronicles and Kings we find Churam or Huram, as we may use the initial letter as a guttural or an aspirate, and Chiram or Hiram, the vowel u or i being indifferently used.

But the Masonic usage has universally adopted the word Hiram.

Now, the Abi and Abiv, used by the King of Tyre, in the book of Chronicles form no part of the name, but are simply inflections of the possessive pronouns my and his suffixed to the appellative Ab.

Ab in Hebrew means father, i is my, and in, iv, or if is his. Abi is therefore my father, and so he is called by the King of Tyre when he is describing him to Solomon, "Hiram my father;" Abif is his father, and he is so spoken of by the historian when he recounts the various kinds of work which were done for King Solomon by "Hiram his father." But the word Ab in Hebrew, though primarily signifying a male parent, has other derivative significations.

It is evident that in none of the passages in which he is mentioned is it intended to intimate that he held such relationship to either the King of Tyre or the King of Israel.

The word "father " was applied by the Hebrews as a term of honor, or to signify a station of preeminence.

Buxtorf[67] says it sometimes signifed Master, and he cites the fourth chapter of Genesis, where Jabal is called the father of cattle and Jubal the father of musicians.

Hiram Abif was most probably selected by the King of Tyre to be sent to Solomon as a skillful artificer of preeminent skill that he might execute the principal works in the interior of the Temple and fabricate the various utensils intended for the sacred services.

He was a master in his art or calling, and properly dignified with a title which announced his distinguished character.

The title of Father, which was given to him, denotes, says Smith,[68] the respect and esteem in which he was held, according to the similar custom of the people of the East at the present day.

I am well pleased with the suggestion of Dr. McClintock that "Hiram my father seems to mean Hiram my counsellor; that is to say, foreman or master workman"[69] Applying this meaning to the passages in Chronicles which refer to this artist, we shall see how easily every difficulty is removed and the Craftsman Hiram placed in his true light.

When King Hiram, wishing to aid the King of Israel in his contemplated building, writes him a letter in which he promises to comply with the request of Solomon to send him timber from Lebanon and wood-cutters to hew it, as an additional mark of his friendship and his desire to contribute his aid in building " a house for Jehovah," he gives him the services of one of his most skillful artisans and announces

---

[67] "Lexicon Talmudicum."
[68] "Cylopaedia of Biblical Literature."
[69] "Cyclopeadia of Biblical, Theological, and Classical Literature."

the gift in these words: "And now I have sent a skillful man, endued with understanding, my master workman Hiram." And when the historian who wrote the Chronicles of the kingdom had recapitulated all the work that Hiram had accomplished, such as the pillars of the porch, the lavers and the candlesticks, and the sacred vessels, he concludes by saying that all these things were made for King Solomon by his master-workman Hiram, in the Hebrew gnasah Huram Abif Lammelech Schelomoh.

Hiram or Huram was his proper name. Ab, father of his trade or master-workman, his title, and i or if, any or his, the possessive pronominal suffix, used according to circumstances.

The King of Tyre calls him Hiram Abi, "my master-workman." When the chronicler speaks of him in his relation to King Solomon, he calls him Hiram Abif " his master-workman." And as all his Masonic relations are with Solomon, this latter designation has been adopted, from Anderson, by the Craft.

Having thus disposed of the name and title of the personage who constitutes the main point in this Masonic Legend, I proceed to an examination of the origin and progressive growth of the myth.

"The Legend of the Temple-Builder," as he is commonly but improperly called, is so intimately connected in the ritual with the symbolic history of the Temple, that we would very naturally be led to suppose that the one has always been contemporary and coexistent with the other.

The evidence on this point is, however, by no means conclusive or satisfactory, though a critical examination of the old manuscripts would seem to show that the writers of those documents, while compiling from traditional sources the Legend of the Craft, were not altogether ignorant of the rank and services that have been subsequently attributed by the Speculative Masons of the present day to Hiram Abif.

They certainly had some notion that in the building of the Temple at Jerusalem King Solomon had the assistance of a skillful artist who had been supplied to him by the King of Tyre.

The origin of the Legend must be looked for in the Scriptural account of the building of the Temple of Jerusalem, The story, as told in the books of Kings and Chronicles, is to this effect.

On the death of King David, his son and successor, Solomon, resolved to carry into execution his father's long-contemplated design of erecting a Temple on Mount Moriah for the worship of Jehovah.

But the Jews were not a nation of artisans, but rather of agriculturists, and had, even in the time of David, depended on the aid of the Phoenicians in the construction of the house built for that monarch at the beginning of his reign.

Solomon, therefore, applied to his ally, Hiram, King of Tyre, to furnish him with trees from Lebanon and with hewers to prepare them, for, as he said in his letter to the Tyrian King, "thou knowest that there is not any among us that can skill to hew timber like unto the Sidonians." Hiram complied with his request, and exchanged the skilled workmen of sterile Phoenicia for the oil and corn and wine of more fertile Judea.

Among the artists who were sent by the King of Tyre to the King of Israel, was one whose appearance at Jerusalem seems to have been in response to the following application of Solomon, recorded in the second book of Chronicles, the second chapter, seventh verse: "Send me now therefore a man cunning to work in gold, and in silver, and in brass, and in iron, and in purple and in crimson, and blue, and that can skill to grave with the cunning men that are with me in Judah, and in Jerusalem, whom David my father did provide." In the epistle of King Hiram, responsive to this request, contained in the same book and chapter, in the thirteenth and fourteenth verses, are the following words: "And now I have sent a cunning man, endued with understanding, of Huram my father's.

The son of a woman of the daughters of Dan, and his father was a man of Tyre, skillful to work in gold and in silver, in brass, in iron, in stone, and in timber, in purple, in blue, and in fine linen, and in crimson; also to grave any manner of graving, and to find out every device which shall be put to him, with thy cunning men, and with the cunning men of my lord David, thy father." A further description of him is given in the seventh chapter of the first book of Kings, in the thirteenth and fourteenth verses, and in these words: "And King Solomon sent and fetched Hiram out of Tyre. He was a widow's son of the tribe of Naphtali-and his father was a man of Tyre, a worker in brass; and he was filled with wisdom and understanding, and cunning to work all works in brass, and he came to King Solomon and wrought all his work." It is very evident that this was the origin of the Legend which was incorporated into the Masonic system, and which, on the institution of Speculative Freemasonry, was adopted as the most prominent portion of the Third Degree.

The mediaeval Masons were acquainted with the fact that King Solomon had an assistant in the works of the Temple, and that assistant had been sent to him by King Hiram.

But there was considerable confusion in their minds upon the subject, and an ignorance of the scriptural name and attributes of the person.

In the Halliwell MS., the earliest known to us, the Legend is not related.

Either the writers of the two poems of which that manuscript is composed were ignorant of it, or in the combination of the two poems there has been a mutilation and the Hiramic Legend has been omitted.

In the Cooke MS., which is a hundred years later, we meet with the first allusion to it and the first error, which is repeated in various forms in all the subsequent manuscript constitutions.

That manuscript says: "And at the makyng of the temple in Salamonis tyme as lit is seyd in the bibull in the iii boke of Regum in tertio Regum capitulo quinto, that Salomoii had iiii score thousand masons at his werke.

And the kyngis sone of Tyry was his master mason." The reference here made to the third book of Kings is according to the old distribution of the Hebrew canon, where the two books of Samuel are caged the mat and second books of Kings.

According to our present canon, the reference would be to the fifth chapter of the first book of Kings.

In that chapter nothing is said of Hiram Abif, but it is recorded there that "Adoniram was over the levy." Now the literal meaning of Adoniram is the lord Hiram.

As the King of Tyre had promised to send his workmen to Lebanon, and as it is stated that Adoniram superintended the men who were there hewing the trees, the old legendist, not taking into account that the levy of thirty thousand, over whom Adoniram presided, were Israelites and not Phoenicians, but supposing that they had been sent to Lebanon by Hiram, King of Tyre, and that he had sent Adoniram with them and viewing the word as meaning the lord Hiram, hastily came to the conclusion that this Lord or Prince Hiram was the son of the King.

And hence he made the mistake of saying that the son of the King of Tyre was the person sent to Solomon to be his, master-mason or master-builder.

This error was repeated in nearly all the succeeding manuscripts, for they are really only copies of each other, and the word Adon, as meaning lord or prince, seems to have been always assumed in some one or other corrupted form as the name of the workman sent by King Hiram to King Solomon, and whom the Freemasons of the present day know as Hiram Abif.

Thus in the Doweled MS., conjecturally dated at A.D. 1550, it is said: "And furthermore there was a Kinge of another region that men called IRAM, and he loved well Kinge Solomon and he gave him tymber to his worke.

And he had a sonn that height (was called) AYNON, and he was a Master of Geometrie and was chief Master of all his Masons, and was Master of all his gravings and carvings and of all manner of Masonrye that longed to the Temple." There can be no doubt that Aynon is here a corruption of Adon. In the Landsdowne MS., whose date is A.D. 1560, the language is precisely the same, except that it says King Iram " had a sonne that was called a man." It seems almost certain that the initial letter a in this name has been, by careless writing, dislocated from the remaining letters, man, and that the true reading is Aman, which is itself an error, instead of Amon, and this a manifest corruption of Adon.

This is confirmed by the York MS., Number 1 which is about forty years later (A.D.1600), where the name is spelled Amon.

This is also the name in the Lodge of Hope MS., dated A.D. 1680.

In the Grand Lodge MS., date of A.D. 1632, he is again called the son of the King of Tyre, but his name is given as Aynone, another corrupted form of Adon.

In the Sloane MS., Number 3,848, A.D. 1646, it is Aynon, the final e being omitted.

In the Harleian MS., Number 1942, dated A.D. 1670, both the final e and the medial y are omitted, and the name becoming Anon approximates still nearer to the true Adon.

In the Alnwick MS., of A.D. 1701, the name is still further corrupted into Ajuon.

In all of these manuscripts the Legend continues to call this artist the son of the King of Tyre, whose name is said to be Hiram or more usually Iram; and hence the corrupted orthography of Amon, Aynon, or Anon, being restored to the true form of Adon, with which word the old Masons were acquainted, as signifying Lord or Prince, we get, by prefixing it to his father's name, Adon-Iram or Adoniram, the Lord or Prince Hiram.

And hence arose the mistake of confounding Hiram Abif with Adoniram, the chief of the workmen on Mount Lebanon, who was a very different person.

The Papworth MS., whose date is A. D. 1714, is too near the time of the Revival and the real establishment of Speculative Masonry to be of much value in this inquiry.

It, however, retains the statement from the Old Legend, that the artist was the son of King Hiram.

But it changes his name to that of Benaim.

This is probably an incorrect inflection of the Hebrew word Boneh, a builder, and shows that the writer, in an attempt to correct the error of the preceding legendists who had corrupted Adon into Anon or Amon, or Ajuon, had in his smattering of Hebrew committed a greater one.

The Krause MS. is utterly worthless as authority.

It is a forgery, written most probably, I think I may say certainly, after the publication of the first edition of Anderson's Constitutions, and, of course, takes the name from that work.

The name of Hiram Abif is first introduced to public notice by Anderson in 1723 in the book of Constitutions printed in that year.

In this work he changes the statement made in the Legend of the Craft, and says that the King of Tyre sent to King Solomon his namesake Hiram Abif, the prince of architects." Then quoting in the original Hebrew a passage from the second book of Chronicles, where the name of Hiram Abif is to be found, he excels it "by allowing the word Abif to be the surname of Hiram the Mason;" furthermore he adds that in the passage where the King of Tyre calls him " Huram of my father's," the meaning is that Huram was "the chief Master Mason of my father, King Abibalus," a most uncritical attempt, because he intermixes, as its foundation, the Hebrew original and the English version.

He had not discovered the true explication, namely, that Hiram is the name, and Ab the title, denoting, as I have before said, Master Workman, and that in, or iv, or if, is a pronominal suffix, meaning his, so that when speaking of him in his relation to King Solomon, he is called Hiram Abif, that is Hiram, his or Solomon's Master Workman.

But Anderson introduced an entirely new element in the Legend when he said, in the same book, that "the wise King Solomon was Grand Master of the Lodge at Jerusalem, King Hiram was Grand Master of the Lodge at Tyre, and the inspired Hiram Abif was Master of Work." In the second or 1738 edition of the Constitutions, Anderson considerably enlarged the Legend, for reasons that will be adverted to when I come, in the next part of this work, to treat of the origin of the Third Degree, but on which it is here unnecessary to dwell.

In that second edition, he asserts that the tradition is that King Hiram had been Grand Master of all Masons, but that when the Temple was finished he surrendered the pre-eminence to King Solomon.

No such tradition, nor any allusion to it, is to be found in any of the Old Records now extant, and it is, moreover, entirely opposed by the current of opinion of all subsequent Masonic writers.

From these suggestions of Anderson, and from some others of a more esoteric character, made, it is supposed, by him and by Dr. Desaguliers about the time of the Revival, we derive that form of the Legend of Hiram Abif which has been preserved to the present day with singular uniformity by the Freemasons of all countries.

The substance of the Legend, so far as it is concerned in the present investigation, is that at the building of the Temple there were three Grand Masters-Solomon, King of Israel; Hiram, King of Tyre, and Hiram Abif, and that the last was the architect or chief builder of the edifice.

As what relates to the fate of Hiram Abif is to be explained in an altogether allegorical or symbolical sense, it will more appropriately come finder consideration when we are treating, in a subsequent part of this work, of the Symbolism of Freemasonry.

Our present study will be the legendary character of Hiram Abif as the chief Master Mason of the Temple, and our investigations will be directed to the origin and meaning of the myth which has now, by universal consent of the Craft, been adopted, whether correctly or not we shall see hereafter.

The question before us, let it be understood, is not as to the historic truth of the Hiramic legend, as set forth in the Third Degree of the Masonic ritual-not as to whether this be the narrative of an actual occurrence or merely an allegory accompanied by a moral signification-not as to the truth or fallacy of the theory which finds the origin of Freemasonry in the Temple of Jerusalem-but how it has been that the Masons of the Middle Ages should have incorporated into their Legend of the Craft the idea that a worker in metal-in plain words, a smith-was the chief builder at the Temple.

This thought, and this thought alone, must govern us in the whole course of our inquiry.

Of all the myths that have prevailed among the peoples of the earth, hardly any has had a greater antiquity or a more extensive existence than that of the Smith who worked in metals, and fabricated shields and swords for warriors, or jewelry for queens and noble ladies.

Such a myth is to be found among the traditions of the earliest religions,[70] and being handed down through ages of popular transmission, it is preserved, with various unnatural modifications, in the legends of the Middle Age, from Scandinavia to the most southern limit of the Latin race.

Long before this period it was to be found in the mythology and the folk-lore of Assyria, of India, of Greece, and of Rome.

Freemasonry, in its most recent form as well as in its older Legend, while adopting the story of Hiram Abif, once called Adon Hiram, has strangely distorted its true features, as exhibited in the books of Kings and Chronicles; and it has, without any historical authority, transformed the Scriptural idea of a skillful smith into that of an architect and builder.

Hence, in the Old Legend he is styled a "Master of Geometry and of all Masonry," and in the modern ritual of Speculative Masonry he is called " the Builder," and to him, in both, is supposed to have been intrusted the super- intendence of the Temple of Solomon, during its construction, and the government and control of those workmen-the stone squarers and masons-who were engaged in the labor of its erection To divest this Legend of its corrupt form, and to give to Hiram Abif, who was actually an historic personage, his true position among the workmen at the Temple, can not affect, in the slightest degree, the symbolism of which he forms so integral a part, while it will rationally account for the importance that has been attributed to him in the old as well as in the new Masonic system.

Whether we make Hiram Abif the chief Builder and the Operative Grand Master of Solomon's Temple, or whether we assign that position to Anon, Amon, or Ajuon, as it is in the Old Legend, or to Adoniram, as it is done in some Masonic Rites, the symbolism will remain unaffected, because the symbolic idea rests on the fact of a Chief Builder having existed, and it is immaterial to the development of the symbolism what was his true name.

The instruction intended to be conveyed in the legend of the Third Degree must remain unchanged, no matter whom we may identify as its hero; for he truly represents neither Hiram nor Anon nor Adoniram nor any other individual person, but rather the idea of man in an abstract sense, It is, however, important to the truth of history that

---

[70] "Vala, one of the names of Indra, in the Aryan mythology, is traced," says Mr. Cox, "through the Teutonic lands until we reach the cave of Wayland Smith, in Warwickshire." "Myhtology of the Aryan Nations," vol., p. 326

the real facts should be eliminated out of the mythical statements which envelop them.

We must throw off the husk, that we may get at the germ.

And besides, it will add a new attraction to the system of Masonic ritualism if we shall be able to trace in it any remnant of that oldest and most interesting of the myths, the Legend of the Smith, which, as I have said, has universally prevailed in the most ancient forms of religious faith.

Before investigating this Legend of the Smith in its reference to Freemasonry and to this particular Legend of Hiram Abif which we are now considering, it will be proper to inquire into the character of the Legend as it existed in the old religions and in the mediaeval myths.

We may then inquire how this Legend, adopted in Freemasonry in its stricter ancient form of the Legend of Tubal Cain, became afterward confounded with another legend of a Temple-Builder.

If we go back to the oldest of all mythologies, that which is taught in the Vedic hymns, we shall find the fire-god Agni, whose flames are described as being luminous, powerful, fearful, and not to be trusted." The element of fire thus worshipped by the primeval Aryans, as an instrument of good or of evil, was subsequently personified by the Greeks: the Vedic hymns, referring to the continual renovation of the flame, as it was fed by fuel, called it the fire-god Agni; also Gavishtha, that is, the ever young.

From this the Greeks got their Hephaestus, the mighty workman, the immortal smith who forged the weapons of the gods, and, at the prayer of Thetis, fabricated the irresistible armor of Achilles.

The Romans were indebted to their Aryan ancestors for the same idea of the potency of fire, and personified it in their Vulcan, a name which is evidently derived from the Sanscrit Ulka, a firebrand, although a similarity of sound has led many etymologists to deduce the Roman Vulcan from the Semitic Tubal Cain.

Indeed, until the modern discoveries in comparative philology, this was the universal opinion of the learned.

Among the Babylonians an important god was Bil-can.

He was the fire-god, and the name seems to be derived from Baal, or Bel, and Cain, the god of smiths, or the master smith.

George Smith, in his Chaldaen Account of Genesis, thinks that there is possibly some connection here with the Biblical Tubal Cain and the classical Vulcan.

From the fragments of Sanchoniathon we learn that the Phoenicians had a hero whom he calls Chrysor.

He was worshipped after his death, in consequence of the many inventions that he bestowed on man, under the name of Diamichius; that is, the great inventor.

To him was ascribed the invention of all those arts which the Greeks attributed to Hephaestus, and the Romans to Vulcan.

Bishop Cumberland derives the name of Chrysor from the Hebrew Charatz, or the Sharbener, an appropriate designation of one who taught the use of iron tools.

The authorized version of Genesis, which calls Tubal Cain " an instructor of every artificer in brass and iron," is better rendered in the Septuagint and the Vulgate as a sharpener of every instrument in brass and iron." Tubal Cain has been derived, in the English lectures of Dr. Hemming, and, of course, by Dr. Oliver, from a generally received etymology that Cain meant worldly possessions, and the true symbolism of the name has been thus perverted.

The true derivation is from kin, which, says Gesenius, has the especial meaning to forge iron, whence comes Kain, a spear or lance, an instrument of iron that has been forged.

In the cognate Arabic it is Kayin.

"This word," says Dr. Goldziher in his work on Mythology Among the Hebrews" which with other synonymous names of trades occurs several times on the so-called Nabatean Sinaitic inscriptions, signifies Smith, maker of agricultural implements[71] and has preserved this meaning in the Arabic Kayin and the Aramaic kinaya, whilst in the later Hebrew it was lost altogether, being probably suppressed through the Biblical attempt to derive the proper name Cain etymologically from kana, " to gain." Here it is that Hemming and Oliver got their false symbolism of "worldly possessions." Goldziher attempts to identify mythologically Cain the fratricide with the son of Lamech.

Whether he be correct or not in his theory, it is at least a curious coincidence that Cain, which I have shown to mean a smith, should have been the first builder of a city, and that the same name should have been assigned to the first forger of metals, while the old Masonic Legend makes the master smith, Hiram of Tyre, also the chief builder of Solomon.

---

[71] He confines the expression to "agricultural" to enforce a particular theory then under consideration. He might correctly have been more general and included all other kinds of implements, warlike and mechanical as well as agricultural.

It will, I think, be interesting to trace the progress of the myth which has given in every age and every country this prominent position among artisans to the smith.

Hephaestus, or Vulcan, kindling his forges in the isle of Lemnos, and with his Cyclops journeymen beating out and shaping and welding the red-hot iron into the forms of spears and javelins and helmets and coats of mail, was the southern development of the Aryan fire-god Agni.

"Hephaestus, or Vulcan," says Diodorus Siculus, "was the first founder in iron, brass, gold, silver, and all fusible metals, and he taught the uses to which fire might be applied by artificers." Hence he was called by the ancients the god of blacksmiths.

The Scandinavians, or northern descendants of the Aryan race, brought with them, in their emigration from Caucasus, the same reverence for fire and for the working of metals by its potent use.

They did not, however, bring with them such recollections of Agni as would invent a god of fire Eke the Hephaestus and Vulcan of the Greeks and Romans. They had, indeed, Loki, who derived his name, it is said by some, from the Icelandic logi, or flame. But he was an evil principle, and represented rather the destructive than the creative powers of fire.

But the Scandinavians, interpolating, like all the northern nations, their folk-lore into their mythology, invented their legends of a skillful smith, beneath whose mighty blows upon the yielding iron swords of marvelous keenness and strength were forged, or by whose wonderful artistic skill diadems and bracelets and jewels of surpassing beauty were constructed.

Hence the myth of a wonderfully cunning artist was found everywhere, and the Legend of the Smith became the common property of all the Scandinavian and Teutonic nations, and was of so impressive a character that it continued to exist down to mediaeval times, and traces of it have ex- tended to the superstitions of the present day.

May we not justly look to its influence for the prominence given by the old Masonic legendists to the Master Smith of King Hiram among the workmen of Solomon? Among the Scandinavians we have the Legend of Volund, whose story is recited in the Volunddarkvitha, or Lay of Volund, contained in the Edda of Saemund.

Volund (pronounced as if spelled Wayland) was one of three brothers, sons of an Elf-king; that is to say, of a supernatural race.

The three brothers emigrated to Ulfdal, where they married three Valkyries, or choosers of the slain, maidens of celestial origin, the attendants of Odin, and whose attributes were similar to those of the Greek Parcae, or Fates.

After seven years the three wives fled away to pursue their allotted duty of visiting battle-fields.

Two of the brothers went in search of their errant wives; but Volund remained in Ulfdal.

He was a skillful workman at the forge, and occupied his time in fabricating works in gold and steel, while patiently awaiting the promised return of his beloved spouse.

Niduth, the king of the country, having heard of the wonderful skill of Volund as a forger of metals, visited his home during his absence and surreptitiously got possession of some of the jewels which he had made, and of the beautiful sword which the smith had fabricated for himself Volund, on his return, was seized by the warriors of Niduth and conducted to the castle.

There the queen, terrified at his fierce looks, ordered him to be hamstrung.

Thus, maimed and deprived of the power of escape or resistance, he was confined to a small island in the vicinity of the royal residence and compelled to fabricate jewels for the queen and her daughter, and weapons of war for the king.[72] It were tedious to recount all the adventures of the smith while confined in his island prison.

It is sufficient to say that, having constructed a pair of wings by which he was enabled to fly (by which we are reminded of the Greek fable of Daedalus), he made his escape, having by stratagem first dishonored the princess and slain her two brothers.

This legend of " a curious and cunning workman " at the forge was so popular in Scandinavia that it extended into other countries, where the Legend of the Smith presents itself under various, modifications In the Icelandic legend Volund is described as a great artist in the fabrication of iron, gold and silver.

It does not, however, connect him with supernatural beings, but attributes to him great skill in his art, in which he is assisted by the power of magic.

The Germans had the same legend at a very early period.

In the German Legend the artificer is called Wieland, and he is represented as the son of a giant named Wade.

---

[72] All these smiths of mythology and folk-lore are represented as being lame, like Hephaestus, who broke his leg in falling from heaven.

He acquires the art of a smith from Minner, a skillful workman, and is perfected by the Dwarfs in all his operations at the forge as an armorer and gold smith.

He goes of his own accord to the king, who is here called Nidung, where he finds another skillful smith, named Amilias, with whom he contends in battle, and kills him with his sword, Mimung.

For this offense he is maimed by the king, and then the rest of the story proceeds very much like that of the Scandinavian legend.

Among the Anglo-Saxons the legend is found not varying much from the original type.

The story where the hero receives the name of Weland is contained in an ancient poem, of which fragments, unfortunately, only remain.

The legend had become so familiar to the people that in the metrical romance of Beowulf the coat of mail of the hero is described as the work of Weland; and King Alfred in his translation of the Consolation of Philosophy by Boethius, where the author allude,, to the bones of the Consul Fabricius, in the passage "ubi sunt ossa Fabricie? " (where now are the bones of Fabricius?), thus paraphrases the question: Where now are the bones of the wise Weland, the goldsmith that was formerly so famed?" Geoffrey of Monmouth afterward, in a Latin poem, speaks of the gold, and jewels, and cups that had been sculptured by Weland, which name he Latinizes as Gueilandus.

In the old French chronicles we repeatedly encounter the legend of the skillful smith, though, as might be expected, the name undergoes many changes.

Thus, in a poem of the 6th century, entitled Gautier a la main forte, or Walter of the strong hand, it is said that in a combat of Walter de Varkastein he was protected from the lance of Randolf by a cuirass made by Wieland.

Another chronicle, of the 12th century, tells us that a Count of Angouleme, in a battle with the Normans, cut the cuirass and the body of the Norman King in twain at a single stroke, with his sword Durissima, which had been made by the smith Walander.

A chronicle of the same period, written by the monk John of Marmontier, describes the magnificent habiliments of Geoffrey Plantagenet, Duke of Normandy, among which, says the author, was " a sword taken from the royal treasury and long since renowned.

Galannus, the most skillful of armorers, had employed much labor and care in making it." Galans, for Walans (the G being substituted for the W, as a letter unknown in the French alphabet), is the name bestowed in general on this skillful smith, and the romances of the Trouveres and Troubadours of northern and southern France, in the 12th and 13th centuries, abound in references to swords of wondrous keenness and strength that were forged by him for the knights and paladins.

Whether the name was given as Volund, or Wieland, or Weland, or Galans, it found its common origin in the Icelandic Volund, which signifies a smith.

It is a generic term, from which the mythical name has been derived.

So the Greeks called the skillful workman, the smith of their folk-lore, Daedalus, because there is a verb in their language daidallo, which means to do skillful or ornamental work.

Here it may not be irrelevant to notice the curious fact that concurrently with these legends of a skillful smith there ran in the Middle Ages others, of which King Solomon was the subject.

In many of these old romances and metrical tales, a skill was attributed to him which makes him the rival of the subordinate artisan.

Indeed, the artistic reputation of Solomon was so proverbial at the very time when these legends of the smith were prevalent, that in the poems of those days we meet with repeated uses of the expression " l'uevre Salemon," or "the work of Solomon," to indicate any production of great artistic beauty.

So fully had the Scandinavian sagas the German chronicles, and the French romances spoken of this mythical smith that the idea became familiar to the common people, and was handed down in the popular superstitions and the folk-lore, to a comparatively modern period.

Two of these, one from Germany and one from England, will suffice as examples, and show the general identity of the legends and the probability of their common origin.[73] Herman Harrys, in his Tales and Legends of Lower Saxony, tells the story of a smith who dwelt in the village of Hagen, on the side of a mountain, about two miles from Osnabruck.

He was celebrated for his skill in forging metals; but, being discontented with his lot, and murmuring against God, he was

---

[73] For many of the details of these two legends, as well as for much that has already been said of the mythological smith of the Middle Ages, I have been indebted to the learned Dissertation of M.M. Depping and Michel. It has been ably translated from the French, with additions by Mr. S.W. Singer, London, 1847.

supernaturally carried into a cavernous cleft of the mountain, where he was condemned to be a metal king, and, resting by day, to labor at night at the forge for the benefit of men, until the mine in the mountain should cease to be productive.

In the coolness of the mine, says the legend, his good disposition returned, and he labored with great assiduity, extracting ore from its veins, and at first forging household and agricultural implements.

Afterward he confined himself to the shoeing of horses for the neighboring; farmers.

In front of the cavern was a stake fixed iii the ground, to which the countryman fastened the horse which he wished to have shod, and on a stone near by he laid the necessary fee.

He then retired.

On returning in due time he would find the task completed; but the smith, or, as he was called, the Hiller, i.e., Hider, would never permit himself to be seen.

Similar to this is the English legend, which tells us that in a vale of Berkshire, at the foot of White Horse Hill, evidently, from the stones which lay scattered around, the site of a Druidic monument, formerly dwelt a person named Wayland Smith.

It is easily understood that here the handicraft title has been incorporated with the anglicized name, and that it is the same as the mediaeval Weland the Smith.

No one ever saw him, for the huge stones afforded him a hiding-place.

He, too, was a Hiller,- for the word in the preceding legend does not mean "the man of the hill," but is from the German hullen, to cover or conceal, and denotes the man who conceals himself.

In this studious concealment of their persons by both of these smiths we detect the common origin of the two legends. When his services were required to shoe a horse, the animal was left among the stones and a piece of money placed on one of them.

The owner then retired, and after some time had elapsed he returned, when he found that the horse was shod and the money had disappeared.

The English reader ought to be familiar with this story from the use made of it by Sir Walter Scott in his novel of Kenilworth.

It is very evident, from all that has been here said, that the smith, as the fabricator of weapons for the battle-field and jewels for the bourdoir, as well as implements of agriculture and household use, was a most important personage in the earliest times, deified by the ancients, and invested by the moderns with supernatural gifts.

It is equally evident that this respect for the smith as an artificer was prevalent in the Middle Ages.

But in the very latest legends, by a customary process of degeneration in all traditions, when the stream becomes muddled as it proceeds onward, he descended in character from a forger of swords, his earliest occupation, to be a shoer of horses, which was his last.

It must be borne in mind, also, that in the -Middle Ages the respect for the smith as a "curious and cunning " workman began by the introduction of a new clement, brought by the Crusaders and pilgrims from the East to be shared with King Solomon, who was supposed to be invested with equal skill.

It is not, therefore, strange that the idea should have been incorporated into the rituals of the various secret societies of the Middle Ages and adopted by the Freemasonry at first by the Operative branch and afterward, in a more enlarged form, by the Speculative Masons.

In all of the old manuscripts constitutions of the Operative Masons we find the Legendof the Craft, and with it, except in one instance, and that the earliest, a reference to Tubal Cain as the one who " found [that is, invented] the Smith Craft of gold and silver, iron and copper and steel." Nothing but the universal prevalence of the mediaeval legend of the smith, Volund or Weland, can, I think, account for this reference to the Father of Smith Craft in a legend which should have been exclusively appropriated to Stone Craft.

There is no connection between the forge and the trowel which authorized on any other ground the honor paid by stone-masons to a forger of metals-an honor so marked that in time the very name of Tubal Cain came to be adopted as a significant and important word in the Masonic ritual, and the highest place in the traditional labors of the Temple was assigned to a worker in gold and brass and iron.

Afterward, when the Operative Art was superseded by the Speculative Science, the latter supplemented to the simple Legend of the Craft the more recondite Legend of the Temple. In this latter Legend, the name of that Hiram whom the King of Tyre had sent with all honor to the King of Israel, to give him aid in the construction of the Temple, is first introduced under his biblical appellation.

But this is not the first time that this personage is made known to the fraternity.

In the older Legends he is mentioned, always with a different name but always, also, as "King Solomon's Master Mason." In the beginning of the 18th century, when what has been called the Revival took place, there was a continuation of the general idea that he was the chief Mason at the Temple; but the true name of Hiram Abif is, as we have already said, then first found in a written or printed record.

Anderson speaks of his architectural abilities in exaggerated terms.

He calls him in one place "the most accomplished Mason on earth,"and in another "the prince of architects." This character has adhered to him in all subsequent times, and the unwritten Legend of the present day represents him as the , Chief Builder of the Temple," the " Operative Grand Master," and the " Skillful Architect " by whose elaborate designs on his trestle-board the Craft were guided in their labors and the edifice was constructed.

Now, it will be profitable in the investigation of historic truth to compare these attributes assigned to Hiram Abif by the older and more recent legendists with the biblical accounts of the same person which have already been cited.

In the original Hebrew text of the passage in the book of Chronicles, the words which designate the profession of Hiram Abif are Khoresh nekhoshet,- literally, a worker in brass.

The Vulgate, which was the popular version in those days and from which the old legendists must have derived their knowledge of biblical history, thus translates the letter of King Hiram to King Solomon: "Therefore I have sent to thee a wise and most skillful man, Hiram the workman or smith, my father "-Hiram fabrem Patrem meum.

Indeed, in the close of the verse in the Authorized Version he is described as being "cunning to work all works in brass." And hence Dr. Adam Clarke, in his, Commentaries, calls him "a very intelligent coppersmith." The error into which the old legendists and the modern Masonic writers have fallen, in supposing him to have been a stone-mason or an architect, has arisen from the mistranslation in the Authorized Version of the passage in Chronicles where he is said to have been "skillful to work in gold and in silver, in brass, in iron, in stone, and in timber." The words in the original are Baabanim vebagnelsim, in stones and in woods,- that is, in. Precious stones and in woods of various kinds.

That is to say, besides being a coppersmith he was a lapidary and a carver and gilder.

The words in the original Hebrew are in the plural, and therefore the translation " in wood and in timber " is not correct.

Gesenius says - and there is no better authority for a Hebraism - that the word eben is used by way of excellence, to denote a precious stone, and its plural, abanim, means, therefore, precious stones. In the same way gnetz, which in the singular signifies a tree, in the plural denotes materials of wood, for any purpose.

The work that was done by Hiram Abif in the Temple is fully recounted in the first book of Kings, the seventh chapter, from the fifteenth to the fortieth verse, and is briefly recapitulated in verses forty-one to fifty.

It is also enumerated in the third and fourth chapters of second Chronicles, and in both books care is taken to say that when this work was done the task of Hiram Abif was completed.

In the first book of Kings (vii. 40) it is said: "So Hiram made an end of dung all the work that he made King Solomon for the house of the Lord." In the second book of Chronicles (iv. 2) the statement is repeated thus: "And Hiram finished the work that he was to make for King Solomon for the house of God." The same authority leaves us in no doubt as to what that work was to which the skill of Hiram Abif had been devoted. "It was,"says the book of Chronicles, " the two pillars, and the pommels and the chapiters which were on the top of the pillars; and four hundred pomegranates on the two wreaths; two rows of pomegranates on each wreath, to cover the two pommels of the chapiters which were upon the pillars.

He made also bases, and lavers made he upon the bases; one sea and twelve oxen under it.

The pots also, and the shovels and the flesh hooks and all their instruments, did Huram his father (Hiram Abif) make to King Solomon, for the house of the Lord, of bright brass." Enough has been said to show that the labors of Hiram Abif in the Temple were those of a worker in brass and in precious stones, in carving and in gilding, and not those of a stonemason.

He was the decorator and not the builder of the Temple.

He owes the position which he holds in the legends and in the ritual of Freemasonry, not to any connection which he had with the art of architecture, of which there is not the slightest mention by the biblical authorities, but, like Tubal Cain, to his skill in bringing the potency of fire under his control and applying it to the forging of metals.

The high honor paid to him is the result of the influence of that Legend of the Smith, so universally spread in the Middle Ages, which recounted the wondrous deeds of Volund, or Wieland, or Wayland.

The smith was, in the mediaeval traditions, in the sagas of the north and in the romances of the south of Europe, the maker of swords and coats of mail; in the Legends of Freemasonry he was transmuted into the fabricator of holy vessels and sacred implements.

But the idea that of all handicrafts smith-craft was the greatest was unwittingly retained by the Masons when they elevated the skillful smith of Tyre, the "cunning" worker in brass, to the highest place as a builder in their Temple legend.

The spirit of critical iconoclasm, which strips the exterior husk from the historic germ of all myths and legends, has been doing much to divest the history of Freemasonry of all fabulous assumptions.

This attempt to give to Hiram Abif his true position, and to define his real profession, is in the spirit of that iconoclasm.

But the doctrine here advanced is not intended to affect in the slightest degree the part assigned to Hiram Abif in the symbolism of the Third Degree.

Whatever may have been his profession, he must have stood high in the confidence of the two kings, of him who sent him and him who received him, as " a master workman; " and he might well be supposed to be entitled in an allegory to the exalted rank bestowed upon him in the Legend of the Craft and in the modern ritual.

Allegories are permitted to diverge at will from the facts of history and the teachings of science.

Trees may be made to speak, as they do in the most ancient fable extant, and it is no infringement of their character that a worker in brass may be transmuted into a builder in stone to suit a symbolic purpose.

Hence this " celebrated artist," as he is fairly called, whether smith or mason, is still the representative, in the symbolism of Freemasonry, of the abstract idea of man laboring in the temple of life, and the symbolic lesson of his tried integrity and his unhappy fate is still the same.

As Freemasons, when we view the whole Legend as a myth intended to give expression to a symbolic idea, we may be content to call him an architect, the first of Masons, and the chief builder of the Temple; but as students of history we can know nothing of him and admit nothing concerning him that is not supported by authentic and undisputed authority.

We must, therefore, look upon him as the ingenious artist, who worked in metals and in precious stones, who carved in cedar and in olive-wood, and thus made the ornaments of the Temple.

He is only the Volund or Wieland of the olden legend, changed, by a mistaken but a natural process of transmuting traditions, from a worker in brass to a worker in stone.

CHAPTER XLIV

THE LELAND MANUSCRIPT

The Leland Manuscript, so called because it is said to have been discovered by the celebrated antiquary John Leland, and sometimes called the Locke Manuscript in consequence of the suppositous annotations appended to it by that metaphysician, has for more than a century attracted the attention and more recently excited the controversies of Masonic scholars.

After having been cited with approbation by such writers as Preston, Hutchinson, Oliver, and Krause, it has suffered a reverse under the crucial examination of later critics.

It has by nearly all of these been decided to be a forgery-a decision from which very few at this day would dissent.

It is in fact one of those "pious frauds" intended to strengthen the claim of the Order to a great antiquity and to connect it with the mystical schools of the ancients.

But as it proposes a theory concerning the origin of the Institution, which was long accepted as a legend of the Order, it is entitled to a place in the legendary history of Freemasonry.

The story of this manuscript and the way in which it was introduced to the notice of the Craft is a singular one.

In the Gentleman's Magazine for September, 1753, the so called manuscript was printed for the first time under the title of "Certayne Questyons with Awnserers to the same, Concernynge the Mystery of Maconrye, wrytenne by the Hande of Kynge Henrye the Sixthe of the Name, and faythfullye copyed by me John Leylande Antiquaries, by the Commaunde of His Highnesse." That is, King Henry the Eighth, by whom Leland was employed to search for antiquities in the libraries of cathedrals, abbeys, priories, colleges and all places where any ancient records were to be found.

The article in the Gentleman's Magazine is prefaced with these words: "The following treatise is said to be printed at Franckfort, Germany, 1748, under the following Title.

Ein Brief Vondem Beruchmten Herr Johann Locke, betreffend die Frey-Maureren.

So auf einem Schrieb-Tisch enines verstorbnen Bruders ist gefunden worden.

That is, A Letter of the famous Mr. John Locke relating to Freemasonry; found in the Desk or Scritoir of a deceased Brother." The claim, therefore, is that this document was first published at Frankfort in 1748, five years before it appeared in England.

But this German original has never been produced, nor is there any evidence before us that there ever was such a production.

The laborious learning of Krause would certainly have enabled him to discover it had it ever been in existence.

But, although he accepts the so-called manuscript as authentic, he does not refer to the Frankfort copy, but admits that, so far as he knows, it first made its appearance in Germany in 1780, in J. G. L. Meyer's translation of Preston's Illustrations.[74] Kloss, it is true, in his Bibliography, gives the title in German, with the imprint of "Frankfort, 12 pages." But he himself says that the actuality of such a document is to be wholly doubted.[75] Besides, it is not unusual with Kloss to give the titles of books that he has never seen, and for whose existence he had no other authority than the casual remark of some other writer.

Thus he gives the titles of the Short Analysis of the Unchanged.Rites and Ceremonies of Freemasons, said to have been printed in 1676, and the Short Charge, ascribed to 1698, two books which have never been found.

But he applies to them the epithet of "doubtful " as he does to the Frankfort edition of the Leland Manuscript.

But before proceeding to an examination of the external and internal evidence of the true character of this document, it will be expedient to give a sketch of its contents.

It has been published in so many popular works of easy access that it is unnecessary to present it here in full.

It is introduced by a letter from Mr. Locke (the celebrated author of the Essay on the Human, said to be addressed to the Earl of

---

[74] "Kunsturkunden der Freimaurerei," I., 14
[75] "Bibliographie der Friemaurerei," No. 329 Understanding

Pembroke, under date of May 6, 1696, in which he states that by the help of Mr. C- ns he had obtained a copy of the MS. in the Bodleian Library, which he therewith had sent to the Earl.

It is accompanied by numerous notes which were made the day before by Mr. Locke for the reading of Lady Masham, who had become very fond of Masonry.

Mr. Locke says: "The manuscript of which this is a copy, appears to be about 160 years old.

Yet (as your Lordship will observe by the title) it is itself a copy of one yet more ancient by about 100 years.

For the original is said to have been the handwriting of K. H. VI.

Where the Prince had it is at present an uncertainty, but it seems to me to be an examination (taken perhaps before the king) of some one of the Brotherhood of Masons; among whom he entered himself, as 'tis said, when he came out of his minority, and thenceforth put a stop to the persecution that had been raised against them." The "examination," for such it purports to be, as Mr. Locke supposes, consists of twelve questions and answers.

The style and orthography is an attempted imitation of the language of the 15th century.

How far successful the attempt has been will be discussed hereafter.

Masonry is described to be the skill of Nature, the understanding of the might that is therein and its various operations, besides the skill of numbers, weights and measures, and the true manner of fashioning all things for the use of man, principally dwellings and buildingd of all kinds and all other things that may be useful to man.

Its origin is said to have been with the first men of the East, who were before the Man of the West, by which Mr. Locke, [76]in his note, says is meant Pre-Adamites, the "Man of the West " being Adam.

The Phoenicians, who first came from the East into Phoenicia, are said to have brought it westwardly by the way of the Red and Mediterranean seas.

It was brought into England by Pythagoras, who is called in the document "Peter Gower," evidently from the French spelling of the name, "Petagore," he having traveled in search of knowledge into Egypt, Syria, and every other land where the Phoenicians had planted Masonry.

---

[76] It will be seen that in this and other places I cite the name of Mr. Locke as if he were really the author of the note, a theory to which I by no means desire to commit myself. The reference in this way is merely for convenience.

Having obtained a knowledge of the art in the Lodges of Masons into which he gained admission, on his return to Europe he settled in Magna Grecia (the name given by the ancients to Southern Italy), and established a Grand Lodge at Crotona, one of its principal cities, where he made many Masons.

Some of there traveled into France and made many Masons, whence in process of time the art passed over into England.

Such is the history of the origin and progress of Masonry which is given in the Leland Manuscipt.

The remainder of the document is engaged in giving the character and the objects of the Institution.

Thus it is said, in relation to secrecy, that Masons have at all times communicated to mankind such of their secrets as might generally be useful, and have kept back only those that might be harmful in evil hands-those that could be of no use unless accompanied by the teachings of the Lodge, and those which are employed to bind the brethren more strongly together.

The arts taught by Masons to mankind are enumerated as being Agriculture, Architecture, Astronomy, Geometry, Arithmetic ,Music, Poetry, Chemistry, Government, and Religion.

Masons are said to be better teachers than other men, because the first of them received from God the art of finding new arts, and of teaching them, whereas the discoveries of other men have been but few, and acquired only by chance.

This art of discovery the Masons conceal for their own profit.

They also conceal the art of working miracles, the art of foretelling future events, the art of changes (which Mr. Locke is made in a note to interpret as signifying the transmutation of metals), the method of acquiring the faculty of Abrac, the power of becoming good and perfect without the aid of fear and hope, and the universal language.

And lastly it is admitted that Masons do not know more than other men, but onlyhave a better opportunity of knowing, in which many fail for want of capacity and industry.

And as to their virtue, while it is acknowledged that some are not so good as other men, yet it is believed that for the most part they are better than they would be if they were not Masons.

And it is claimed that Masons, greatly love each other, because good and true men, knowing each other to be such, always love the more the better they are.

"And here endethe the Questyonnes and Awnsweres." There does not appear to be any great novelty or value in this document The theory of the origin of Masonry had been advanced by others before its appearance in public, and the characteristics of Masonry had been previously defined in better language.

But no sooner is it printed in the Gentleman's Magazine for the month of September, and year 1753, than it is seized as a bonne bouche by printers and writers, so that being first received with surprise, it was soon accepted as a genuine relic of the early age of English Masonry and incorporated into its history, a position that it has not yet lost, in the opinion of some.

The forgeries of Chatterton and of Ireland met a speedier literary death.

Of the genuine publications of this document, so much as this is known.

It was first printed, as we have seen, in the Gentleman's Magazine, in September, 1753.

Kloss records a book as published in 1754, with no place of publication, but probably it was London, with the title of A Masonic Creed, with a curious letter by Mr. Locke.

This, we can hardly doubt, was the Leland Manuscript .pt with a new title.

The republications in England pursued the following succession.

In 1756 it was printed in Entick's edition of the Constitutions and in Dermott's Ahiman Rezon; in 1763 in the Freemasons Pocket Companion, in 1769, in Wilkinson's Constitutions of the Grand Lodge of Ireland, and in Calcott's Candid Disquisition; in 1772, in Huddesford's Life of Leland, and in Preston's Illustrations of Masonry, - in 1775, in Hutchinson's Spirit of Masonry and in 1784, in Northouck's edition of the Constitutions.

In Germany it first appeared in 1776, says Krause, in G. L. Meyer's translation of Preston; in 1780, in a translation of Hutchinson, published at Berlin; in 1805, in the Magazinfiir Freimaurer of Professor Seehass; in 1807, in the collected Masonic works of Fessler; in 1810, by Dr. Krause in his Three Oldest Documents,and in 1824, by Mossdorf in his edition of Lenning's Encyclopedie.

In France, Thory published a translation of it, with some comments of his own, in 1815, in the Acta Latomorum.

In America it was, so far as I know, first published in 1783, in Smith's Ahiman Rezon of the Grand Lodge of Pennsylvania; it was also published in 1817, by Cole, in his Ahiman Rezon of Maryland, and it has been copied into several other works.

In none of these republications, with one or two exceptions, is there an expression of the slightest doubt of the genuineness of the document.

It has on the contrary been, until recently, almost everywhere accepted as authentic, and as the detail of an actual examination of a Mason or a company of Masons, made by King Henry VI., of England, or some of his ministers, in the 15th century.

Of all who have cited this pretended manuscript, Dr. Carl Christian Friederich Krausse is perhaps the most learned, and the one who from the possession of great learning, we should naturally expect would have been most capable of detecting a literary forgery, speaks of it, in his great work on The Three Oldest Documents Of the Fraternity of Freemasons, as being a remarkable and instructive document and as among the oldest that are known to us.

In England, he says, it is, so far as it is known to him, accepted as authentic by the learned as well as by the whole body of the Craft, without a dissenting voice.

And he refers as evidence of this to the fact that the Grand Lodge of England has formally admitted it into its Book of Constitutions, while the Grand Lodge of Scotland has approved the work of Lawrie, in which its authenticity is supported by new proofs.

And Mossdorf, whose warm and intimate relations with Krause influenced perhaps to some extent his views on this as well as they did on other Masonic subjects, has expressed a like favorable opinion of the Leland Manuscript.

In his additions to the Encyclopedie of Lenning, he calls it a remarkable document, which, notwithstanding a singularity about it, and its impression of the ancient time in which it originated, is instructive, and the oldest catechism which we have on the origin, the nature, and the design of Masonry.

The editor of Lawrie's History is equally satisfied of the genuine character of this document, to which he confidently refers as conclusive evidence that Dr. Plot was wrong in saying that Henry VI. did not patronize Masonry.

Dr. Oliver is one of the most recent and, as might be expected from his peculiar notions in respect to the early events of Masonry, one of the most ardent defenders of the authenticity of the manuscript, although he candidly admits " that there is some degree of mystery about it, and doubts have been entertained whether it be not a forgery." But, considering its publicity at a time when Freemasonry was beginning- to excite a considerable share of public attention, and that the deception, if there was one, would have been publicly exposed by the opponents of the Order, he thinks that their silence is presumptive proof that the document is genuine.

"Being thus universally diffused," he says, "had it been a suspected document, its exposure would have been certainly attempted if a forgery, it would have been unable to have endured the test of a critical examination.

But no such attempt was made, and the presumption is that-the document is authentic." But, on the ther hand there are some writers who have as carefully investigated the subject as those whom I have referred to, but the result of whose investigations have led them irresistibly to the conclusion that the document never had any existence until the middle of the 18th century, and that the effort to place it in the time of Henry VI. is, as Mounier calls it, " a Masonic fraud." As early as 1787, while the English Masons were receiving it as a document of approved truth, the French critics had begun to doubt its genuineness.

At a meeting of the Philalethes, a Rite of Hermetic Masonry which had been instituted at Paris in 1775, the Marquis de Chefdebien read a paper entitled Masonic -Researches for the use of the Primitive Rite of Narbonne.[77] In this paper he presented an unfavorable criticism of the Leland Manuscript. In 1801 M. Mounier published an essay On the Influence attributed to the Philosophers, the Freemasons and the Illuminate in the French Revolution, in which he pronounces the document to be a forgery and a Masonic fraud.[78]

Lessing was the first of the German critics who attacked the genuineness of the document.

This he did in his Ernst und Falk, the first edition of which was published in 1778.

Others followed, and the German unfavorable criticisms were closed by Findel, the editor of the Bauhutte, and author of a History of Freemasonry, first published in 1865, and which was translated in 1869 by Bro. Lyon.

He says: -'There is no reliance, whatever, to be placed on any assertions based on this spurious document; they all crumble to dust.

Not even in England does any well-informed Mason of the present day, believe in the genuineness of this bungling composition." In England it is only recently that any doubts of its authenticity have been expressed by Masonic.

---

[77] "De l'Influence attribuee aux Philosophes, aux Franc-Macons et aux Illumines sur la Revolution de France," per F.F. Mounier. critics.
[78] "Recheres Maconniques a l'usage des Freres du Regime Premitifde Narbonne."

The first attack upon it was made in 1849, by Mr. George Sloane, in his New Curiosities of Literature. Sloane was not a Freemason, and his criticism, vigorous as it is, seems to have been inspired rather by a feeling of enmity to the Institution than by an honest desire to seek the truth.

His conclusions, however, as to the character of the document are based on the most correct canons of criticism.

Bro. A. F. A. Woodford is more cautious in the expression of his judgment, but admits that " we must give up the actual claim of the document to be a manuscript of the time of King Henry VI., or to have been written by him or copied by Leland." Yet he thinks " it not unlikely that we have in it the remains of a Lodge catechism conjoined with a Hermetic one." But this is a mere supposition, and hardly a plausible one But a recent writer, unfortunately anonymous, in the Masonic Magazine,[79] of London, has given an able though brief review of the arguments for and against the external evidence of authenticity, and has come to the conclusion that the former has utterly failed and that the question must fall to the ground.

Now, amid such conflicting views, an investigation must be conducted with the greatest impartiality. The influence of great names especially among the German writers, has been enlisted on both sides, and the most careful judgment must be exercised in determining which of these sides is right and which is wrong.

In the investigation of the genuineness of any document we must have resort to two kinds of evidence, the external and the internal.

The former is usually more clear and precise, as well as more easily handled, because it is superficial and readily comprehended by the most unpracticed judgment.

But when there is no doubt about the interpretation, and there is a proper exercise of skill, internal evidence is freer from doubt, and therefore the most conclusive.

It is, says a recent writer on the history of our language, the pure reason of the case, speaking to us directly, by which we can not be deceived, if we only rightly apprehend it.

But, although we must sometimes dispense with external evidence, because it may be unattainable, while the internal evidence is always existent, yet the combination of the two will make the conclusion to which we may arrive more infallible than it could be by the application of either kind alone. If it should be claimed that a particular

---

[79] Vol. vi., No. 64, October, 1878, p. 148

document was written in a certain century, the mention of it, or citations from it, by contemporary authors would be the best external evidence of its genuineness.

It is thus that the received canon of the New Testament has been strengthened in its authority, by the quotation of numerous passages of the Gospels and the Epistles which are to be found in the authentic writings of the early Fathers of the Church.

This is the external evidence.

If the language of the document under consideration, the peculiar style, and the archaic words used in it should be those found in other documents known to have been written in the same century, and if the sentiments are those that we should look for in the author, are in accord with the age in which he lived, this would be internal evidence and would be entitled to great weight.

But this internal evidence is subject to one fatal defect.

The style and language of the period and the sentiments of the pretended author and of the age in which he lived may be successfully imitated by a skillful forger, and then the results of internal evidence will be evaded.

So the youthful Chatterton palmed upon the world the supposititious productions of the monk Rowley and Ireland forged pretended plays of Shakespeare.

Each of these made admirable imitations of the style of the authors whose lost productions they pretended to have discovered.

But when the imitation has not been successful, or when there has been no imitation attempted, the use of words which were unknown at the date claimed for the document in dispute, or the reference to events of which the writer must be ignorant, because they occurred at a subsequent period, or when the sentiments are incongruous to the age in which they are supposed to have been written, then the internal evidence that it is a forgery, or at least a production of a later date, will be almost invincible.

It is by these two classes of evidence that I shall seek to inquire into the true character of the Leland Manuscript If it can be shown that there is no evidence of the existence of the document before the year 1753, and if it can also be shown that neither the language of the document the sentiments expressed in it, nor the character attributed to the chief actor, King Henry VI. are in conformity with a document of the 15th century, we shall be authorized in rejecting the theory that it belongs to such a period as wholly untenable, and the question will admit of no more discussion.

But in arriving at a fair conclusion, whatever it may be, the rule of Ulpian must be obeyed, and the testimonies must be well considered and not merely counted.

It is not the number of the whole but the weight of each that must control our judgment.

Those who defend the genuineness of the Leland Manuscript are required to establish these points: 1. That the document was first printed at Frankfort, in Germany, whence it was copied into the Gentleman's Magazine for September, 1753. 2. That the original manuscript was, by command of King Henry VIII., copied by John Leland from an older document of the age of Henry VI. 3. That this original manuscript of which Leland made a copy, was written by King Henry VI. 4. That the manuscript of Leland was deposited in the Bodleian Library. 5. That a copy of this manuscript of Leland was made by a Mr.C-ns, which is said to mean Collins, and given by him to John Locke, the celebrated metaphysician. 6. That Locke wrote notes or annotations on it in the year 1696, which were published in Frankfort in 1748, and afterward in England, in 1753.

The failure to establish by competent proof any one of these six points will seriously affect the credibility of the whole story, for each of them is a link of one continuous chain. 1. Now as to the first point, that the document was first printed at Frankfort in the year 1748.

The Frankfort copy has never yet been seen, notwithstanding diligent search has been made for it by German writers, who were the most capable of discovering it, if it had ever existed.

The negative evidence is strong that the Frankfort copy may be justly considered as a mere myth.

It follows that the article in the Gentleman's Magazine is an original document, and we have a right to suppose that it was written at the time for some purpose, to be hereafter considered, for, as the author of it has given a false reference, we may conclude that if he had copied it at all he would have furnished us with the true one.

Kloss, it is true, has admitted the title into his catalogue, but he has borrowed his description of it from the article in the Gentleman's Magazine, and speaks of this Frankfort copy as being doubtful.

He evidently bad never seen it, though he was an indefatigable searcher after Masonic books.

Krause's account of it in that it first was found worthy of Locke's notice in England; that thence it passed over into Germany-" how, he does not know "- appeared in Frankfort, and then returned back to England, where it was printed in 1753.

But all this is mere hearsay, and taken by Krause from the statement in the Gentleman's Magazine.

He makes no reference to the Frankfort copy in his copious notes in his Kunsturkunden, and, like Kloss, had no personal knowledge of any such publication.

In short, there is no positive evidence at all that any such document was printed at Frankfort-on-the-Main, but abundant negative evidence that it was not.

The first point must therefore be abandoned. 2. The second point that requires to be proved is that the Manuscript, was, by command of King Henry VIII., copied by John Leland, from an older document of the age of Henry VI.

Now, there is not the slightest evidence that a manuscript copy of the original document was taken by Leland, except what is afforded by the printed article in the Gentleman's Magazine, the authenticity of which is the very question in dispute, and it is a good maxim of the law that no one ought to be a witness in his own cause.

But even this evidence is very insufficient.

For, admitting that Locke was really the author of the annotations (an assertion which also needs proof), he does not say that he had seen the Leland copy, but only a copy of it, which had been made for him by a friend.

So that even at that time the Leland Manuscript had not been brought to sight and up to this has never been seen.

Amid all the laborious and indefatigable researches of Bro. Hughan in the British Museum, in other libraries, and in the archives of lodges, while he has discovered many valuable old records and Masonic Constitutions which until then had lain hidden in these various receptacles, he has failed to unearth the famous Leland Manuscript.

The hope of ever finding it is very faint, and must be entirely extinguished if other proofs can be adduced of its never having existed.

Huddesford, in his Life of Leland, had, it is true, made the following statement in reference to this manuscript: "It also appears that an ancient manuscript of Leland's has long remained in the Bodleian Library, unnoticed in any account of our author yet published.

This Tract is entitled Certayne Questyons with Awnsweres to the same concernynge the mystery of Maconrye.

The original is said to be the handwriting of K. Henry VI., by order of his highness K. Henry VIII.[80] And he then proceeds to dilate

---

[80] Huddesford's "Life of John Leland," p. 67

upon the importance of this " ancient monument of literature, if its authenticity remains unquestioned." But it must be remembered that Huddesford wrote in 1772, nineteen years after the appearance of the document in the Gentleman's Magazine, which he quotes in his Appendix, and from which it is evident that he derived all the knowledge that he had of the pseudomanuscript.

But the remarks on this subject of the anonymous writer in the London Masonic Magazine, already referred to, are so apposite and conclusive that they justify a quotation.

"Though Huddesford was keeper of the Ashmolean Library, in the Bodleian, he does not seek to verify even the existence of the manuscript, but contents himself with 'it also appears' that it is from the Gentleman's Magazine of 1753.

He surely ought not to have put in here such a statement, that an ancient manuscript of Leland has long remained in the Bodleian, without inquiry or collation.

Either he knew the fact to be so, as he stated it, or he did not; but in either case his carelessness as an editor is to my mind, utterly inexcusable.

Nothing would have been easier for him than to verify an alleged manuscript of Leland, being an officer in the very collection in which it was said to exist.

Still, if he did not do so, either thebmanuscript did exist, and he knew it, but did not think well, for some reason, to be more explicit about it, or he knew nothing at all about it, and by an inexcusable neglect of his editorial duty, took no pains to ascertain the truth, and simply copied others, by his quasi recognition of a professed manuscript of Leland.

But it is utterly incredible that Huddesford could have known and yet concealed his knowledge of the existence of the manuscript.

There is no conceivable motive that could be assigned for such concealment and for the citation at the same time of other authority for the fact. It is therefore a fair inference that his only knowledge of the document was delved from the Gentleman's Magazine.

There is therefore, no proof whatever that Leland ever copied any older manuscript. Referring to certain obvious mistakes in the printed copy, such as Peter Gower for Pythagoras, it has been said that it is evident that the document was not printed from Leland's original transcript, but rather from a secondary copy of an unlearned.

Huddesford adopts this view, but if he had ever seen the manuscript of Leland he could have better formed a judgment by a collation of it with the printed copy than by a mere inference that a man of Leland's learning could not have made such mistakes.

As he did not do so, it follows that he had never seen Leland's Manuscript.

The second point, therefore, falls to the ground.

3. The third point requiring proof is that the original manuscript of which Leland made a copy, was written by King Henry VI.

There is a legal rule that when a deed or writing is not produced in court, and the loss of it is not reasonably accounted for, it shall be treated as if it were not existent.

This is just the case of the pretended manuscript in the handwriting of Henry VI.

No one has ever seen that manuscript, no one has ever had any knowledge of it; the fact of its ever having existed depends solely on the statement made in the Gentleman's Magazine that it had been copied by Leland.

Of a document "in the clouds" as this is, whose very existence is a mere presumption built on the very slightest foundation, it is absurd to predicate an opinion of the handwriting.

Time enough when the manuscript is produced to inquire who wrote it.

The third point, therefore, fails to be sustained. 4. The fourth point is that the manuscript of Leland was deposited in the Bodleian Library.

This has already been discussed in the argument on the first and third point.

It is sufficient now to say that no such manuscript has been found in that library.

The writer in the London Masonic Magazine, whom I have before quoted, says that he had had a communication with the authorities of the Bodleian Library, and had been informed that nothing is known of it in that collection. Among the additional manuscripts of the British Museum are some that were once owned by one Essex, an architect, who lived late in the last century.

Among these is a copy of the Leland Manuscript evidently a copy made by Essex from the Gentleman's Magazine, or some one of the other works in which it had been printed.

I say evidently, because in the same collection is a copy of the Grand Mystery, transcribed by him as he had transcribed the Leland Manuscript, as a, to him perhaps, curious relic.

The original Leland Manuscript is nowhere to be found, and there the attempt to prove the fourth point is unsuccessful. 5. The fifth point is that a copy of Leland's MS. was made by a Mr. C-ns, and given by him to Locke.

The Pocket Companion printed the name as "Collins," upon what authority I know not.

There were only two distinguished men of that name who were contemporaries of Locke-John Collins, the mathematician, and Anthony Collins, the celebrated skeptical writer.

It could not have been the former who took the copy from the Ashmolean Library in 1696, for he died in 1683.

There is, however, a strong probability that the latter was meant by the writer of the prefatory, since he was on such relations with Locke as to have been appointed one of his executors,[81] and it is an ingenious part of the forgery that he should be selected to perform such an act of courtesy for his friend as the transcription of an old manuscript.

Yet there is an uncertainty about it, and it is a puzzle to be resolved why Mr. Locke should have unnecessarily used such a superabundance of caution, and given only the initial and final letters of the name of a friend who had been occupied in the harmless employment of copying for him a manuscript in a public library.

This is mysterious, and mystery is always open to suspicion.

For uncertainty and indefiniteness the fifth point is incapable of proof. 6. The sixth and last point is that the notes or annotations were written by Mr. Locke in 1696, and fifty-two years afterward printed in Frankfort-on-the-Main.

We must add to this, because it is a part of the story, that the English text, with the annotations of Locke, said to have been translated into German, the question-was it translated by the unknown brother in whose desk the document was found after his death?-and then retranslated into English for the use of the Gentleman's Magazine.

It is admitted thar if we refuse to accept the document printed in the magazine in 1753 as genuine, it must follow that the notes supposed to have been written by are also spurious.

The two questions are not necessarily connected.

Locke may have been deceived, and, believing that the manuscript presented to him by C-ns, or Collins, if that was really his

---

[81] It is strange that the idea that the Collins mentioned in the letter was Collins, the friend and executor of Locke, should not have suggested itself to any of the defenders or oppugners of the document. The writer in the "London Masonic Magazine" intimates that he was "a book-collector, or dealer in MSS." Locke

name, did take the trouble, for the sake of Lady Masham, to annotate it and to explain its difficulties.

But if we have shown that there is no sufficient proof, and, in fact, no proof at all, that there ever was such a manuscript, and therefore that Collins did not transcribe it, then it will necessarily follow that the pretended notes of Locke are as complete a forgery as the text to which they are appended.

Now if the annotations of Locke were genuine, why is it that after diligent search this particular one has not been found? It is known that Locke left several manuscripts behind him, some of which were published after his death by his executors, King and Collins, and several unpublished manuscripts went into the possession of Lord King, who in 1829 published the Life and Correspondence of Locke.

But nowhere has the notorious Leland Manuscript appeared.

"If John Locke's letter were authentic," says the writer already repeatedly referred to, "a copy of this manuscript would remain among Mr. Locke's papers, or at Wilton house and the original manuscript probably in the hands of this Mr. Collins, whoever he was, or in the Bodleian." But there are other circumstances of great suspicion connected with the letter and annotations of Locke, which amount to a condemnation of their authenticity.

In concluding his remarks on what he calls "this old paper," Locke is made to say: "It has so raised curiosity as to induce me to enter myself into the fraternity; which I am determined to do (if I may be admitted) the next time I go to London, and that will be shortly." Now, because it is known that at the date of the pseudo-letter, Mr. Locke was actually residing at Oates, the seat of Sir Francis Masham, forechose lady he says that the annotations were made, and because it is also known that in the next year he made a visit to London, Oliver says that there "he was initiated into Masonry." Now, there is not the slightest proof of this initiation, nor is it important to the question of authenticity whether he was initiated or not, because if he was not it would only prove that be had abandoned the intention he had expressed in the letter.

But I cite the unsupported remark of Dr. Oliver to show how Masonic history has hitherto been written - always assumptions, and facts left to take care of themselves.

But it is really most probable that Mr. Locke was not made a Freemason in 1697 or at any other time, for if he had been, Dr. Anderson, writing the history of Masonry only a few years afterward, would not have failed to have entered this illustrious name in the list of "learned scholars " who had patronized the Fraternity.

It appears, from what is admitted in reference to this subject, that the Leland Manuscript, having been obtained by Mr. Collins from the Bodleian Library, was annotated by Mr. Locke, and a letter, stating the fact, was sent with the manuscript and annotations to a nobleman whose rank and title are designated by stars (a needless mystery), but who has been subsequently supposed to be the Earl of Pembroke. All this was in the year 1696. It then appears to have been completely lost to sight until the year 1748, when it is suddenly found hidden away in the desk of a deceased brother in Germany.

During these fifty-two years that it lay in abeyance, we hear nothing of it.

Anderson, the Masonic historian, could not have heard of it, for he does not mention it in either the edition of the Constitutions published in 1723, or in that more copious one of 1738. If anyone could have known of it, if it was in existence, it would have been Anderson, and if he had ever seen or heard of it he would most certainly have referred to it in his history of Masonry during the reign of Henry VI.

He does say, indeed, that according to a record in the reign of Edward IV. "the charges and laws of the Freemasons have been seen and perused by our late Sovereign, King Henry VI., and by the Lords of his most honourable Council, who have allowed them and declared that they he right good, and reasonable to be holden as they have been drawn out and collected from the records of ancient times," etc.[82] But it is evident that this is no description of the Leland Manuscript which does not consist of "charges and laws," but is simply a history of the origin of Masonry, and a declaration of its character and objects.

And yet the fact that there is said to have been something; submitted by the Masons to Henry VI. and his Council was enough to suggest to the ingenious forger the idea of giving to his pseudo-manuscript a date corresponding to the reign of that monarch.

But he overleaped the bounds of caution in giving the peculiar form to his forgery.

Had he fabricated a document similar to those ancient constitutions, many genuine manuscripts of which are extant, the discovery of the fraud would have been more difficult.

But to continue the narrative: The manuscript, having been found in the desk of this unknown deceased brother, is forthwith

---

[82] Anderson's "Constitutions," edition of 1738, p. 75

published at Frankfort, Germany, in a pamphlet of twelve pages and in the German language.

Here again there are sundry questions to be asked, which can not be answered.

Had the tale been a true one, and the circumstances such as always accompany the discovery of a lost document, and which are always put upon record, the replies and explanations would have been ready.

Was the letter of Locke, including of course the catechism of the Leland Manuscript, which was found in the desk of the unknown brother, the original document, or was it only a copy? If the latter, had it been copied in English by the brother, or translated by him into German? If not translated by trim, by whom was it translated? Was the pamphlet printed in Frankfort merely a German translation, or did it also contain, in parallel columns, the English original, as Krause has printed the English documents in his Kunsterkunden, and as, in fact, he has printed this very document? These are questions of very great importance in determining the value and authenticity of the Frankfort pamphlet, And yet not one of them can be answered, simply because that pamphlet has never been found, nor is it known that anyone has ever seen it.

The pamphlet next makes its appearance five years afterward in England, and in an English translation in the Gentleman's Magazine for September, 1753.

Nobody can tell, or at least nobody has told, how it got there, who brought it over, who translated it from the German, how it happened that the archaic language of the text and the style of Locke have been preserved.

These are facts absolutely necessary to be known in any investigation of the question of authenticity, and yet over them all a suspicious silence broods.

Until this silence is dissipated and these questions answered by the acquisition of new knowledge in the premises, which it can hardly now be expected will be obtained, the stain of an imposture must remain upon the character of the document.

The discoverer of a genuine manuscript would have been more explicit in his details.

As to internal evidence, there is the most insuperable difficulty in applying here the canons of criticism which would identify the age of the manuscript by its style.

Throwing aside any consideration of the Frankfort pamphlet on account of the impossibility of explaining the question of translation, and admitting, for the time, that Mr. Locke did really annotate a copy of a manuscript then in the Bodleian Library, which copy was made for him by his friend Collins, how, with this admission, will the case stand? In Mr. Locke's letter (accepting, it as such) he says: "The manuscript, of which this is a copy, appears to be about 160 years old." As the date of Locke's letter is 1696, this estimate would bring us to 1536, or the thirty-first year of the reign of Henry VIII.

Locke could have derived his knowledge of this fact only in two ways: from the date given in the manuscript or from its style and language as belonging, in his opinion, to that period.

But if he derived his knowledge from the date inserted at the head of the manuscript, that knowledge would be of no value, because it is the very question which is at issue.

The writer of a forged document would affix to it the date necessary to carry out his imposture, which of course would be no proof of genuineness.

But if Locke judged from the style, then it must be said that, though a great metaphysician and statesman, and no mean theologian, he was not an archaeologist or antiquary, and never had any reputation as an expert in the judgment of old records.

Of this we have a proof here, for the language of the Leland Manuscript is not that of the period in which Leland lived.

The investigator may easily satisfy himself of this by a collation of Leland's genuine works, or of the Cranmer Bible, which is of the same date.

But it may be said that Locke judged of the date, not by the style, but by the date of the inanuscript itself.

And this is probably true, because he adds: "Yet (as your Lordship will observe by the title) it is itself a copy of one yet more ancient by about 100 years: For the original is said to have been in the handwriting of K. H. VI." Locke then judged only by the title - a very insufficient proof as I have already said, of authenticity.

So Locke seems to have thought, for he limits the positiveness of the assertion by the qualifying phrase "it is said." If we accept this for what it is worth, the claim will be that the original manuscript was written in the reign of Henry VI., or about the middle of the 15th century.

But here again the language is not of that period. The new English, as it is called, was then beginning to take that purer form which a century and a half afterward culminated in the classical and vigorous style of Cowley.

We find no such archaisms as those perpetrated in this document in the Repressor of over-much Blaming of the Clergy, written in the same reign, about 1450, by Bishop Pecock, nor in the Earl of Warwick's petition to Duke Humphrey, written in 1432, nor in any other of the writings of that period.

It is not surprising, therefore, that the glossary or list of archaic words used in the document, by which from internal evidence we could be enabled to fix its date, has, according to Mr.

Woodford, "always been looked upon with much suspicion by experts." If I may advance an hypotheses upon the subject I should say that the style is a rather clumsy imitation of that of Sir John Mandeville, whose Voiage and Travails was written in 1356, about a century before the pretended date of the Leland Manuscript.

An edition of this book was published at London in 1725.

It was, therefore, accessible to the writer of the Leland document.

He being aware of the necessity of giving an air of antiquity to his forgery, and yet not a sufficiently skillful philologist to know the rapid strides that had taken place in the progress of the language between the time of Mandeville and the middle of the reign of Henry VI., adopted, to the best of his poor ability, the phraseology of that most credulous of all travelers, supposing that it would well fit into the period that he had selected for the date of his fraudulent manuscript.

His ignorance of philology has thus led to his detection.

I am constrained, from all these considerations, to endorse the opinion of Mr. Halliwell Phillips, that "it is but a clumsy attempt at deception, and quite a parallel to the recently discovered one of the first Englishe Mercurie." But the strangest thing in this whole affair is that so many men of learning should have permitted themselves to become the dupes of so bungling an impostor.

PART TWO

CHAPTER I

PRELIMINARY OUTLOOK

If the reader has bestowed any attention on the preceding part of this work, he will have been enabled to discover that what I have designated as " Prehistoric Masonry " is nothing more than a collection of legends and traditions derived from various sources and, apparently, invented at different periods during the Middle Ages, when the Fraternity of Freemasons was a thoroughly Operative association, composed of architects and builders, with a few unprofessional men of rank and wealth, who had been accepted by the Craft as patrons or honorary members.

It is, however, only in compliance with the usage of historians that I have consented to adopt the use of this term "prehistoric" in reference to the present subject, and not because I have considered it to be an absolutely correct one when applied to the history of Freemasonry.

Anthropologists have divided the chronological series of events in every nation or race into two distinct periods-the prehistoric and the historic.

The former includes the time when the inhabitants of a country were in a condition of utter barbarism, from which they gradually raised themselves to a higher state of civilization.

Of the fact even of the existence of such a primitive people we have no evidence, except certain myths and legends, in which they appear to have embodied their ideas of religious belief, and, at a somewhat later period in their progress toward civilization, some fragmentary records, to be found principally in the hieroglyphic monuments of ancient Egypt and in the cuneiform inscriptions of old Assyria.

But when a nation or race began, by the natural process of advancement, to emerge from this lower sphere of intellectual debasement to a higher one, its first labor was to preserve the evidences of its existence and the memorial of its transactions in written records.

All before this era of emergence from oral traditions to records has been called by anthropologists the "prehistoric period" - all after the historic.

Now it is very evident that no such division can, in strictness, be applied to the history of Freemasonry.

Viewed as an association of builders, when there ceases to be a record of the association, it must be supposed that it did not exist.

There are no legends or traditions whose existence can be traced to a period anterior to that which contains historic records of the society.

These legends and traditions, all of which have been given in the first part of this work, were not, like the primeval myths of the prehistoric nations, the outgrowth of an uneducated religious sentiment wholly unconnected with and independent of any record of real events which occurred, or were occurring, at the same time.

On the contrary, they sprang up in the Middle Ages, at the very time when Freemasonry was making its indelible record in the history of Europe.

They were fabricated by Freemasons who had long before been recognized in history as an association of some importance.

They were not the spontaneous growth of some primitive body of builders, known to us only by these legends which had been orally transmitted from the earliest prehistoric times.

They were the inventions of a later period, most of the facts which they detailed being borrowed from historical records, principally from the Bible or from ecclesiastical historians, and they were indebted for their fabrication partly to a desire to magnify the antiquity of the Institution and partly to the influence of that legendary spirit which prevailed in the Middle Ages, and which we find still more extensively developed in the legends of the Saints which have been accepted by the Roman Catholic Church.

These Masonic legends differ also in another respect from the prehistoric myths of antiquity.

As soon as a nation began to make its history, its myths were relegated to their proper place in the region of rnythology and the history continued to be written without any admixture with them.

They were considered as things of the past.

They had their inevitable influence upon the religion of the people, but they were not intruded into its political history.

But from the very time of the fabrication of the Masonic legends and traditions, they were accepted as a part of the annals of the association and were incorporated into it as a portion of its true history.

As such they have been maintained almost to the present day.

In this way we have two histories of Freemasonry which have always been presenting themselves to our consideration with the assumption of an equal claim to our credence.

We have in the first place, the authentic history, gathered from the records of all the building guilds and confraternities from the time of Numa, and which, assuming various forms at different periods, finally has culminated in the Speculative Freemasonry of the present day.

And then we have a mass of legends and traditions fabricated in the Middle Ages, and some others of a later day.

These have been obtruded into the authentic history, have grown up alongside of it, and have presented and sought to preserve a different and, of course, an apocryphal form of history.

Looking at the time and manner of the fabrication of these legends and the persistent way in which for some centuries they have traveled down the stream of pari passu with the authentic history, it would perhaps have been better to designate them as " extra- historic," rather than "prehistoric" something not before history, but something outside of history.

Yet, as they have been made to assume the appearance of prehistoric legends, and have claimed, however incorrectly, to be traditions of the origin and progress of the Institution at a time when there were no written records of its existence, I have felt myself excusable, and perhaps even justifiable, in tolerating temporarily this mistaken view, under the protest of this explanation, and of adopting the usage of historians in their treatment of the histories of nations.

As a matter, therefore, of convenience I have used the term "pre-historic," although I am well convinced that there is no such thing as a "prehistoric Freemasonry." There is, unquestionably, a prehistoric architecture.

The art of building, so as to secure shelter from the inclemencies of the seasons and protection from the incursions of wild beasts, was practiced at a period long antecedent to the existence of any written records of the existence of the arts.

The Troglodytes must have made alterations for their greater comfort, convenience, and security in the rude caves which they made their homes, and the lake-dwellers of prehistoric Helvetia exhibited, as we may judge from their remains, considerable skill and ingenuity in the construction of their lacustrine houses.

But architecture, when it is not united with and practiced by an organized craft, guild, or fraternity, is not Freemasonry.

Therefore prehistoric architecture and prehistoric Freemasonry are two entirely different things.

Of the former we have monumental records; of the latter we have no evidence, and the term is used only as a facon deparler, as a matter of convenience, and as a concession to common usage in the treatment of historical subjects.

There is one very marked difference in character between the prehistoric myths of antiquity and the legends of Freemasonry, which, for the reason just assigned, I have placed in the supposititious prehistoric period of that institution.

The myths of the earliest peoples found their origin and groundwork in an enforced observance of the contending powers of nature.

The nomadic races, wandering over the wide plains and lofty mountains of the East, were necessarily struck by the alternate changes of darkness and light, of night and day.

They saw and they feared the dark sky with its diadems of glittering stars and its murky clouds; these they beheld dispersed by the rosy dawn, before which stars and clouds and darkness fled as the wild game flees before the hunter.

Then they beheld the glorious sun, ushered in by the dawn, traverse the sky, at length to be destroyed in the far West by the recuperated forces of night, which again reigned supreme over the earth, until it was anew dispersed by the ever-renewing dawn.

This perpetually recurring elemental strife gave rise to the formation of myths, which formulated fables of the wars of these opposing forces of nature, just as, later, men in the historic period described the battles of contending armies.

These simple myths[83] were undoubtedly the first acts of the human mind. As time passed onward and the intellect became more cultivated, the myths were developed into a definite form of religious faith, The forces of nature were impersonated as actual, living dieties.

The primitive Aryans, out of the fire which descended from the clouds in the forked lightning, and the fire which they brought by friction out of the wood, both of which they deemed to be identical, made their god Agni.[84] At a later period their Greek descendants symbolized the all-healing and purifying sun, whose rays disperse the morbific influences of malaria, as Herakles destroying the hydra of the Lernaean marshes, or as the light-diffusing Phoebos Apollo, who pictured the solar rays by his flowing locks of golden hair and his quiver filled with arrows.

Thus it was that the simple nature-myths of the primeval nations, Aryan and Semitic, were in the progress of time resolved into a system of complicated mythology that became the popular religion of the ancient nations.

But this mythology was perfectly separated from political and national history.

The prehistoric mythology of Greece and Rome was always distinct from Grecian and Roman authentic history.

Though in the earliest period when history began to emerge from tradition there was, undoubtedly, some confused admixture of the two, yet, as each nation began to keep its records, the two streams were made to flow in different channels, and the mythical and the historical elements were not permitted to intermingle.

The priests preserved the fromer in their temple services, and the poets only referred to them in their epics and in their odes; the philosophus and the historians confined their instructions to the latter.

But it has not been so with the legends, which may be called the myths, of Freemasonry.

Springing into existence not at any early, prehistoric period, but receiving their form at the very time when Masonry was already an historical institution, these traditions have traveled down

---

[83] Goldziher says that the myth is the result of a purely psychological operations, and is, together with language, the oldest act of the human mind. "Mythology Among the Henrews," ch. i., p. 3.

[84] In the old Vedic faith, Agni is sometimes addressed as the one great god who makes all things, sometimes as the light which fills the heavens, sometimes as the blazing lightning, or as the clear flame of earthly fire. "Con. Aryan Mythology," vol. ii., p. 190.

contemporaneously with its authentic narratives, not in two independent and separated streams, but in one commingled current.

At the period when the speculative element of Masonry withdrew itself from the alliance which it had always maintained, the traditions contained in the Legend of the Craft, which constitute the great body of Masonic myths, were incorporated into and made an inseparable part of the true history.

Nothing was rejected; everything was accepted as authentic; and indeed other legends borrowed from or suggested by Rabbinical and Talmudic reveries were added.

Hence has arisen that inextricable and deplorable confusion of tradition and history, of false and true, of apocryphal and authentic, that we find in all the so-called histories of Freemasonry which were written in the 18th century.

Nor did this false method of writing cease with the expiration of that period.

It was continued into the 19th century, and its influence is still felt, not only in the opinions entertained by the masses of the Fraternity, but in the statements made in annual addresses before lodges, by men not always unlearned or unscholarly, but who do not hesitate to advance traditions and legends as a substitute for the true history of the Order.

Of this mode of writing Masonic history, let us take at random a single passage from one of the works of the most eminent of the writers of this school.

"The Druidical Memoranda," says Dr. Oliver,[85] "were made in the Greek character, for the Druids had been taught Masonry by Pythagoras himself, who had communicated its area a to them, under the name he had assigned to it in his own country.

This distinguished appellation (Mesouraneo), in the subsequent declension and oblivion of the science, during the dark ages of barbarity and superstition, might be corrupted into MASONRY, as its remains, being merely operative, were confined to a few hands, and these artificers and working Masons." Here are no; less than five positive assertions, of which but one rests on the slightest claim of authority, while the whole of them are absolutely unhistorical. 1.The statement that the Druids used the Greek character in their secret writing is made on the authority of a casual remark of Caesar but later authorities, much better than Caesar, on the subject of Druidism have shown that the character used by them was the old Irish Oghum alphabet. 2. The assertion that the

---

[85] "Antiquities of Freemasonry," Period I., ch. i., p. 17

Druids practiced or were acquainted with Masonry is altogether untenable.

It is known that the dogmas and practices of their religion were antagonistic to those of Masonry 3. The statement that they were taught Masonry by Pythagoras is met by the simple fact that philosopher never visited Britain. 4. All that is said about the Greek word Mesoureneo, as the term under which Masonry was known to Pythagoras and communicated by him to the Druids, is a mere fable.

It had its origin in a whimsical etymology first proposed by Hutchinson, and which has never been accepted by competent philologists. 5. The implied doctrine contained in the close of the paragraph, that the first form of Masonry was Speculative, and that the Operative branch was merely what remained after the declension and decay of the science, to be practiced by working Masons, is in direct violation of all historic truth, which makes the Speculative element an after-thought and a development out of the Operative.

When history is thus caricatured, what chance is there that the unlearned shall find the truth; and what labor must be imposed on the learned in striving to extract the pure gold of facts from the worthless ore of tradition in which it has been imbedded? The mode of writing Masonic history which was adopted in the 18th century, and which, with some honorable exceptions, has been pursued almost to the present day, was one which was by no means calculated to elicit truth or to satisfy the inquiring mind.

A groundwork for the history of Freemasonry was found in the Legend of the Craft.

All the statements in that old document were accepted as authentic narratives of events that had actually occurred.

Hence the origin of the institution was placed at a period anterior to the flood.

All the patriarchs were declared to have been Masons; Noah and his sons were said to have been the means of transmitting its tenets from the antediluvians to the post-diluvians.

Its progress was traced from Noah to Moses, who was said to have practiced its mystic rites in the wilderness.

From Moses it was made to pass over to Solomon, who, in some incomprehensible way, was supposed to have organized, as its first Grand Master, an association which, however, according to the preceding history, appears to have been in existence thousands of years before.

From the King of Israel it was made to pass over from Palestine to Europe, and is landed with little respect, or at least with no accounting for the lapse of time, in the kingdom of France, and in the time of Charles Martel.

From him it crosses the Channel, and is reorganized in England in the reign of King Athelstan and by his brother Edwin.

Such is the history of Freemasonry that for a century and a half has claimed and received almost universal belief from the Craft.

And yet, perhaps there never was a history of any kind that could present so few claims to belief. It is fragmentary in its details. Centuries are passed over with no connecting link.

From Abraham, who, it is said, "had learned well the science and the art (that is, Geometry and Operative Masonry), to Moses, who is called the Grand Master of the Jewish Masons, a period of more than four centuries passes with the most inefficient and unsatisfactory account, if it can be called an account at all, of how this science and art were transmitted from the one to the other.

From Moses to Solomon there occurs a vast chasm of fifteen centuries, with scarcely an attempt to fill it up with a consecutive series of intervening events.

And so the fragmentary history goes on in intermittent leaps from Solomon to Zerubbabel, from Zerubbabel to Augustus, from Augustus to Charles Martel, and finally from him to Athelstan.

It is contradictory in its statements.

Claiming for the Institution a purely Hebrew character, it intermixes with strange inconsistency the labors and the patronage of Jewish patriarchs and Pagan monarchs, and finds as much of true Masonry in the works of the idolatrous Nebuchadnezzar as in those of King Solomon.

But perhaps the most important fault of these 18th century historians of Freemasonry is the entire absence of all citation of authority for the records which they have made.

They assume a statement to suit their theory, but give no evidence or support from contemporary profane or sacred writers that it is a genuine fact and not a bare assumption.

The scholar who is seeking in his historical studies for truth and truth only, finds himself thus involved in a labyrinth of doubts, from which all the canons of criticism fail, however skillfully applied, to extricate him.

He knows not when the writer is acting on the results of his own or some Predecessor's invention, or when he is reciting events that have really occurred.

We are not to attribute to those writers who have thus made a romance instead of a history any willful intention to falsify the facts of history.

At first led astray by a misinterpretation of the Legend of the Craft, they had on this misinterpretation framed a theory of the antiquity of Freemasonry in a wrong direction, and then, as has occurred thousands of times before, they proceeded to fit the facts to the theory, and not, as they should have done, the theory to the facts.

The doctrines of the new school of anthropology, which does' not admit that the origin of the whole human family is to be found solely in the Semitic race, were, in their day, unknown.

If Freemasonry was older than the era of the revival and the establishment. of the Grand Lodge of England, its antiquity was to be sought only in the line of the Jewish patriarchs.

Thus it became venerable, not only by its age but by its religious character.

To this line they wished, therefore, to confine the direction of its rise and progress, and they thought that they could find the proofs of this line of progress in their own interpretation of the Legend of the Craft, and the application to it of certain passages of Holy Writ.

They succeeded in this, at least to their own satisfaction, because "the wish was father to the thought." But as they recognized the symbolic character of Freemasonry, and as they found some of the most important and expressive of these symbols prevailing in the Pagan associations of antiquity, they thought it necessary to account for this contemporary prevalence of the same ideas in two entirely different systems of religion in such a way as not to impair the validity of the claim of Masonry to a purely Semitic origin.

This they did by supposing, that while the Divine truths inculcated by Speculative Masonry were preserved in their purity by those of the descendants of Noah who had retained the instructions which they had received from their great ancestor, there was at some era, generally placed at the time of the attempted building of the Tower of Babel, a secession of a large number of the human race from the purer stock.

These seceders rapidly lost sight of the Divine truths which they had received at one time, and fell into the most grievous religious errors.

Thus they corrupted the purity of the worship and the orthodoxy of the faith, the Principles of which had been originally communicated to them.

In this way there sprung up two streams of Masonry, distinguished by Dr. Oliver as the "Pure" and the "Spurious." The former was practiced by the descendants of Noah in the Jewish line, the latter by his descendants in the Pagan line.

It is thus that these theorists account for the presence of a Masonic element, though a perverted one, in the mysteries of the ancient Pagan nations.

There was afterward a union of these two lines, the Pure and the Spurious, at the building of the Temple of Jerusalem, when King Solomon involved the assistance and the cooperation of the heathen and idolatrous workmen of the King of Tyre.

The Spurious Freemasonry did not, however, cease to exist in consequence of this union at the Temple of the Jewish and Tyrian Freemasons. It lasted, indeed, for many centuries subsequent to this period.

But the Jewish and Tyrian cooperation had effected a mutual infusion of their respective doctrines and ceremonies, which eventually terminated in the abolition of the two distinctive systems and the establishment of a new one, which was the immediate forerunner of the present Institution.

This delightful romance, in which the imagination has been permitted to run riot, in which assumptions are boldly advanced for facts, and in which statements are made which there is no attempt to corroborate by reference to authority, has for years been accepted by thousands upon thousands of the Fraternity, and is still accepted by the masses as a veritable history of the rise and progress of Freemasonry.

In my younger days, when my researches were directed rather to the deign and to the symbolism of the Order than to its history, which I was willing to take from older and more experienced heads, I had been attracted by the beauty and ingenuity of this romantic tale, and gave, without hesitation, my adhesion to it.

But when my studies took an historical direction, and I began to apply the canons of criticism to what I was reading on this subject, I soon found and recognized that the landscape which I had viewed with so much pleasure was, after all, only a wonderful mirage. I have, therefore, been compelled to abandon this theory and to seek for one more plausible and more consistent with the facts of history.

I have come to this conclusion, I admit, with great reluctance, because I was unwilling to throw aside the picture which I had so long admired and which was the work of masters whose labors I respected and whose memory I venerated.

But I am forced to say, with Aristotle, that though Plato and Socrates be my friends, yet truth is a greater friend and one that I must value above them both.

When we look at the course pursued by these Masonic historians of the early part of the 18th century, it is lamentable to think how many glorious opportunities of preserving facts in the history of the Institution have been lost by the mistaken direction of their views.

We have in the History of St. Mary's Lodge, by Bro. J. Murray Lyon, a fair sample of what might have been done by Dr. Anderson, if he had pursued a similar plan in the composition of the two editions of the Constitutions compiled by him.

In 1723 he must have had access to many documents of great importance bearing on the history of Masonry in the latter part of the 17th and in the beginning of the 18th century.

There were undoubtedly minutes of lodges which were accessible to him, but the lodges are now extinct and the records perhaps forever lost.

In these he would have found authentic evidence of the manners and customs, the organization and the regulations, of the Operative Masons, and could have accurately defined the line through which Operative Masonry passed in its transmission and transmutation to a purely Speculative system.

But on these subjects he has maintained unbroken silence.

In the first edition he has not said a single word of the actual condition of Freemasonry at the time of his writing.

But he has wasted pages in an inaccurate and unauthentic history of the rise and progress of architecture, which had been already written by far better authority, because a professional architect with equal ability can write history of his own science more skillfully than can a doctor of divinity.

Even of the four lodges which in 1717 organized the Grand Lodge of England, a few lines comprise the brief account that he gives.

He tells us their names and the locality in which they held their meetings, and no more.

And yet these lodges must have had their history, there must have been a minute-book of some kind, however brief and imperfect might have been the records.

And these minute-books, only three or four, must have been in existence before Anderson began the compilation of his book, and from his position in the Order must have been accessible to him.

And yet he has treated these invaluable records-invaluable to the future Masonic historian and which should have been invaluable to him with a silence bordering almost on contempt.

Comparing this treatment of the early English records with the manner in which Lyon has treated those of Scotland, we can not too much deplore this neglect of the real duties of a historian.

The result of this difference of treatment of the same subject by two different historians has been that while we are made by Lyon familiar with the true history of the Scottish Lodges in the 17th century with their regulations, their usages, their modes of reception, and almost everything that appertains to their internal organization we are, so far as we can gather anything from Anderson, absolutely as ignorant of all that relates to the English Lodges of the same period as if no such bodies had ever existed.

Such neglect of opportunities never to be recalled, such obdurate silence on topics of the deepest interest, and such waste of time and talent in the compilation of a jejune history of architecture instead of an authentic narrative of the Masonic history which was passing before his eyes, or with which he must have been familiar from existing documents, and from oral communication with many of the actors in that history, is to be not only deeply regretted, but to be contemplated almost as a crime.

Anderson's compilation has been that which gave form and feature to all subsequent histories of Freemasonry until a recent period.

Smith, Calcott, Preston, and Oliver have followed in his footsteps, only pouring, as it were, from one vial into another, so that all the treatment of early Freemasonry anterior to the year 1717, as treated by English and French writers, has been almost wholly without the nessecary element of authenticity.

These historians have dealt in hypotheses, suggestions, assumptions, and romantic legends, so as to lead the scholar who studies their pages in search of historical light into an inextricable web of doubt and confusion.

The Germans have done better, and bringing the Teutonic instinct of laborious research to the investigation of Masonic history, they have made many approximations to the discovery of truth.

And later English Masons forming a school of iconoclasts, have begun, by the rejection of anachronisms and improbabilities, to give to that history a shape that will stand the crucial test of critical examination.

It must be evident to the reader, from what has been said, that the history of Freemasonry, upon which this book is about to enter, will be treated in a method that seeks to approach that accuracy with which authentic history should always be written.

From the causes already assigned, there must often be an embarrassment in finding proper evidence to authenticate the material offered to the inspection of the reader.

But in no case will assumption be presented in the place of facts.

When the supposed occurrence of events can not be proved by contemporaneous authority, such events will not be recorded as historical.

It may be conjectured that such events may have occurred, and such a conjecture is entirely legitimate, but its value will be determined by its plausibility.

It will be a matter of logical inference, and not of historical statement.

Thus one of the great errors of Anderson will be avoided, who continually presents his conjectures as facts, without discrimination, and thus leaves his reader in doubt as to when he is writing history and when indulging in romance or in assumptions.

Pursuing this method, I am compelled to reject the universally received hypothesis that Freemasonry received its organization at the Temple of Solomon.

I reject it because there is no historical evidence of the fact.

The only authorities on this subject are the books of Kings and Chronicles.

That of Josephus need not be referred to, because it is simply a compilation of Jewish history made up out of the Scriptural account.

Now, the account of the events that occurred at the building of the Temple is very briefly related in those books, and it gives us no authority for saying that there was any organization of the builders, at that edifice, at all like the one described in our Masonic histories.

Similar objections may be urged against all other propositions or theories which seek to connect the rise of the Masonic Institution from bodies which were not architectural in their character.

I fall back, therefore, upon that theory which since the time of the Abbe Grandidier has been gradually gaining strength, and which connects the Speculative Masonry of our own times with the Operative Masonry of the Middle Ages.

Never abandoning, for a moment, the predominant idea that Freemasonry, in whatever aspect it may be viewed, whether as Operative or Speculative, whether as ancient or modern, has always been connected in some way with the art of building and with a guild organization, I shall proceed to trace its early history not in religious communities or in social fraternities, but solely in the associations which have been organized for the pursuit and practice of architecture.

Finding; such associations among the ancient Romans I shall endeavor to pursue the course of these associations, from their birth in the imperial city and in the time and under the fostering care of Numa, to their dissemination with the Roman legions into the conquered provinces of Gaul, Germany, and Britain; their subsequent establishment in these countries of confraternities which they called Colleges of Workmen (Collegia Fabrorum), out of which, after the decay of the Empire and the extinction of the armies, was developed in the gradual course of civilization the societies of Traveling Freemasons, who sprang from the school of Como in Lombardy.

Thence, by slow but certain steps, we shall advance to the time of the Operative or Stonemasons of Germany, France, and Britain, who were a development and result of the Comacine Fraternity.

And lastly this will bring us to the era when the Operative system was wholly abandoned as a practice, and when the society was delivered up to the pursuit of a Speculative Philosophy, still, however, retaining the evidence within itself of its architectural parentage, by the selection of its symbols and its peculiar language as well as by many features of its internal organization.

The connection, according to this theory, of Freemasonry with the art of building, a connection that has never, even in its Speculative form, been wholly severed, will necessarily lead to digressions in the course of this history upon the subjects of Roman, Byzantine, and Gothic architecture.

These subjects will have to be discussed, not as architectural studies, but solely in their close relationship to Freemasonry, and in respect to the reciprocal influences that were exerted upon Freemasonry and its followers by the varying systems of architecture and that produced on them by the skill and intelligence of the Freemasons.

There will be no attempt to write a history of Architecture and to call it, as Dr. Anderson has unfortunately done, a history of

Freemasonry, but the effort will be made to write a history of Freemasonry in its connection with, and its reference to, Architecture.

"Every Freemasons" said the Chevalier Ramsay, in his visionary hypothesis, "is a Templar." The truer doctrine is that in the olden time every Freemason was an architect, using this word in its purest and primitive meaning, to signify a builder.

Mr. Hallam says, in his History of the Middle Ages, that "the curious subject of Freemasonry has unfortunately been treated of only by panegyrists or calumniators, both equally mendacious." And he thinks that it would be interesting to know more of the history of the Craft during a period in which they were literally architects.

The desire here expressed, is the object and the design of this work to gratify.

Whether the object has been successfully achieved can be determined only when the work is finished.

Let me say, in concluding this preliminary essay-and I say it lest there should be any misconception of my views-that the theory which I shall seek to establish is not that the Freemasons of the present day are in direct and uninterrupted descent from the Roman Colleges of Artificers, but that these latter associations brought, by the Roman legions from the civilization of the Empire, into the comparatively unenlightened provinces of Gaul, Germany, and Britain, those sentiments of architectural beauty as well as those principles of architectural skill, which gave rise to the establishment of associations of builders, who in time constituted themselves into the form of guilds.

These guilds, or fraternities, at a very early period assumed an important place in the history and practice of the building art, and associated themselves together for the purpose of disseminating the principles and practice of building over certain parts of Europe.

Thence arose the association known as "Travelling Freemasons," who, starting from their school in Lombardy, perambulated the continent and erected many important edifices, mostly of a religious character, such as monasteries and cathedrals.

From these the Stonemasons of Germany, of France, and of England borrowed the system of guild-formation, that is to say, the usages and regulations of a guild in the practice of their profession.

These Operative Masons at various times admitted into the mem- bership and privileges of their guild many persons of rank, influence, and learning, who were not professionally connected with the building art.

These honorary admissions accomplished two objects: they were received as gratifying compliments by the non- professional members, and at the same time secured their good wishes and protection for the guild.

But eventually a schism took place between the Operative Masons and the honorary members.

The former adhered to the Operative Craft, but the latter, eliminating altogether the Operative element, formed a new guild or fraternity of Speculative Masons whose only connection with architecture or building was that they preserved much of its technical language and implements, but consecrated them to symbolical purposes.

Having thus abandoned the professional practice of the craft of building, and assumed a merely ethical character, they became the Freemasons or the Speculative Masons of the present day.

Such is a brief outline of the plan which will be pursued in the future prosecution of this history of the rise and progress of the Order of Freemasonry.

CHAPTER II

THE ROMAN COLLEGES OF ARTIFICERS

It will be evident, from what has been said in the preceding chapter, that the plan upon which it is intended to write the history of Freemasonry in the present work will utterly preclude any search for the origin of the Institution among the purely religious associations of antiquity, whether they be of Jewish or of Gentile character.

Hence I reject as untenable either of the hypotheses which traces the rise of the Order to the Patriarchal religion, the ancient Mysteries, the workmen at the Temple of Solomon, the Druids, the Essenes, or the Pythagoreans.

If we contemplate the Speculative Freemasonry of the present day as the outgrowth of the Operative system which prevailed in the Middle Ages, we must look for the remote origin of the former in the same place in which we shall find that of the latter.

Now, the mediaeval Operative Masons, known as the Steinmetzen of Germany, the Tailleurs de pierre of France, and the Freemasons of England, were congregated and worked together under the form and regulations of a Guild.

But as all institutions in their gradual growth and development are apt to preserve some of the most important features of their original construction, notwithstanding all the changes and influences of surrounding circumstances to which they are subject in the course of time, we may very legitimately come to the conclusion that whatever was the original body or prototype from which the Masonry of the Middle Ages derived its existence, or of which it was a continuation, that prototype must have had some of the forms of a guild.

It is true that when the operative Masons organized themselves into an association, at some period between the 10th and the 17th centuries, which period is not at this time and in this place to be accurately determined, they may as an original body have assumed a form, independent of all previous influences.

But we know that such is not the fact, and the Masons of that period were the successors of other bodies that had preceded them, and that they only developed and improved the principles of art that had already been long in existence.

Then the body of men-the association, the sodality-of which they were the outgrowth must have some features in its form and character that were imitated by the body of Masons who succeeded them, who pursued the same objects, and only developed and improved the same principles.

Now, what were the features that must distinguish and identify the original, the exemplar, of which the more modern Freemasonry was an outgrowth? I answer to this question that those features, to which we must look for an identification of the original body, are at least two in number: First, the original body must have had the form and character of a sodality, a confraternity, or what in more modern times would be called a Guild.

And secondly, that this sodality, confraternity, or guild must have consisted of members who were engaged in the practice of the art of building.

The absence of either of these two features will make a fatal break in the process of identification, by which alone we are enabled to trace a connection between the original and the copy.

We can easily find in the records of ancient history numerous instances of sodalities or confraternities, but as they had no reference to the art of building, it is clear that not one of them could have been the exemplar or source of mediaeval Masonry.

The members of those religious associations of antiquity, which were called the " Mysteries," and to which Speculative Masonry is thought, not altogether incorrectly, to bear a great similitude, were undoubtedly united in a sodality or confraternity- They had admitted into their association none but those who had been duly chosen, and reserved to themselves the power of rejecting those whom they did not deem worthy of a participation in their rites; they had ceremonies of initiation; they adopted secret methods of recognition; and in many other ways secured the isolation of an exclusive society.

They were in every respect a confraternity, and their organization bore a very striking resemblance to that of the modern Freemasons.

And hence it is that some writers have professed to find in these religious Mysteries of the ancient pagans an origin to which they might trace the Masonic Institution.

But the hypothesis is untenable, because these religious associations had no connection with architecture or the art of building.

Freemasonry, which always has been either an operative art or been closely connected with it, could not, by any possible contingency, have derived its origin from what was a wholly religious association.

The Society of Dionyiac Artificers, who flourished in Asia Minor, did indeed unite with the observance of the Mysteries of Dionysus the practice of architecture.

Hence the compiler of Lawrie's History of Masonry has pretended to trace the origin of our modern system to the connection of the Pagan Dionysiacs with the Jewish builders at the construction of King Solomon's Temple.

There would be a great deal of plausibility in this theory, if it could be proved that the Dionysiacs as architects were contemporaneous with Hiram of Tyre and Solomon of Israel.

But unfortunately the authentic annals of chronology prove that they were only known as builders of temples, palaces, and theaters about seven hundred years after the era of the building of the Temple at Jerusalem.

So, too, of the Essenes, we may say that the doctrine can not be sustained which attributes to them the continuation and preservation of the Masonry of the Temple builders, and which assigns to them the origin of the modern Speculative system.

Leaving out of the question the fact that it is impossible to account for the lapse of time which occurred between the construction of the Temple and the first appearance of the Essenes, about the era of the Maccabees, we meet with the insurmountable objection that the Essenian sect was wholly unconnected with architecture.

So, too, of all the other schemes of tracing Masonry to the Druids, the Pythagoreans, or the Rosicrucians, we always have the invincible obstacle in our way, that all of these were associations not devoted to, nor pursuing the art of building.

It is impossible to trace the origin of a fraternity of working Masons, all of whose ideas, principles, pursuits, usages, and customs prominently and exclusively connected them with the cultivation of architecture and the art of building, not theoretically but practically to any other and older sodality which knew nothing of architecture and whose members never were engaged in the construction of edifices.

But if we should discover in long-past time a sodality, whose members were builders and who were congregated together for the purpose of pursuing their professional labors, in a society which partook of the main features of a modern guild, we should be encouraged to make the inquiry whether such a sodality may not have given birth, and suggested form, to the mediaeval associations of Operative Masons, from whom afterward sprang, in direct succession, the Speculative Masons of the 18th century.

Now just such a sodality will be found in the Roman Colleges of Artificers -the Collegia Fabrorum-which are said to have been instituted by Numa, the successor of Romulus, and, therefore, the second king of Rome.

That the establishment of these colleges of workmen of various crafts was one of the numerous reforms instituted by Numa, among his subjects, is a fact that has not been denied by historians.

The evidence of the existence of these colleges in the later days of the empire and of their dispersion into various provinces, is attested by numerous inscriptions in votive tablets and other monuments that remain to the present day.

The important relation which it is supposed that the Roman colleges bore to mediaeval stonemasonry, makes it proper that something more than a mere glance should be given at the history of their origin and progress as well as at their character and deign.

Of Numa himself, a few words may be said.

He was undoubtedly one of those great reformers who, like Confucius, Moses, Buddha, and Zoroaster, have sprung up at different periods in the world's history and have changed the character and the religion of the people among whom they lived and placed them on the first steps of the march of civilization.

That such was the career of Numa, is testified by the fact that he so transformed the military disorder of the heterogeneous multitude that had been left by Romulus, into the orderly arrangements of a well-regulated municipality, that, as Livy says, that which the neighboring nations had hitherto called a camp, they now began to designate as a city.

Numa, who was a native of Cures, a considerable city of the Sabines, was, on account of his nationality, selected, through the influence of the Sabine population of Rome, to succeed Romulus, and was called to the throne, according to the generally received chronology, 686 years before the Christian era.

Having borne in his private life the character of a wise and just man, with no distinction as a warrior, he cultivated, when he assumed the reins of government, all the virtues of peace. He found the Romans a gross and almost barbarous people.

He refined their manners, purified their religion, built temples, instituted festivals, and established a regular order of priesthood.

As Plutarch says, the most admirable of all his institutions was his distribution of the citizens according to their various arts and trades.

Before his accession to the throne, the different craftsmen had beer, confusedly mixed up with the heterogeneous Roman and Sabine population and had no laws or regulations to maintain their rights or to secure their skill from the rivalry of inexperienced charlatans.

But Numa divided the several trades into distinct and independent companies, which were designated as Collegia or colleges.

Plutarch names but eight of these colleges, namely: musicians, goldsmiths, masons, dyers, shoemakers, tanners, braziers, and potters, but he adds that the c4her ar6mcen were also divided into companies, so that the exact number of colleges that were instituted by Numa cannot be learned from the authority of Plutarch.

If we suppose that the other artificers alluded to by him comprehended all the remaining crafts, which were united in another college, which was afterward developed into new societies, the whole number which, according to Plutarch, were originally instituted by Numa would amount to nine.

But as, besides the Collegia, such as those of the augurs and priests which were specially established by legal authority, there were many others formed by the voluntary association of individuals, the number of the colleges of handicraftsmen became in the later days of the republic, and especially of the Empire, greatly increased.

There were, among the Greek sodalities or fraternities which they called etaireiai.

They were established by Solon, and Gaius thinks that the Roman colleges borrowed some of their regulations from them.

But this could not have been the case in reference to any regulations established by Numa, since Solon lived about a century after him. The Greek etaireiai were, however, not confined to craftsmen but, according to the law of Solon, cited by Gaius,[86] they comprehended brethren assembled for sacrifices, or sailors, or people who lived together and used the same sepulcher for burial, or who were companions of the

---

[86] Gaius, lib. iv., ad Legem duodecium tabularum

same society, or who, inhabiting the same place, were united in the pursuit of any business, which last division might be supposed to refer to workmen of the same craft.

All of these were permitted to make regulations for their own government, provided they were not forbidden by the laws of the state.

Among the Romans a college generally signified any association which, being permitted by the state and recognized as an independent association, devoted itself to some determined object.

Its recognition by the state gave to the college the character of a legal personage, such as is now called a corporation.

If we examine the laws which were made for the establishment and the government of the colleges, we shall be impressed with their similarity to those which have always existed among the Masonic Lodges, both Operative and Speculative.

The identity of regulations are amply sufficient to warrant us in believing that the regulations of the one were derived from, or at least had been suggested by, the other.

The laws and usages by which the workmen at the Temple of King Solomon were distributed into classes and regulated, which have been given by Masonic historians, and by none more extensively than by Dr. Oliver, are all supposititious and apocryphal; but those that describe the government of the Roman colleges or guilds of craftsmen have been recorded by various historians, and especially in the different codes of the Roman law and have, therefore, all the character and value of authenticity.

Whatever conclusions we may think proper to deduce in connecting these colleges with the modern Masonic guilds, must of course be judged according to their logical weight, but the facts on which these conclusions are based are patent and have an authentic record.

It was required by the Roman law that a college should not consist of less than three members.

It is hardly necessary to remind the reader that a Lodge can not be composed of less than three Masons.

As in Freemasonry there are "regular Lodges" which have been established by competent authority, and "clandestine Lodges" which have been organized without such authority, and whose members are subject to the severest Masonic penalties, so there were legal colleges - Collegia licita - which were formed by authority of the government and illegal colleges - Collegia illicita - which assembled under no color of law and which were strictly prohibited.

Illicit colleges, says Ulpian[87] are forbidden, under the same penalties as are adjudged to men violating public places or temples; and Marcian[88] says that they must be disso;ved by virtue of the decrees of the Senate, but their members when they separate are permitted to divide the common property.

According to the Justinian code, no college of any kind was permitted to assemble unless by an act of the Senate, or a decree of the emperor.[89] Each college was permitted to make its own internal regulations, provided that they were not in contravention of the laws of the state.

The regulations were proposed by the officers, and after due deliberation adopted or rejected by a vote of the members, in which a majority ruled.

The members of a college (sodales), says Gaius,[90] were permitted to make their own regulations if they did not contravene the public law; and he shows that the same privilege was granted by Solon to the Greek eltaireiai or fraternities.

The colleges had also the right of electing their officers, and of receiving members by a vote of the body on their application.

The applicants for admission were required to be freemen; but the Justinian code permitted slaves to be received into a college if it was done with the consent of the Domini or Masters; but not otherwise, under a penalty of one hundred pieces of gold to be inflicted on the Curatores or Wardens.[91] As in the mediaeval Lodges of Freemasons we find that distinguished persons not belonging to the Craft were sometimes admitted, so a similar usage prevailed in the Roman colleges.

To them the law had granted the privilege of selecting from the most honorable of the Roman families, persons who were not connected with the Craft, as patrons and honorary members. That they exercised this privilege is evident from inscriptions and some remaining lists of members.[92] We have also the authority on this point of Pliny, who in his correspondence when he mas governor of Bithynia with the Emperor Trajan, shows by implication that it was the usage of the colleges of builders to admit non-professional persons into their guild.

---

[87] Ulpian, "de Officis Pro Consulis," lib. ii, p. 7
[88] "De Jud. Pub.," lib. ii.
[89] "Digest," lib. xlvii., tit. xxii., 1
[90] "Ad Legem," xii., tab. lib. iv.
[91] "Digest," ut supra
[92] Krause, "Kunsturkunden," iv., p. 136

A conflagration having destroyed a great part of the city of Nicomedia, Pliny applied to the Emperor for permission to establish a College of Workmen-COLLEGIUM FABRORUM, to consist of one hundred and fifty men; and knowing that it was the custom in these colleges to admit persons who were not of the Craft, he adds: " I will take care that no one not a workman shall be received among them, and that they shag not abuse the privileges conceded to them by their establishment."[93] Each college had also its arca, or common chest, in which the funds of the guild were kept.

These funds were collected from the monthly contributions of the members, and were, of course, devoted to defraying the expenses of the college.

At a later period when these societies, or sodalities had become objects of suspicion to the government, in consequence of their sometimes engaging in political intrigues, they were forbidden to assemble.

But there is a decree of the Emperor Severus, cited by Marcianus, which, while it forbids the governors of provinces to permit COLLEGIA SODALITIA or confraternities, even of soldiers, in the camps, yet allows the poorer soldiers to make a monthly contribution in a common chest, provided they did not meet more than once a month, lest under this pretext they should form an illicit college.

The permission thus given to make monthly contributions (what in modern Freemasonry we should call "monthly dues") was most probably derived from the custom long before practiced by the Colleges of Workmen.

The members of the colleges were exempt by Constantine from the performance of public duties; but this exemption appears to have applied to all craftsmen as well as to those who were united in corporations.

And the reason assigned was that they might have better opportunities of acquiring skill in their professions or trades and of imparting it to their children.

And therefore this immunity from public employments was confined in the colleges to those members who were really craftsmen, and in the code of Theodosius[94] it was expressly declared that this immunity should not be granted promiscuously to all who had been received in the colleges, but only to the craftsmen.

---

[93] Ego attendum ne quis nisi faber, recipiatur, neve jure concesso in aliud utatur. Pliny, "Epistolae," lib. x., ep. 42
[94] "Cod. Theodos. de excus. Artificum," lib. v.

Patrons and honorary members were not to be included in the exemption.

The meetings of a college were held in a secluded hall called a Curia, which was the name originally given to the Senate-house, but afterward came to signify any building in which societies met for the transaction of business or for the performance of religious rites.

Each of these corporations, says Smith, had its common hall, called Curia, in which the citizens met for religious and other purposes.[95] In the old inscriptions we frequently meet with this word in connection with a college, as the Curia Saliorum, or the Hall of the College of the Priests of Mars, and Curia, Dendrophororum, or the Hall of the College of Woodcutters.[96] Krause says that they sometimes met in private houses he does not give his authority for this statement, but it was probably in cases where the college was too poor to afford the expense of owning or hiring a common hall or Curia.

Officers were elected by the members to preside or to perform other duties in the college.

There seems to have been some variety at different periods and under different circumstances in the titles of these officers.

The officer who presided was called the Magister, or Master.

It would seem that in some of the legionary colleges he was called the Prefectus or Prefect.

In the Justinian code he is styled the Curator.[97] Corresponding in some sense to our Masonic Wardens were the Decuriones, whose number was not however confined to two.

In a list of the officers and members of a college, which has been preserved and which is given by Muratori, there are seven Decuriones.

A Decurio denoted, as the word imports among the Romans, one who commanded or ruled over ten men.

Hence Dr. Krause supposes that the members of a college were divided into sections of about ten, over each of which a Decurio presided.

It will be remembered that Sir Christopher Wren states in the Parentalia talia, while describing the regulations that prevailed among the Traveling Freemasons of the Middle Ages that " the members lived in a camp of huts reared beside the building on which they were employed

---

[95] "Dict. Greek and Roman Antiq.," citing Dionysius of Halicarnassus, ii., 23
[96] This was one of the orginal colleges of Numa. There is some dispute about their occupation; but the one given above is the most plausible
[97] "Digest," lib. xlvii., tit, xxii

that a surveyor or Master presided over and directed the whole and that every tenth man was called a Warden and overlooked those who were under his charge." This is at least a coincidence, and it may give some color to the hypothesis of Krause, that the Decuriones of the Roman colleges presided over sections of ten men.

Reference has been made to a list of the officers of a college, which has been preserved by the celebrated Italian antiquary, Muratori, in his work on inscriptions.

Similar lists are to be found in the works of Gruter, who has made the best collection of ancient inscriptions.

These lists, like those published at this day by the Masonic Lodges, were intended to preserve the names of the officers and members for the information of the government.

In the list published by Muratori we find the following names and titles of officers, which will give us a very good idea of the manner in which the internal government of a Roman College of Artificers was regulated.

In this list first appears the names of fifteen Patrons, who, as has already been said, were not craftsmen.

The last of these is called the Bisellarius of the college.

There is some difficulty in coming to an exact understanding of the meaning of this word.

A bisellium was a double seat-a seat capable of holding two-as Hesychius calls it, " a distinguished and splendid seat," remarkable for its size and grandeur.

It might be compared to the "Oriental chair" appropriated to the use of the Worshipful Master in our modern Lodges.

It was, in short, a chair of state, capable of holding, two persons; though it is evidenced from several specimens which were found at Pompeii and which were accompanied by a single footstool, that it was occupied only by one.

These chairs were used in the theaters and other public places at Rome and in the provinces as seats of honor.

The privilege of occupying a bisellium was granted as an honor by a decree of the Senate or an edict of the emperor, and the person to whom the privilege was granted was called a Bisellarius.

Its form was like that of a modern ottoman, but larger and higher, and there was also a stool or suppedaneum, on which the feet rested.

Krause says that some of the colleges had several Bisellarii among their members, and he thinks the word is equivalent to honorary member But as the Patrons were generally persons of wealth and distinction, selected by the college to defend and promote its interests, it is not likely that of the fifteen named in Muratori's list only one should have been elected an honorary member.

But as the privilege of a Bisellarims was a dignity conferred as an honor on certain persons, it is more probable that of the fifteen the last one only had arrived at this honor, and that the record of it was made in the list, just as in the present day titles are appended to the names of persons in catalogues.

The next officers mentioned in this list are seven Decuriones.

Then follow the names of the following officers: An Haruspex, a Soothsayer and Diviner, who may be considered as equivalent to our modern chaplain, and whose duty it was to attend to the sacrifices and conduct the religious services of the college; a Medicus, or Physician; a Scriba Perpetuus, or Permanent Secretary, and a Scriba, or Secretary. Against the names of two of the members is written the word immunes, or exempt, to show that for some reason, not explained, these members were relieved from the payment of the monthly contribution.

In this list no title of Magister or Master appears. The same occurs in an inscription on a marble plinth, which has been preserved by Gruter. It is dedicated on the front side by the College of Carpenters (Collegium Fabrorum Tignariorum) to the Emperor M. Aurelius Antoninus.

On the other side are forty names, many of which have the title affixed of Honoratus, or Honorary.

The last six names have the title of Scriba, or Secretary, attached to each; hence Krause thinks it probable that each Decuria, or section of ten men, had its Master, who was a Decurio, its Secretary and its Patron, and, besides, its own property, obtained from bequests or donations.

If this be true, a college would not appear to have been a single lodge, but rather an aggregation of lodges.

The mediaeval division, described by Wren, where in a building the workmen were divided into tens, each having its own warden, would precisely meet this ancient condition of the Decuriae.

In the time of the Empire, when the government began to be suspicious of the revolutionary tendencies of the craftsmen, care was taken to place officers over the colleges who might have a control of their arts.

These officers differed at different times and in different places.

Sometimes he was called a Precurator, or Superintendent; sometimes a Prapositus, or Overseer, and sometimes a Prefectus, or Prefect.

In fact, the legionary colleges, which accompanied the legions and which were principally concerned in the fabrication of weapons, as armorers and smiths, had an officer over them who was called the Prefectus Fabrum, or Prefect of the Workmen.

But originally the title of Magister, or Master, was applied to him who wasover the Decuriones, and who controlled all the acts, the labors, and the hours of rest of the members of the college, as well as their sacrifices and other religious ceremonies.

There is abundant evidence of this in the inscriptions, and from them also we learn that the Master was chosen annually, and afterward with all the other officers quinquennially.

But sometimes he was elected for life, a custom that was observed at a long subsequent period by the French Lodges, whose Venerables were chosen ad vitam.

Thus we meet with such inscriptions as Magister quinquennatis Collegium Fabrorum Tignariorum and Magister quinquennatis Collegium Auriﬁcum, that is, Quinquennial Master of the College of Carpenters and Quinquennial Master of the College of Goldsmiths.

Sertorius also refers to certain peculiar powers of the Magister Collegium, or Master of the College.

There can be no doubt that this was a well-recognized title of the presiding, officer of those sodalities.

But the Patrons, who were selected from the most wealthy and influential families of Rome, and who were not craftsmen, seemed to have exercised very important powers.

Chosen that they might protect the interests of the society, no regulation was enacted, no contracts were made, and no work undertaken without their sanction.

The kings, prelates, and nobles so often recorded as Grand Masters by Dr. Anderson in his history of early English Masonry, may very well be supposed to correspond in position and duties to these Patrons of the Roman Colleges.

Dr. Krause thus describes the internal organization of these colleges: "It was only the Masters who could undertake any work.

The members of the Decuria, (or sections) who corresponded to the Fellow Crafts of the present day, worked under them; and under these and under the Master, were the Alumni or Apprentices, who were still being instructed in the schools (attached to the college) and whose names, as they were not yet members of the college, are not mentioned in any of the Inscriptions."[98] That there was a distinction of ranks among the members of a college is very evident from several of the inscriptions, and from passages in the code. It, besides, in the nature of things that in every trade or craft there should be some well skilled and experienced in the Mystery, who will take the highest place; others with less knowledge who must be subordinate to these; and finally scholars or apprentices who are only beginning to learn the principles of their art.

As in the Lodges of Operative Masons, in the Middle Ages, there were Masters, journeymen, and Apprentices, so must there have been in the colleges of Rome, a similar division of ranks.

The passage in the Justinian code, already referred to, provides that slaves could be received in the colleges only with the consent of their masters; if received without this consent the Curator or Master of the College was liable to a penalty of one hundred pieces of gold.

This would indicate that in the Roman colleges, the distinction of bond and free so much insisted on in the modern Masonic system, was not recognized among the craftsmen of Rome.

But it must be remembered that among the Romans, a condition of servitude did not always imply the debasement of ignorance.

Slaves were sometimes instructed in literature and the liberal arts, and many of them were employed in trade and in various handicrafts.

It was these last who were to be conditionally admitted into the Colleges of Artificers.

It is evident that with the prosecution of their craft, the members of the colleges connected the observance of certain religious rites.

In the list from Muratori, heretofore cited, it is seen that among the officers designated was a Haruspex or Sacrificer.

This semi-religious character, first introduced in their establishment by the pious Numa, continued to prevail to the latest days of the Empire. It was in the spirit of paganism, which connected the transaction of all private as well as public business with sacrificial rites.

Hence every college had its patron deity, which was called its Genius, under whose divine protection it was placed.

---

[98] Krause, "Kunsturkunden," iv., 165

The Curia, or hall of the college, was often built in the near vicinity of the temple of this god, and meetings of the guild were sometimes held in the body of the temple.

Sacrifices were offered to him; festival days were kept in his honor, and were often celebrated by public processions.

Among the paintings discovered at Pompeii is one that represents a procession of the College of Carpenters.

Krause gives ample proof that the Colleges of Artificers made use of symbols derived from the implements and the usages of their craft.

We need not be surprised at this, for the symbolic idea was, as we know, largely cultivated by the ancients.

Their mythology, which was their religion was made up out of ii great system of symbols. Sabaism, their first worship, was altogether symbolic, and out of their primitive adoration of the simple forces of nature, by degrees and with the advancement of civilization was developed a multiplicity of deities, every one of which could be traced for his origin to the impersonation of a symbol.

It would, indeed, be strange if, with such an education, the various craftsmen had failed to have imbued their trades with that same symbolic spirit which was infused into all their religious rites and their public and private acts.

But it is interesting to trace, as I think we may, the architectural symbolism of the mediaeval builders to influences which were exerted upon them by the old builders of Rome, and which they in turn communicated to their successors, the Speculative Masons of the 18th, and perhaps the 17th century.

This is, I think, one of the most important links in the chain that connects the Roman colleges with modern Freemasonry.

Nothing of the kind can be adduced by those who would trace the latter institution to a Jewish or Patriarchal source.

The Jews were not an aesthetic people.

They rejected as vainly superstitious the use of painting and sculpture in their worship.

Though we find among them a few symbols of the simplest kind, symbolism was not cultivated by them as an intellectual science.

Christian iconography, which succeeded the Jewish and the Pagan, has been more indebted for its eminently symbolic character to the latter than to the former influences.

It is the same with the symbolism that has always been cultivated in Masonry, both in its Operative and in its Speculative form.

It has been indebted for its warmth and beauty rather to the Roman colleges than to the Jewish Temple.

The most important of these colleges in the present inquiry were the Collegian Fabrorum, which has generally been translated the Colleges of Artificers.

The word Faber, in the Latin language, means generally one who works in any material, but the signification is limited by some adjoining word.

Thus faber tignarius meant a carpenter, faber ferrarius a blacksmith, faber aurarius a goldsmith, and so on.

But it was very generally used to designate one who was employed in building-a stone-cutter or mason.

We meet in Gruter, and elsewhere, with many inscriptions in which the word can only bear this meaning.

In the passage above cited from Pliny, we see that when he asks the imperial consent to establish a society of artisans to reconstruct the burned edifices of Nicomedia, for which purpose builders only could be of use, he calls the desired society a Collegium Fabrorum, which may be fairly interpreted a College or Guild of Masons.

There were, of course, colleges of other trades, such as the Collegium Pistorum, or College of Bakers, the Collegium Sutorum or College of Shoemakers, of whom a votive tablet was found at Osma in Castile,[99] and many others.

But, as Dalloway says, the Fabri were "workmen who were employed in any kind of construction and were subject to the laws of Numa Pompilius."[100] It is to these Collegia Fabrorum, or Roman guilds of Masons or Builders, that Dr. Krause, whose opinion on this subject I adopt with some modifications, has sought to trace the origin of the Mediaeval corporations of stonemasons and the more recent Lodges of Freemasons.

In concluding this survey of the character and internal organization of these Roman colleges, the prototypes of the modern Masonic guilds, it will not be inappropriate to cite the language on this subject of the latest and most classical writers on the antiquities of Greece and Rome.

The following brief description is taken from Guhl and Komer's able work on The Life of the Greeks and .Romans.'[101]

---

[99] Don Cean-Bermudez, "Sumario de las Antiguedas Romanas que hay in Espana," Madrid, 1832, p. 179.
[100] "Master and Freemason," p. 400
[101] Hueffer's Translation from third German edition, New York, 1875, p. 519

Mechanics guilds (Collegia Opipium) existed at an early period, their origin being traced back to King Numa.

They were nine in number, viz., pipers, carpenters, goldsmiths, dyers, leather- workers, tanners, smiths, and potters, and another guild combining, at first, all the remaining handicrafts, which afterward developed into new, separate societies.

Amongst these later guilds, frequently mentioned in inscriptions, we name the goldsmiths, bakers, purple-dyers, pig dealers sailors, ferry men, physicians etc.

They had their separate inns (curia, schola), their statutes and rules of reception and expulsion of members, their collective and individual privileges, their laws of mutual protection and their widows' fund, not unlike the mediaeval guilds.

There was, however, no compulsion to join a guild.

In consequence, there was much competition from freedmen-foreign, particularly Greek, workmen who settled in Rome, as also from the domestic slaves who supplied the wants of the large families-reasons enough to prevent the trades from acquiring much importance.

"They had, however, their time-honored customs, consisting of sacrifices and festive gatherings at their inns, on which occasions their banners (vexilla) and emblems were carried about the streets in procession.

A wall-painting at Pompeii is most likely intended as an illustration of a carpenters' procession.

A large wooden tray (ferculum) surmounted by a decorated baldachin is being carried on the shoulders of young workmen.

On the tray stands a carpenters bench in miniature, with two men at their work, the figure of Daedalus being seen in the foreground." In reading this brief description, the principal details of which have already been given in our preceding pages, the reader can hardly fail to be struck with the far closer resemblance the usages of Freemasonry bear to those Roman colleges or guilds, than they do those of the Jewish workmen at the Temple, as we learn them from the very imperfect and unsatisfactory allusions contained in the Bible or in the Antiquities of Josephus. One can barely fail to see that the derivation of Masonry from the former is a far more reasonable hypothesis than a derivation from the latter.

Though but indirectly and remotely connected with this subject, one fact may be mentioned that shows how much the spirit of the guild organization, itself the spirit of Freemasonry, had imbued the common life of the Romans.

The benefit societies of the present day, which are said to be and most probably are but coarse imitations of the Masonic Lodges, were not unknown to the ancient Romans.

They had their burial clubs, called Collegia Tenuirom, the literal meaning of which is Guilds of the Poor.

They were, as their name imports, societies formed by the poorer classes, from whose funds, derived from annual contributions, the expenses of the burial of a member were defrayed and a certain sum was paid to the surviving family.[102] Having shown that there existed among the Romans guild-like associations of craftsmen, presenting a very close resemblance in their usages and purposes to the guilds or corporations of Stonemasons of the Middle Ages, who are admitted to have been the predecessors of the Speculative Freemasons of the 18th century and of the present day, the further connection of these two institutions can be identified only by tracing the progress of the Roman colleges from their rise in the reign of Numa, to their dissolution at the time of the decline and fall of the Empire, and their absorption into the architectural associations which sprang up in those parts of Europe which had once been Roman provinces.

The inquiry into this difficult but interesting topic must be the appropriate subject of the following chapter.

---

[102] Hueffer's Translation from third German edition, New York, 1875, p. 591

CHAPTER III

GROWTH OF THE ROMAN COLLEGES

It has been shown in the preceding chapter that Numa, in his sagacious efforts to improve the civilization of the early Romans, and to reconcile the heterogeneous elements of which the population was composed had instituted colleges or guilds of mechanics.

I do not intend to complicate this question by any reference to the theory of Niebuhr and his disciples who have ignored the existence of any true history at that period, but who deem every theory connected with regal Rome as merely mythical and traditionary.

I content myself with the fact that when Roman history began to present itself under the authentic form of records, the preexistence of these guilds was fully recognized.

It is sufficient for the present purpose to accept the generally received opinion, and while it is not denied that in primitive Rome such guild formations prevailed, we may safely attribute their origin to some early reformer, who may be represented by the name of Numa as well as by any other.

In treating the subject of the rise and progress of these colleges or guilds, I shall pursue the course of Roman history as it has been generally received by scholars.

As we advance to later times we shall find ourselves amply fortified by the contemporaneous authority of classical writers, and by numerous monuments and inscriptions.

Except the mere question whether they were first established by Numa or by somebody else, in what Niebuhr would call prehistoric Rome-a question of but little or no importance in reference to their connection with the mediaeval guilds-there is no statement concerning them that is not a part of authentic history.

It has therefore been proved that these colleges were guild-like in their organization; that they had all the legal rights of a corporation; that they elected their own members; that they were governed by certain officers chosen by the votes of the society; that they were supported by monthly contributions; that they had a guild-chest or common fund, which was the property of the corporation; that they had a tutelary deity, in honor of whom they performed religious rites; that they had honorary members not belonging to the Craft, who, as patrons of the colleges, and being selected from the wealthiest and most influential families of the Republic or the Empire, protected their interests; and finally, that they had, like our modern corporations, laws, regulations, usages, and a jurisdiction which were all sanctioned by the authority of the state.

In tracing the progress of the Colleges of Artificers, through the reigns of the seven kings the long period of the Republic and the rise and fall of the Empire, we need not dwell upon the age of Romulus.

Though the narrative of his reign was accepted as authentic by Dionysius and Plutarch, by Livy and Cicero, the incredulity of modern scholars, stimulated by their researches, has led to the very general opinion that the first of the Roman kings was a mythical personage, and that his history was founded, as Niebuhr says, on a heroic lay.

Yet even he admits that portions of the nar- rative are to be accepted as matters of fact.

Made up as it has been of traditions, which were believed from the earliest periods, the reign and the character of Romulus may be considered as an expoltation of that of the time in which he is supposed to have lived.

From these traditions we learn that he was, as the founder of an empire might well be supposed to be, a warlike king, who was engaged in constant contests with the inhabitants of neighboring and rival cities.

Though claimed to have been a legislator of the highest order, who exercised his skill in the organization of a new state, the necessity of defending his territory from aggression and of increasing its limits, gave him but little opportunity or inclination to cultivate the arts of peace.

He is said to have created those religious institutions of the Romans, which were afterward developed into greater maturity by Numa and some of his successors.

But he discouraged the cultivation of the arts, and interdicted the citizens from the practice of all mechanical and sedentary trades, which were left to foreigners and slaves, while the free Romans were confined to agricultural labors and warlike pursuits.

His successor, Numa, was, on the contrary, distinguished for his pacific character.

During his long reign of forty-three years, the state over which he ruled enjoyed an uninterrupted flow of peace.

There were no domestic dissensions and no foreign wars.

He was not only a king but a philosopher, and by an anachronism which Niebuhr attempts, but vainly, to explain, he was considered as a disciple of the sage Pythagoras.

He established the religious institutes; and pontifical regulations, whose cruder form had been attributed to Romulus; he built several temples, especially that of Janus; he reformed the calendar; instituted public markets and festivals; encouraged the pursuit of agriculture and the mechanic arts; and created the brotherhoods or corporations of the trades and handicrafts- men, which continued to exist through the whole history of the Roman state under the name which he had originally given them of Colleges of Artificers.

Tullus Hostilius was the successor and the contrast of Numa.

He was a warlike monarch, and his reign was marked by a series of military successes. He was not Eke his predecessor, of a religious turn of mind, and it was only in moments of trepidation, says Livy,[103] that he made vows to build temples or had recourse to expiatory sacrificial rites.

Heineccius[104] thinks it probable that he abolished the craft associations which had been instituted by Numa, because they were calculated to divert the citizens from military pursuits and to deprive him of the services of active soldiers.

Ancus Martius, the fourth king, was the grandson of Numa.[105]

He revived the institutions of his grandfather and brought the Romans back from the warlike habits of the previous reign to a cultivation of the arts of peace.

With this view he caused the sacred institutes of Numa to be written out by the Pontifex Maximus upon tablets and to be exhibited to the inspection of the public. Under his reign, the colleges must have revived from the oppression they had experienced under his predecessor.

The history of the next king, Tarquinius Priscus, if we are to judge from the legends upon which it is founded, afford no reason for believing that his reign was unfavorable to the craft associations.

---

[103] "In re trepida," lib., i., 27
[104] "De Collegiis et corporibus opificum."
[105] Sir George Cornwall Lewis, "An Inquiry into the Credibility of the Early Roman History," ii., 465

He is said to have been a patron of architecture and of a constructive character.

He is said to have adorned the Forum, to have formed the Circus Maximus, to have constructed the Cloaca, or sewers, to have laid the foundations of the temple of Jupiter Capitolinus, and to have built a stone wall around the city.

All these labors would have required the aid of architects and builders, and we suppose that the corporations or colleges of these craftsmen were encouraged by a monarch so well disposed to the cultivation of the arts of construction.

Servius Tullius, the sixth king, has had the reputation of a reformer.

He was the first to make a census of the people, and to distribute them into classes.

Florus says that he made the division in curia and colleges and that things were so ordered that all distinctions of property, station, age, occupation, and office must have been well marked.

In this reign the colleges and craftsmen took a recognized position among the classes of the community.

Tarquinius Superbus, the last of the race of Roman kings, whose name has been stained by the record of his tyranny, was the enemy of the people.

His life was that of a despot.

He surrounded himself with a body-guard to protect his person; he prohibited all assemblies of the peace e4her in the country or in the city, so that no opportunity might be afforded them of consulting on the affairs of the state; he occupied them in forced labors for the construction of the sewers and the completion of the Circus; he repealed all the popular laws of his predecessor; abolished the equitable distribution into classes which had been made by the census; and suppressed the colleges and craft sodalic, As the natural and expected result of this oppressive course, the people rose to the assertion of their liberties.

Tarquin and his family were perpetually banished, the monarchy ceased to exist, and the republic rose on its ruins.

For a time after the expulsion of the King the Patricians ruled over the Plebeians with a hand not always light.

Dissensions sprang up between the oppressors and the oppressed, and the Colleges of Artificers became a subject of suspicion and dislike to the former class, because as these associations were wholly made up out of the latter, they were supposed to be the fomenters of discontent and bodies in which seditious factions would be nourished.

Nevertheless, one of the first acts of the Consular government was to re-establish the mild and beneficent laws of Servius Tullius, and to permit the assemblage of the people, whence resulted the restoration of the colleges.

The severity of a famine which occurred in the Year of the City 276, is attributed by Dionysius of Halicarnassus to the fact that the number of women, children, slaves, and handicraftsmen who were unproductive classes, was three times greater than that of the citizens who were engaged in agricultural pursuits.

Though history, such as it was at that time, is silent on the subject, yet it must be evident that the continual discords for many of the early years of the Republic, between the Patricians and the Plebeians, must have seriously affected the interests of the Colleges of Artificers and secured to them only intermittent periods of spasmodic activity.

But when the people had extorted from the Senate the Tribuneship by which they became a part of the governing power, and the right of holding offices of honor and of entering the priesthood, the colleges of handicraftsmen appear to have been more firmly established.

The laws of the Twelve Tables, which were adopted in the Year of the City 302, confirmed their privileges, a decree which Gaius in his Commentary on these laws thinks was suggested by and copied from the decree of Solon in reference to similar associations among the Greeks.

In the Year of the City 687, the Senate had suppressed the colleges, but eight years afterward they were restored by the Tribune Publius Clodius.

From that time the Roman citizens began to pay much attention to the arts and to mechanics.

But though the craftsmen were united in the Tribes and had the right of voting, they were not highly respected and were not permitted to serve in the army except on extraordinary occasions, such as domestic seditions.[106] Yet a great many new colleges were created, some by legal enactment and some by voluntary association.

Such, for example, were the colleges of Ship Carpenters, of Smiths, and especially the Collegia Sirucloram, or Colleges of Builders, who were the same as the Fabrii Cementarii, or as it must be literally translated, the Stonemasons.

---

[106] "Signonio de ant. jur. civil. Rom."

But these guilds or Colleges of Artificers were not confined to the city of Rome. They spread into the provinces and the municipal cities, or those which had been invested with the right of Roman citizenship.

For a long time these corporations of workmen pursued a quiet and exemplary course, engaged in the lawful pursuit of the various trades and handicrafts.

But the number in time greatly increased; Clodius, the Tribune, in abrogating the decree of the Senate which had suppressed them, unfortunately had extended the privilege to slaves and foreigners of creating new colleges or of uniting with the old ones.

Hence many of these sodalities gradually degenerated into factions and political clubs, and thus became dangerous to the state.

In addition to this fault, the classical writers speak in terms of denunciation of the sumptuous feasts in which many of the colleges indulged.

They carried this species of dissipation to such an extent, that Varro complains that the extravagant banquets of the colleges had greatly enhanced the price of food at Rome.

These follies were of gradual growth.

The colleges continued to exercise their functions during the existence of the Republic, and were found in a flourishing condition at the advent of the Empire.

It is not to be supposed that in a change of government from the simplicity of a democracy to the corruptions of a monarchy, based on a revolution, the faults of political intrigue and extravagant conduct would not increase rather than abate.

Hence we find the emperors generally opposed to the increase of these sodalities, and there are frequent decrees suspending or suppressing them.

But it must be remarked that this opposition appears to have been directed rather against the creation of new corporations than to the suppression of the old ones.

To properly appreciate the true condition of the Roman Colleges of Workmen, we must advert to the fact that while there were a certain number of them which had existed from the earliest period, being the continuation of the primitive system which had been established by Numa, and which had, except at intermittent periods of suspicion been tolerated and even patronized by the government, there were many others which had sprung up in later times, and which were formed by the voluntary association of individuals.

These bodies were for the most part the creation of political factions, whose revolutionary designs were sought to be concealed in the exclusiveness of secret consultations, or sometimes of less worthy craftsmen who, not having been admitted into the fellowship of the old college, were willing to set up a rivalry in business.

Hence had arisen a distinction well recognized in the decrees of the Senate, or of the emperors, and constantly referred to in the various codes of Roman law.

This distinction was into lawful and unlawful colleges, or, to use the legal terms, into Collegia licita and Collegian illicita.

The voluntary associations, to which allusion has just been made, were of the latter class. They were illicit or illegal colleges, and held a somewhat similar position to the old and lawful colleges that, in modern times, an unincorporated society does in its privileges and franchises to a corporation.

The analogy goes so far at least as this, that the illicit colleges, like the unincorporated societies of the present day, had no recognition in law-in other words, possessed no rights which the law recognized.

But, in another respect, the analogy fails.

The illicita colleges were not only not recognized, but were actually discountenanced by the state, an interference to which our unincorporated associations are not subjected.

If the law does not protect them, it does not persecute them.

They are allowed, if guilty of no violation of the laws, to continue without let or hindrance.

But this was not the happy lot of the illegal colleges.

They were repeatedly denounced and suppressed by the state, which looked upon them always as associations of a dangerous character.

It has been supposed that it was the policy of the Empire to destroy the corporations of craftsmen which had been originally instituted by Numa, and decrees and laws have been quoted to prove the statement.

If such had been the case, we should meet with an insurmountable difficulty in tracing back the corporations of builders of the Middle Ages, to the Roman colleges.

The total and permanent suppression at any time of these, would naturally destroy the links of that chain of continuity which is absolutely necessary to identify the one with the other in the progress of history.

But we can not find any evidence that the primitive colleges, and especially those of the builders, ever were suppressed.

The decrees of the Senate and of the emperors were directed against the new, and not against the old, associations of craftsmen.

Thus Suetonius tells us that Julius Caesar abolished " all colleges except those which had been anciently constituted; " the same author informs us that Augustus " dissolved all colleges except the old and legitimate."[107] The same reservation is made in all references through the Digest of Justinian, to any decrees or enactments which affected these corporations.

It is only Collegia illicita against which the penalties of law are to be enforced.

"It is permitted to assemble for religious purposes," says the Digest, " provided that by this the decree of the senate prohibiting illicit colleges is not contravened." Ulpian says that " illicit colleges are forbidden under the same penalties as are adjudged to armed men who take possession of temples or public places." There was a very wholesome dread, both in the times of the republic and under the emperors, of those illegal associations, voluntarily assembled, too often for the promotion of factions or the encouragement of political opinions which were dangerous to the state.

When the greater part of the city of Nicomedia had been destroyed by fire, Pliny,[108] who was then the governor of Bithynia, applied to Trajan for permission to organize for the purpose of rebuilding a College of Masons (Collegium.Fabrorum), which should not consist of more than one hundred and fifty artisans, and in which he would take care, by the exclusion of every person who was not a Mason, that the purposes of the new college should not be diverted into an improper direction.

There is a good deal of suggestive history in this passage of Pliny's letter to the Emperor.

It indicates, in the first place, that it was not unusual to create new Colleges of Masons[109] for special purpose, which purposes being accomplished, the colleges were dissolved.

---

[107] "Cunta Collegia praetor antiquitus constituta distraexit" and "Collegia praetor antiqua et legitima dissolvit" are the expressions of the Roman biographer

[108] See the 42nd and 43d Epistles for the correspondence on this subject between Pliny and the Emperor Trajan

[109] I cannot hestitate to translate the words "Collegium Fabrorum" into the English "College of Masons." The whole tenor of the classical writings and especially the inscriptions show that it was not usual to add to the generic word faber the distinctive one marmoriarius to show that he was a worker in stone or in marble.

Pliny would hardly have asked permission to perform an act of such importance, if it had not been sanctioned by previous custom.

But this brings us very near to the similar custom of the Stonemasons in the Middle Ages, who, we know, were accustomed to create their temporary or especial Lodges of workmen, when any building was to be undertaken.

We see in this, if not a proof of the direct continuation of the mediaeval Masons from the Roman colleges (which Mr. Findel is unwilling to admit), at least a very exact imitation in an interesting point, by the former of the customs of the latter.

And in the next place, we learn from this epistle of Pliny that it was not unusual to admit into these colleges of workmen members who were not of the Craft, and that this was often done for an evil purpose On this fact, indeed, was based the objection of the state to illicit colleges.

Voluntary associations were often formed which, assuming the name and pretending to practice the professions of the regular colleges, consisted really, in great part, of non-operatives who met together in secret to concoct political and insurrectionary schemes.

If the illicit colleges had confined themselves to a rivalry in work with the regular bodies, it is not likely that the state would have meddled with the contests between regular and irregular workmen, or, as in after times they were called, Freemasons and Cowans.

Government does not at this day, in any country, interfere between constitutional and clandestine Lodges of Masons.

It leaves, as it is probable that it would have done in Rome, the settlement of the controversy to the Masonic law.

But it was the admission of these non-operative members into the illicit colleges, who converted them from bodies of honest work.men into political clubs, that made all the evil and awoke the suspicions and the interference of the state.

Trajan consequently declines to permit the creation of a new and temporary college at Nicomedia, and he assigns the reason for his refusal in these words.

He says, in reply to Pliny: "You have suggested the establishment of a College of Masons (Collegia Fabrorum) at Nicomedia, after the example of many other cities.

But we should not forget that this province, and especially its cities, have been greatly troubled by this kind of factions.

Whatever name we may, give to them for any cause, bodies of men, however small in number, who are drawn together by the same design, will become political clubs." The last two words are in the original hetaria. This from the Greek, among which people hetaria, or helairiai were associations originally instituted for convivial purposes or for mutual relief, like our benefit societies.

They became, in later times, very common in the Greek cities of the Roman Empire, but, as Mr. Kennedy says, " were looked on with suspicion by the emperors as leading to political combinations."[110] I think, therefore, that we may safely arrive at the conclusion that the primitive colleges of artisans, who derived their origin from the time of Numa, and to which we may trace the idea of the mediaeval guilds of Masons, were generally undisturbed by the government, whether regal, republican, or imperial, and continued their existence and their activity to a very late period in the history of the empire.

The persecutions, suppressions, and dissolutions of colleges of which we read, refer only to those illegal and irregular ones, which, not confining their operations within the legitimate limits of their craft, were voluntary associations made up, for the most part, of non-operative members, who were engaged in factious schemes against the powers of the state.

This point being settled, we may next direct our attention to the condition of these colleges, and especially the Colleges of Masons, or Collegia Fabrorum (for with them only are we concerned), in the empire and in the provinces until the final overthrow of the Roman power The Romans in the earlier portion of their history, were without any taste or refinement.

The people were entirely military in their character, and they cultivated the rude arts of war rather than the polished ones of peace.

Architecture, therefore, was in a debased condition.

The principles of building extended only to the construction of a shelter from the weather, their houses were of the rudest form, and, as their name imported, were merely coverings from the sun and rain.

"These sheds of theirs," says Spence, " were more like the caves of wild beasts than the habitations of men; and rather flung together, as chance led them, than formed into regular streets and openings.

Their walls were half mud; and their roofs pieces of boards stuck together."[111] The builders of the college established by Numa could at that time have been occupied only in the most inglorious part of their profession.

---

[110] Smith, "Dictionary of Greek and Roman Antiquities," article Eranoi.
[111] Spence, "Polymatis," Dialogue V., p. 36

They were engaged in works of utility and absolute necessity, and could have had no knowledge of or inclination for ornament.

The most bungling carpenter or bricklayer of the present time must have greatly surpassed them in skill.

During that period the colleges furnished no architects to the army.

The only workmen that we find there were the smiths and the carpenters; they were soldiers who exercised with but little need of skill the mysteries of these trades, being employed in the renovation of weapons and in needful repairs about the camp.

It was not until centuries afterward that workmen were supplied by the colleges and authorized by the state to accompany the legions in their campaigns and in their occupation of conquered provinces.[112] It was not until about the era of Augustus-that monarch who boasted that he had found Rome a city of brick and left it a city of marble-that the Romans began to exhibit a fondness for the fine arts, and especially for architecture.

Marcellus, the conqueror of Syracuse, had, two centuries before, implanted the seeds of a refined taste in his countrymen, and invited the invectives of the ascetic Cato, by the works of Grecian art which he brought to Rome from the spoliation of the city which he had conquered.

To him, therefore, has been attributed the introduction of the arts into Rome.

But it is to Augustus that architecture was indebted for the high position as an art that it assumed among the Romans, and from the period of his reign must we date the rise of the Colleges of Builders, as associations of architects, whose cultivated and encouraged genius produced its influence upon the conquered provinces into which they migrated with the Roman legions.

Pittacus says, in his Lexicon of Roman Antquities,[113] that those workmen who at first confined their labors to the city of Rome, afterward spread over the whole of Italy and then into the various provinces of the empire, furnishing everything that was needed by the army.

The government seems to have taken especial care of these colleges, for besides the officers elected by the members themselves, the state placed over them other officers, whose duty it was to give them a general superintendence.

---

[112] Pittacus, "Lexicon Antiquitatum Romanorum," article Fabri
[113] "Lexicon Antiquitatum Romanorum," article Collegium.

In the provinces this duty was entrusted to the proconsul or government.

Thus we have seen that Pliny, as governor of the province of Bithynia, proposed to create a College of Builders, over which he was to exercise a control such as would regulate it in the admission of its members.

In the municipal cities this officer was called sometimes a Procurator, and sometimes a Praepositus.

In every legion the artisans were under the government of a Prefect, who was styled the Prefectus Fabrum, or Prefect of the Artisans.

I am not willing to confound this officer with the Prefect of the Camp, who was, like our modern quartermaster, of a purely military character.

There is an inscription copied by Reinesius, in which occur the words Faber et Praef. Fabr. Leg., XX., i.e., Artificer and Prefect of the Artificers.

This would seem to imply that the Prefect himself was sometimes, if not always, an artificer and one of the Craft." Under the officer appointed by the state, as the general superintendent of the artificers of the college, was a subordinate one, appointed also by the state or perhaps by himself, whose duty it was to inspect and to direct the labors of the workmen, and to see that everything was done in an artistic and workmanlike manner.

He was, in fact, what in later times the Freemasons called the Magister Operis, or Master of the Work.

When, therefore, we meet in Gaul, in Britain, or in any other province which had been penetrated by the legions, with a monument of the labors of these Roman Masons, which some wellpreserved inscription attests to have been the work of a Collegium Fabrorum, or College of Masons, we may suppose that it was accomplished in the following manner.

In the first place the men the materials, the site, the character of the building, and all other matters relating to the general design, were determined by the Proconsul, Procurator, Commander of the Legion, or whomsoever had been appointed by the state or the empoeror as superintendent of the artificers and the colleges.

The workmen being then assembled, commenced their labors by congregating themselves, or being congregated, into a college, if such a college did not already exist, and they were placed under the immediate, control and direction of a subordinate officer, who was an artificer or an architect, and who regulated their labors, made designs or plans, and corrected the errors of the workmen.

In all this we see a great analogy to the method pursued by the operative Stonemasons of the Middle Ages.

First, there was a prelate, nobleman, or man of wealth and dignity, who had formed the design of building a cathedral, an abbey, or a castle.

In the old English Constitutions this great personage is always refered to as " the Lord" and the work or building was called "the Lord's work." Having congregated in huts or temporary dwellings around the site of the edifice they were about to erect, they formed a Lodge, which was under the control of a Master.

And then there was the architect or Master of the Works, who was responsible for the faithful performance of the task.

The convenience of military operations, such as the establishment or removal of camps, and the passage of armies from one place to another, required that the legions should carry with them in their marches architects and competent workmen to accomplish these objects.

Bergerius, who wrote a treatise "On the Public and Military Roads of the Roman Empire",[114] estimates, with perhaps some extravagance, that the number of architects and workmen engaged in the Roman states in the repairs of roads, the construction of bridges and other works of a similar kind, exceeded those employed in the building of the Pyramids of Egypt and the Temple of Solomon.

Of these a great number were distributed among the legions; accompanied them in their marches; remained with them wherever they were stationed; created their colleges and proceeded to the erection of works, sometimes of a temporary and sometimes of a more permanent character.

Dr. Krause says, citing as his authority the Corpus Juris and the inscriptions, that in every legion there were corporations or colleges of workmen who were employed for building and other purposes needed in military operations.

Hence, in tracing the advance of the Roman legions into different colonies, we are also tracing the advance of the Roman architects and builders who accompanied them.

---

[114] "De publicis et militaribus Imperii Romani Viis," contained in vol. x. of the "Thesaurus Antiq. Rom." of Graevius.

And when the legion stopped in its progress and made any colony its temporary home, they exercised all the influence of a conquering army of civilized soldiers over a country of barbarians.

Of all these influences of civilization the one that has been the most patent was that of the architects who substituted for the rude constructions which they found in the countries which had been invaded, the more refined principles of building.

The monuments of the edifices erected in Spain, in Gaul, and in Britain have, for the most part, disappeared under the destructive agencies of time; but their memorials remain to us in ruins, in inscriptions, and in the history of the improved condition of architecture, among these barbarous and uncultivated peoples.

It was, it is true, developed in subsequent times, and greatly modified by the instructions of Byzantine artists, but the first growth and outspring of the architecture practiced by the mediaeval guilds of Freemasons must be traced to the introduction of the art into the Roman provinces by the Colleges of Builders which accompanied the Roman legions in the stream of conquest which these victorious armies followed.

Having thus presented the details of the history of these Roman Colleges of Builders from their organization by Numa, through the successive eras of regal, of republican, and of imperial Rome; having shown their continued existence and eventually their spread .into the municipal or free cities and into the conquered provinces, impressing everywhere the evidences of an influence on the art of building, it is proper that we should now pause to examine the memorials of their labors in the different provinces and colonies.

It is thus that we shall be enabled to establish the first link in that chain which connects the Freemasonry of the mediaeval and more recent periods of Europe with the building corporations of Rome.

CHAPTER IV

THE FIRST LINK: SETTLEMENT OF ROMAN COLLEGESOF ARTIFICERS IN THE PROVINCES OF THE EMPIRE

The first link of the chain which connects the Roman Colleges of Artificers with the building corporations of the Middle Ages, is found in the dispersion and settlement of the former in the conquered colonies of Rome.

It has been satisfactorily shown that the Masons at Rome were incorporated into colleges, where the principles of their art were diligently studied and taught to younger members who stood for that purpose in the place occupied by the Apprentices in the Stonemasons' lodges at a long subsequent period.

We have seen that an immunity from all public services was granted by the Emperor Constantine to workmen, and among others to architects for the express reason that they might have the opportunity of acquiring a knowledge of their professions and of imparting it to their disciples.

Now, these architects, one of whom was always appointed to a legion with workmen from the colleges under him, carried the skill which they had been enabled to acquire at home, with them into the colonies or provinces which they visited, and there, if they remained long enough, which was usually the case, as the legions were for the most part stationed for long periods, they erected, besides the military defences constructed for the safety of the army, and the roads which they opened for its convenience, more permanent edifices, such as temples.

Of this we have abundant evidence in the ruins which still remain of some of these structures, ruins so dilapidated as to supply us with only meagre and yet sufficient evidence of their former existence and even splendor, but more especially in the numerous inscriptions on stone or marble tablets, hundreds of which, in every province, have been collected by Gruter, Muratori, Reinesius and other writers who have devoted themselves to the study of Roman antiquities.

Thus we shall find in Spain, in Gaul, and in Britain abundant evidences, of the kind referred to, of these labors of the Roman architects, while these provinces were under Roman domination.

It can not be denied that this must have exercised a certain influence on the original inhabitants and have introduced a more refined taste and a superior skill in the art of building.

Nor was the influence thus exerted of an altogether ephemeral nature.

When the Roman domination ceased, and the legions were withdrawn to sustain the feeble powers of a decaying empire, threatened by the barbarian hordes of the north with extinction, not all the Romans who had come with the legions, or since their advent immigrated into the country, left with them.

A very long series of years had passed, and many of these architects and builders had been naturalized, as it were, and were unwilling to depart from the homes which they had made.

They remained, and continued to perpetuate among the people with whom they were domiciliated the skill and the usages which they had originally brought from Rome.

M. Viollet-le-Duc says, in his Dictionary of Architecture,[115] that in the Middle Ages the workmen of the southern cities of Europe preserved the Roman traditions, and that in them the corporations or colleges did not cease to exist, but that these bodies were not established in the northern cities until the time of the affranchisement of the communes.

Even if this were the fact, it would only be lengthening the chain of connection, for it is fair to suppose that the corporations of the north, at whatever later period they were established, must have adored the system of confraternities from the southern cities where they had long existed as a part of the Roman tradition.

So that even in this view the chain is uninterrupted which binds the corporations of builders of the Middle Ages with those of Rome.

But I think that it will hereafter be shown to be historically true that the traditions and the usages of the Roman colleges were well

---

[115] "Dictionnaire Raisonne de lArchitecture de XI me au XVI me siecle," tome vi., p. 346

preserved in the early period of English architecture, and that out of these traditions sprang, in part, the regulations of the Saxon guilds.

But this is a question for future consideration when we come to the investigation of the post-Roman architecture of Gaul and England.

The evidences of the influence of the Roman colleges on the province of Spain are very abundant, arising from the peculiar relations of that province to the Empire.

Upon the expulsion of the Carthaginians from Spain, which occurred 206 B.C., it was erected into a Roman province, at least so much as had been conquered by the Romans under the Scipios, which did not include more than half of the peninsular.

Thenceforward it was governed sometimes by one proctor and sometimes by two, and two legions were always kept stationary in the province.

The influence of this political arrangement was of the most important character.

The soldiers intermarried with the native- women, and thus became so estranged from Italy that when the legions were disbanded. Many of them refused to return home, and continued their residence in Spain.[116] A little more than a century after its conquest, such a system of internal communication had been established by the opening of roads and especially the military one of Pompey over the Pyrences, that the country was laid open to travelers, many of whom settled there.

In the time of Strabo, a portion of the province had been so Romanized in manners as to have become almost Roman.

The great privilege of citizenship had been granted to many of the inhabitants, and they had even forgotten their native language.

Spain, thus becoming more intimately connected with the Empire than any of the other provinces, furnished, as it is well known, some distinguished names to Latin literature, such as Lucanus, the poet, the older and the younger Seneca, Columelle, Quintilian, and the epigrammatist, Martial.

In the reign of Augustus many considerable colonieswere founded, represented by the modern cities of Zaragossa, Merida, Badajoz, and many others.

In these cities the art of building flourished, and they were adorned with some of the finest productions of Roman architecture, of many of which the magnificent ruins still remain, while temples, theaters, baths, circuses, and other public edifices, which had been

---

[116] Niebuhr, "Lectures on Roman History," ii., p. 208

erected by the Roman masons, have perished through the waste of time and the destructive influences of invasions and intestine wars.

It is well known that while Spain was, from the earliest times, an object of the grasping ambition of foreign peoples, and that it was in turns invaded and conquered by the Phoenicians, the Greeks, the Romans, the Goths, and the Arabs, all of whom were attracted by the delights of the climate, the fertility of the soil, and the richness of the mines, the Romans, from the longer duration of their domination and from the more solid character of the edifices which they constructed, have left a greater number of architectural monuments, and these in a greater state of preservation, than the other nations who preceded or followed them.[117] But the invasion of the Goths, after the departure of the Romans, and the subsequent more permanent occupation of the peninsular by the Saracenic Arabs or Moors, so completely withdrew the architects of Spain from all communication with those of the rest of Europe, and so completely obliterated all effects of the earlier Roman influence, that it is impossible to trace a continued and uninterrupted connection between the Roman Colleges of Masons, who left behind such wonderful evidences of their skill, and the medaevel guilds or corporations of the Middle Ages, who in other countries were their successors.

It is a curious historical fact that while of all the Boman provinces Spain was the one in which the Roman domination was most firmly, established, it was also the one in which, after the decay of the Empire, all the results of that domination were the most thoroughly obliterated.

Spain has, therefore, been alluded to on the present occasion not with any intention of making it a part of that train of succession which, beginning with the colleges of Numa, ended in the mediaeval guilds of Stonemasons, but because it furnishes a very complete instance of how these Roman Colleges of Artificers extended their labors and introduced their art into foreign countries.

In the three other provinces of the western empire, the two Gauls and Britain, the connection of the Roman colleges with the guilds or corporations which subsequently sprang up may be more readily traced. Cisalpine or Citerior Gaul was the name given by the classical writers to that part of Gallia which was south of the alpine mountains, and which constituted what is more familiarly known as northern Italy.

---

[117] Don Caen-Bermudez, "Sumario de las Antiguedades Romanas que hay in Espana," Madrid, 1852, p. 2

Deriving its first settlement, if we may trust to the authority of Livy, which, however, Niebuhr rejects, by an immigration of the Gauls beyond the mountains, in the time of Tarquinius Priscus, these people were for centuries engaged in struggles with the Romans, whose attempts to subdue them were always unsuccessful.

When Hannibal, the Carthaginian general, invaded Italy and sought the destruction of Rome and the Roman power, many of them willingly became his allies. But about two hundred years before the Christian era, the two most important tribes, the Insubrians and the Boians, were subdued by the Roman legions under the Consuls C. Cornelius Cethegus and Q. Minucius Rufus, and from that time to the reign of Augustus, Cisalpine Gaul came slowly but surely under the Roman domination.

When it was established as a Roman province, it was rapidly filled with a Roman population, and became one of the most valuable of the Roman possessions.

Most of the towns received that political status known as the Jus Latii, or the Latinitas, by which they were placed in a middle position between strangers and the Roman citizens, and the pure right of citizenship was bestowed on their magistrates, which was, in the time of Caesar, extended to all the inhabitants, the larger towns being made municipalities.

Fifty years before Christ all Cisalpine Gaul had been invested with the right of citizenship, and consisted of Roman communities organized after the Roman fashion.

This would necessarily indicate the introduction among the peace of Roman civilization and refinement.

Among the arts that were encouraged, that of architecture was not the least, and we have ample evidence in still remaining monuments and in inscriptions that the Roman architects or members of the colleges were industriously employed in the labors of their Craft.

The proofs of this are to be found in the modern cities of northern Italy, which are the successors of the Cisalpine colonies, and which have preserved in their museums or in private collections the memorials and relics of their ancient prosperity and refinement.

Thus Mutina, now the modern Modena, was one of the most flourishing of the Lombard towns. Ciccro did not hesitate to call it "the strongest and most splendid colony of the Roman people." It was so wealthy as to have been able to support for a long time the large army of Brutus.

It fell at length into decay, but was never abandoned, and again rose to prosperity in the Middle Ages under the name of Modena by which it is still known.

Although the magnificent architectural remains of the ancient city were employed in the construction of the cathedral and other public buildings of the modern one, or were buried under the depositions of alluvial soil, yet the Museum of Modena contains a valuable collection of sarcophagi and of inscriptions which have been excavated at various times and which furnish the evidence of the existence and the labors of the Roman architects and builders under the empire.

There was another town of Cisalpine Gaul, called Aquileia, which was built by the Romans to defend the fertile plains of Italy on the northeast from the incursions of barbarians.

Two centuries before Christ it was settled by several thousand colonists from Rome and became a place of great commercial prosperity.

In the 5th century it was plundered and burnt by Attila, King of the Huns; but though it never again became a place of importance, it was always inhabited, and in the 6th century was the See of a bishop, and, to borrow the language of Mr. Bunbury,[118] " It maintained a sickly existence throughout the Middle Ages." At the present day it is an obscure village, with only a cathedral.

Although it contains no vestiges of Roman edifices, the site, says the same writer, it abounds with remains of antiquity, coins, engraved stones, and other minor objects as well as shads and capitals of columns, fragments of frieze, etc., the splendor and beauty of which sufficiently attest the magnificence of the ancient city." Among the inscriptions found there arc some which relate to the temple and the worship of Belenus, a local sun-god whom the Romans identified with Apollo.

All the works of which we have these memorials must have been effected by the Roman architects, who, with their colleges, were surely among the six or seven thousand who emigrated from Rome and built up the city.

Bononia, or the modern Bologna, was built, it is supposed, by the Tuscans, and was raised to the rank of a Roman colony about two centuries before Christ.

It continued to be an important and flourishing city under the empire.

---

[118] Smith's "Dictionary of Greek and Roman Geography."

Though it suffered decay, it was able, in the 5th century, to withstand successfully the attacks of Alaric.

It never lost the continuity of its existence, but after the fall of the empire regained, in a great measure, its prosperity, and at length assumed, in the Middle Ages, a preeminence among the cities of northern Italy which it still retains.

It is not probable that it had soon lost as traditions of those arts which it practiced when a Roman colony, and which are attested by fragments of sculpture and traditions which have been preserved.

The modern city of Ivrea, which is an important place, was the ancient Eporedia, a Roman colony founded about one hundred years before Christ.

The strength of its position, as commanding two important passes of the Alps, gave it great military value, and it does not, therefore, appear to have been subjected to any great process of decay.

As late as the close of the 4th century it was a considerable town and occupied, as a military station, by a portion of a legion.

The modern city still contains a fine Roman sarcophagus and some other remains of its ancient splendor.

But the most interesting of all the cities of Cisalpine Gaul, in a reference to the connection of the Roman colleges, which labored in them, with the sodalities of the Middle Ages which succeeded them, is Comum, an important city at the foot of the Alps and on the borders of the Lake of Como.

The present name of the city is como It is supposed to have been the birthplace of both the elder and the younger Pliny, the latter of whom made it his favorite residence, and established in it a school of learning.

It was under the empire a flourishing municipality, and its prosperity was secured by the beauty and convenience of its position at the extremity of the lake, for it became the point of embarkation for travelers who were proceeding to cross the Rhactian Alps.

It retained its prosperity to the close of the Roman Empire.

In the 4th century a fleet was stationed there for the protection of the lake.

Cassiodorus speaks of it in the 6th century as one of the military bulwarks of Italy, and extols the richness of the palaces with which the shores of the lake in its vicinity were adorned.

It continued to retain its importance in the Middle Ages, and it is from there that the "Masters of Como," the Traveling Freemasons, proceeded to traverse Europe in the 10th century, and to erect cathedrals, monasteries, and palaces in the various countries which they visited.

But this body, whose acts form the most valuable portion of the historical testimony of the connection between the Roman Colleges of Artificers and the corporations of Freemasons in the Middle Ages, will be hereafter discussed and described in a more extended manner For the present, this simple allusion to them must suffice We next come to the consideration of the architectural condition of Transalpine Gaul, or Gaul proper, under the Roman domination.

This subject may be briefly discussed, as the early condition of Roman architecture in Gaul will be more diffusely treated in a subsequent chapter.

The name of Transalpine Gaul was given by the Romans to that country which extended from the Pyrenean mountains to the river Rhine, within which limits modern France is embraced.

It was first conquered by the Roman arms under Julius Caesar, and remained a province of the empire until its final decline.

The Gauls represented to have been a ferocious and sanguinary people, though at the time of the conquest Caesar found an improvement in the manners of some of the tribes.

But their progress toward civilization and refinement was rapid after they came under the dominion of the Romans.

Caesar had formed a legion of Gaulish soldiers whom he armed and drilled after the Roman fashion, and subsequently when he had arrived at the Dictatorship he made them Roman citizens, and sent Roman colonies to several of the cities.

Under the Emperor Augustus, Gaul became rapidly Romanized.

Schools were established in the large towns, and the Latin language and the Roman law were adopted.

In religion there was a compromise and there was a mixture of Gallic and Roman worship, though wherever the Romans made a permanent settlement, temples were erected to the Roman deities.

Architectural works were pursued with great energy but with little prudence.

Temples and other public buildings, together with bridge, roads and aqueducts, were erected over all the country.

These must have cost immense sums, and as the expansion was wholly defrayed by the inhabitants without aid from the mother government, great distress began to prevail among the people, which led to several mutinies.

But though the embellishments of the Roman architects had impoverished the colonists, the influences of refinement in art continued long after these troubles to prevail, and in Gaul we find an almost uninterrupted connection between the architecture of the Roman colleges and that of the mediaeval Freemasons.

That part of Gaul which lay along the shore of the Mediterranean Sea, and which the Romans emphatically called the Province (Provincia), had been civilized and Romanized long before the conquest of the other parts of the country.

It was in the towns of this province that the most extensive operations in architecture were exhibited.

It must be remarked however, that all over Gaul outside of the Provincia, as well as within it, there are ample evidences of the splendid style of architecture that was cultivated by the architects who accompanied the legions, or the colonists who went from Rome to settle in Gaulish towns.

Baeterrae, now Beziers received a colony of soldiers of the seventh legion, who constructed a causeway, of which some traces still exist.

There are also the vestiges of an amphitheater and the remains of an aqueduct.

Arelate, now known as Arles, was a city of the Provincia.

The Roman remains are very numerous there; among them an obelisk of Egyptian granite which was excavated some centuries ago, and in 1675 was set up in one of the public squares.

The amphitheater was estimated as capable of holding twenty thousand persons.

There is also an old cemetery which contains many ancient tombs, both Pagan and Christian.

Nemausus, the modern Nimes, which was also a city of the Provincia, contains many remains of the skill of the old Roman architects and the splendor of their works.

The amphitheater, not quite as large as that of Arles, is in a good state of preservation.

There is also a temple still existing which, as Arthur Young says, in his Travels in France is beyond comparison the most light, elegant, and pleasing building that he ever beheld.

Under the modern name of "Maison Carree" it is now used as a museum of painting and antiquities.

But the noblest monument that the Romans have left in Gaul is the aqueduct now called the Pont du Gard, which is between three and four leagues from Nimes.

The bridge on which the aqueduct is laid is still solid and strong, and in says Mr. George Long, " a magnificent monument of the grandeur of Roman conceptions, and of the boldness of their execution." It is useless to extend these descriptions farther.

All over Gaul were cities colonized by the Romans, who imparted to the native inhabitants a portion of their skill, their taste, and their refinement.

Temples, amphitheaters, theaters, aqueducts, and public and private buildings of every kind are to be found in all the large and many of the small cities of modern France, which, sometimes well preserved and sometimes in ruins, always indicate that the spirit of architectural - enterprise was imparted to the people under the Roma government and by Roman architects and builders.

How well that spirit was preserved and how it became afterward developed in the Freemasonry of the Middle Ages will remain to be elucidated in our further historical researches.

Britain was twice invaded by Caesar, but on neither occasion did he stay long enough in the island to effect any influence on the inhabitants.

Augustus afterward planned an expedition to Britain, but the plan was never consummated.

It was not until the time of Claudius that any serious attempt at conquest was made.

Under his orders an army was led by Aulus Plautus into the southeastern part of the island.

The city of Camalodunum, now Malden, was taken.

Claudius, who had visited Britain to partake of the triumphs of the victory, returned to Rome and assumed the surname of Britannicus in attestation of his success, leaving his general, Plautus, to complete the conquest, which, however, he did not accomplish.

Vespasian soon after subdued the Isle of Wight and took twenty of the oppida or British towns.

His son Titus also distinguished himself in many battles with the native tribes.

But though the island was at this time penetrated to some extent by the Roman legions, and the southern coasts were occupied by them, the island was not yet conquered.

The struggle between the independent spirit of the natives and the ambitious designs of their Roman invaders lasted for nearly half a century, and the subjection of the whole island was not achieved until the reign of Domican.

Thereafter Britain took the form and felt all the influences of a Roman province, but unlike Spain and Gaul, a discontented one.

It is hardly germane to the objects of the present work to trace, with any particularity of detail, the progress of the Roman power under the various emperors who governed the island from the date of its conquest to the final withdrawal of the Roman armies in the beginning of the 5th century.

It is sufficient to say that during the period of time intervening between these two epochs, Britain had become completely Romanized.

Colonies were founded, cities possessing the right of Roman citizenship were established, legions were distributed in various places, veteran soldiers and immigrants from the imperial city had made permanent settlements, so that, as Gildas says, it was to be viewed not as a British but as a Roman island.

"Britain," says Sharon Turner, "was not now in the state in which the Romans had found it.

Its towns were no longer barricaded forests, nor its houses wood cabins covered with straw, nor its inhabitants naked savages with painted bodies or clothed with skins.

It had been, for above three centuries, the seat of Roman civilization and luxury.

Roman emperors had been born and others had reigned in it. The natives had been ambitious to obtain and hence had not only built houses, temples, courts, and market-places in their towns, but had adorned them with porticoes, galleries, baths, and saloons, and with mosaic pavements, and emulated every Roman improvement.

They had distinguished themselves as legal advocates and orators and for their study of the Roman poets.

Their cities had been made images of Rome itself, and the natives had become Romans." It can not be doubted that the skill and experience of the Roman architects who accompanied the legions or who came from Rome to Britain after its conquest had been imparted to the native Britons, and that the chain of connection between the Roman colleges and the local Colleges of Artificers in the island was well established.

Of this, numerous inscriptions and the remains of Roman buildings, found everywhere in modern England, furnish ample evidence.

In Dorchester, which was the Roman Durnovaria, besides the remains of the old Roman ruins and several camps, those of what was probably an amphitheater attest its former importance and the labors of the Roman builders.

In Dover, the ancient Dubris, there is now an octagon tower attached to a church, and which is almost built of Roman bricks.

It is supposed to have been a lighthouse in the time of the Romans.

London, or Londinium, was a very old city, and was the capital of ancient Britain as it now is of modern England 'Though not invested by the Romans with the rights of a municipality, it was always, as Tacitus says, from the abundance of its trade, a place of great importance.

The remains of Roman monuments which have been found in London show that it contained many splendid buildings.

When the foundations of an old wall which bordered the river were laid open, several years ago, it was found to be composed of materials that had been previously used in the construction of ancient buildings.

"The stones of which this wall was constructed," says Mr. Charles Roach Smith,[119] "were portions of columns, friezes, cornices, and also foundation-stones.

From their magnitude, character, and number, they gave an important and interesting insight into the obscure history of Roman London, in showing the architectural changes that had taken place in it." Architectural fragments, and the remains of tessellated pavements in great number have been discovered, which attest the magnificence of the Roman city, and traces of temples have also been found.

It has been said that London was the station of a cohort of native Britons, which was contrary to the usage of the Roman Emperors, who never stationed auxiliaries in their native countries, but we know that a colony of veterans had been established at Camalodunum or Malden not far off, and there are inscriptions which attest the presence, at various times, of the soldiers of the second, sixth, and twentieth legions in the city.

---

[119] Dr. William Smith's "Dictionary of Greek and Roman Geography."

It is easy, therefore, to trace, as we must, the construction of these magnificent works to Roman architects, supplied by the legions or the colonies.

Eboracum, or York, is familiar to the Masonic scholar from the important part that it plays in the traditional history of English Freemasonry.

It was a town of much importance ill the times of the Romans, and seems to have been a favorite place of residence.

It was the permanent station of the sixth or victorious legion.

The Emperors Severus and Constantius died there, and it is said to have been the birthplace of Constantine the Great.

Among the memorials of the Roman domination which have been found at York are numerous remains of temples, baths, altars, votive tablets, and even private residences.

Of the many inscriptions that have been preserved, one dedicated to the Egyptian god Serapis, and a tablet or slab containing the carved figure of a man with a cap and chlamys, or short mantle, who is stabbing a bull, indicate the introduction by the Romans of the worship of a foreign god as well as the cultivation of the mystical rites of Mithras.

In the beginning of the 5th century, the Roman Empire being imminently threatened with downfall, the legions and the Roman authority, which had ruled and protected Britain for so long a period, were withdrawn.

The people were left to defend themselves from the incursions of the Danes and other barbarous invaders from the opposite shores of the Continent.

Many changes took place in the laws, the language, and the habits of the island.

In time, after many wars, Britain became Anglo-Saxon England.

But, as on the retirement of the Romans, many voluntarily remained, because they had become habituated to the country and, in numerous cases, had been connected by intermarriages with the natives, Britain did not altogether lose the influence of the seed that had been sown.

Especially in the art of building, although there was a deterioration, all the effects of the Roman civilization were not lost.

And it will not, I think, be difficult to trace the development of the system of trade guilds which afterward existed among the Anglo-Saxons and the English to the suggestions of the similar guilds of the Roman colleges.

But the consideration of this question must be postponed to a future chapter.

What has been here attempted has been to show that the Roman colleges, sending their architects to the colonies and (cities established 'in the conquered provinces of the Roman Empire, had secured, in an uninterrupted succession, not only the principles of architecture but the comprehensive and well-regulated system of work which, beginning at the earliest period of Roman history in the Colleges of Artificers, was to be carried throughout its acquired dominions by its legions and its colonists, and finally to be developed in a modern form in the corporations of operative Masons of the Middle Ages, and finally in the lodges of Speculative Masons of the present day.

So far the first and second links of this chain of connection have been shown; we her close the history with the fall of the Roman dominion over the provinces at the beginning of the 5th century.

As we proceed in our investigations our inquires must bring us successively to the condition of architecture and its gradual growth into new systems and various styles in all the countries which were once under the Roman dominion.

We shall, I believe, find the principles of architecture changing from the influences of different causes exerted at different times, Architecture will be constantly changing its features.

The Roman, the Byzantine, the Gothic, and other styles will succeed and displace each other, but the system of cooperative or guild labor, which is the true connecting chain between the ancient and the modern methods of building, will always prevail and show, in every successive age, the unweakened influence of the old Roman guild or college.

CHAPTER V

EARLY MASONRY IN FRANCE

With the condition of Masonry in Gaul, which afterward became France, immediately subsequent to the decadence of the Roman Empire, and afterward up to the Middle Ages, we are by no means as familiar as we are with its condition during the same period in Germany and in Britain.

French Masonic writers have been too speculative in their views, and have given too loose a rein to their imaginations, to permit us to attach any value to the authenticity of what they present as historical statements.

This is a fault, which it is but fair to say has been shared by the English writers of what has been called Masonic history.

Clavel and Thory are hardly to be considered more reliable as historians than Anderson and Oliver.

In the works of each of these distinguished writers we find many statements which are hardly plausible, and which, although offered as historical facts, are wholly unsupported by any authentic authority.

But recently in England a new school of Masonic history has sprung up, which is rapidly clearing away the cobwebs of absurdity and inconsistency, of doubt and error which had been woven around the pure form of history by the older writers of the last and the beginning of the present century.

In France, no such school has been established.

In that country there have been no Hughans, Woodfords, or Lyons to exhume from their sepulcher, on the shelves of national or private libraries, the old charters and capitularies which might throw some light on the real condition of the Masonic sodalities which were left behind in Gaul on the retreat of the Roman legions, and which were afterward developed, by a gradual but uninterrupted growth, into the building corporations of the Middle Ages.

If the scholars of France supply us with no valuable assistance in our inquiries on this subject, we shall look in vain for aid from English or German writers.

These have, in general, thought it a task sufficiently arduous to seek the elucidation of the Masonic history of their own countries, and have not, therefore, found either time or inclination to labor, to any great extent, in other fields.

Even Findal, who is somewhat exhaustive in his account of the early and mediaeval Masonry of Britain, and more especially of Germany passes over that of France without notice.

Indeed he begins his chapter on French Masonry with the year 1725 as his starting-point, and thus entirely ignores all the events that preceded the organization of the modern lodges in Paris after the revival, as it is called, which took place in London in the year 1717.

Hence his history is not really that of Masonry in France, but only that of the French Grand Lodge.

From Kloss, another German writer of eminence, we derive no better information.

He wrote in two volumes a History of Freemasonry in France, Drawn from Authentic Documents, but his theory is that the Institution was introduced into France from England, and he goes, like Findal, no farther back than to the organization of a French lodge in 1715, under the auspices of the Grand Lodge of England.

It will be seen, when we come to the consideration of the origin of the Grand Lodge of Speculative Masons in France, that there is great question of the correctness of this date, for the researches of Bro. Hughan have led to the doubt whether there was a legal lodge in France, deriving its authority from the English Grand Lodge before the year 1732.

This, however, is not germane to the present inquiry.

It is altogether in vain that we look in the pages of French Masonic writers, such as Thory and Clavel, for any documentary history of French Freemasonry anterior to the beginning of the 8th century.

Thory, in his Acta, Lalomorum, commences his annals, so far as they relate to France, with the year 1725, and the establishment of a lodge in Paris by the titular Earl of Derwentwater.

Not a single word does be say of the condition of the association, either as Operative or Speculative, previous to that date.

Clavel, in his Histoire Pictitresaite, gives a very loose and indefinite account of the origin of Freemasonry in France.

He traces it, and in so far he is correct, to the Roman Colleges of Artificers through the architects of Lombardy, and passes very rapidly on to the connection of the French operative Masons with the building corporations of Germany and the Grand Lodge of Strasburg.

But he does not attempt to show how that connection was effected.

There is no objection to the theory which he propounds.

His principal fault, as an historian, lies in his extreme generalization and in the meagerness of his details.

Taking as his point of departure the Roman colleges, he leaps almost at a bound from them to the mediaeval corporations.

He devotes no attention to the period which immediately succeeded the fall of the empire, nor to the influences exerted on, or the methods pursued by, the Roman and Gallic Masons who were left in Gaul on the departure of the legions, and which led to the gradual development of the guilds, sodalities, or lodges which sprang up in time as the successors of the Roman colleges.

But another falling of Clavel as an historian, and one which produces the most unsatisfactory results upon the minds of his readers. is that he produces no documents, does not even refer to any, and cites no authority to corroborate any of the statements that he makes.

Even in a writer of acknowledged care and attention to the credibility and genuineness of the facts that he records, such a method of treating an historical narrative would be objectionable.

But what little claim Clavel's unsupported assertions have to our respect, and how far they are from necessarily demanding our belief, may be learned from the fact that he cites as an undoubted instance of the existence of a Masonic lodge in the year 1512, what is now known to have been merely a convivial society of literary men who met at Florence in that year under the title of the " Society of the Trowel."[120] Its symbols were the trowel, the square, the hammer, and the level, and its patron saint was St. Andrew. Vasari describes it as a festive association of Florentine artists, who met annually to dine together. He describes the origin of its existence and its title to the merely accidental circumstance that certain painters and sculptors, dining together in a garden, observed in the vicinity of their table a mass of mortar in which a trowel was sticking. Some rough practical jokes passed thereupon, such as casting

---

[120] It counted some of the most distinguished inhabitants of Florence among its members.

portions of the mortar on each other and the calling for the trowel to scrape it off. They then resolved to dine together annually, and as a memorial of the ludicrous event that had led to their organization as a dinner-club they called themselves the Societi della Cuechiara, or the Society of the Trowel. The allusion to an implement of operative masonry in the title of the society, led Clavel, as it has done Reghellini, Lenning, and some others, to believe that it was a Masonic organization.

But a reference to the authority of Vasari, in his Lives of the Painters would have shown that the apparently professional title was actually selected by a mere accident and in reference to a jocular proceeding which suggested the name.

There is hardly any necessity to refer to the writings of the Chevalier Ramsay, as throwing any light on the early history of Masonry in France.

His theory is that Freemasonry originated among the Crusaders and was introduced into France by the Templars, who brought it with them on their return from Palestine.

This hypothesis is now generally, perhaps I should say universally, admitted to be untenable.

It comprises a history, or the figment of a history, not founded on facts nor supported by any documentary evidence, but one that was simply invented to sustain a preconceived theory.

The theory was first invented and then the history was written.

Hence it has been rejected by all scholars and has fallen into utter extinction together with the system of Strict Observance that was founded in it.

In this work, which seeks to trace Freemasonry back to the Colleges of Artificers of Rome, it can of course have no place.

Rebold is a pleasing exception to the rest of his countrymen who have treated or attempted to treat this subject, though it is to be regretted that he has not thought proper to corroborate his statements by a reference to authorities, or by what would have been most valuable, the citation of any old records or constitutions.

On the whole, however, he is more satisfactory than any other writer of early French Masonic history, and gives a fuller account of the institution as it existed when Gaul emerged from the dominion of Rome.

His history,[121] briefly analyzed, is to the following effect lie says that Masonry was introduced into Gaul by the Roman confraternities of builders, one of which was attached to each legion of the army.

He describes the vicissitudes to which these architects were subjected during the repeated conflicts of the Romans with the hordes of barbarians, whose alternate defeats and successes were followed by the destruction or the renewal of the labors of the Masons.

At length, in the year 426, the victorious arms of Clovis, King of the Franks, put an end to the Roman domination, and the armies of the empire left, forever, the soil of Gaul.

But the confraternities of builders, which had come into the country with the Roman legions, remained there after their departure.

They, however, underwent material alterations in their organization, and developed a new system, which Rebold thinks became the basis of that Freemasonry which existed for a long time afterward in France.

Moller, in his Memorials of German Gothic Architecture,[122] when referring to the fact that the Roman architecture of the 5th and 6th centuries prevailed at a much later period in Italy, Spain, Gaul, and Britain, explains the circumstance as follows: "The conquerors did not exterminate the old inhabitants, but left to them exclusively, at least in the first periods of their invasion, the practice of those arts of peace, upon which the rude warrior looked with contempt.

And even at a later time, the intimate connection with Rome, which the clergy, then the only civilized part of the nation, entertained, and the unceasing and generally continued use of the Latin language in the divine service, gave considerable influence to Roman arts and sciences.

This must have been so much more the case, from the constant obligation of all freemen to devote themselves to war; whereby the practice of the arts was left almost exclusively to the clergy." The corporations of builders which had been attached, some to the legions and some to the governors of the provinces, under whose orders they had constructed many great edifices, then began to admit into their bosom a large number of native Gauls who had been converted to Christianity.

The most important modification, however, to which they were compelled to submit, was this that being originally a general association of artisans, whose central sect and school of instruction was at Rome,

---

[121] "Histoire des Trois Grandes Loges de Franc-macons en France," Paris, 1864.
[122] Translation by W.H. Leeds, London, 1836, p. 17.

they were obliged to abandon this relation on the retreat of the Roman armies from Gaul, and the severance of all political connection between the province and the imperial, government.

The builders, as well as the other craftsmen, then divided themselves into a variety of sodalities, each being occupied with the cultivation of a different art or trade.

It is here that Rebold should have cited some authority for his statement of a fact that is contrary to what has always been supposed to be the true character of the Roman colleges.

The division into different trades, which he supposes to have been a forced necessity in Gaul, was in existence, if history be correct, from the first organization of the colleges by Numa, when they were ten in number, which was subsequently increased to a large extent under the empire These sodalities of different trades, he says, subsequently gave rise to the corporations or guilds of the Middle Ages.

Of these sodalities, that of the builders, or Masons, being the most important, and the one most needed in the countries where they were left after the departure of the Romans, especially in Gaul and Britain, were alone enabled to retain the ancient organization and the ancient priveleges while they had possessed under the domination of the Romans.

But amid the continued invasions of barbarians, and the wars and political disturbances that followed, the confraternities of builders were at last everywhere without occupation. The arts and architecture among then; paralyzed by international contests, found a refuge only in the monasteries, where they were successfully cultivated by the ecclesiastics who had been admitted into the fraternity of Masons.

Among the most celebrated architects of France who were the products of those rnonastic schools of architecture, Rebold mentions St. Eloi, Bishop of Noyon; St. Fereol, of Limoges; Dalmac, of Rodez; and Agniola, of Chalons, all of whom flourished in the 7th century.

But he says that there were among the laity, also, architects not less distinguished, under whose direction numerous edifices were built in Gaul and in Britain at a later period.

The most distinguished of those whom Rebold has described as architects and as the disciples of the monastic schools of architecture was St. Eloi, or Eligius.

But St. Eloi was not an architect, but a goldsmith, having regularly served an apprenticeship to that trade, even after his appointment by Clothaire II. to the position of treasurer, or master of the mint.

Subsequently, when fifty-two years of age, he was elevated to the bishopric of Noyon, for which he was obliged to prepare himself by two years of study and admission to ecclesiastical orders.

As a prelate be patronized, as many others had done, the architects by the erection of churches and monasteries.

But his connection with Operative Masonry is rather through the guild organizations than through any close connection with the craft of building.

He organized the monks of his abbey, according to St. Croix,[123] into a guild or school of smiths, for whom he drew up a code of regulations.

According; to the same authority the statutes for the government of the craftsmen of Paris, prepared in the 14th century by Stephen Boileau, were but a transcript of those of St. Eloi.

Whittington says that St. Eloi belonged, properly, to the class of professional artists who were magnificently patronized and held in high estimation by him.[124] The writer of his life in the Spicilegium describes him as a very skillful goldsmith and most learned in all constructive arts."[125] It is very evident that Rebold has so far given us the early history of architecture in France rather than that of Freemasonry.

In this respect, his work follows, in its spirit, that of Dr. Anderson in the first and especially in the second edition of the Book of Constitutions.

To the student of Masonic history such annals are of value only because of the traditional relations that exist between the Operative and the Speculative systems.

Well-authenticated history leaves us no room to doubt that the Romans introduced architecture into France, or, to speak more correctly, into Gaul at a very early period, and many magnificent ruins are still remaining in the older cities as Arles, Avignon, Nimes, and other ancient places, which are the vestiges of the labors of builders and architects under the Roman domination.

In fact, when the barbarians began their invasions into Gaul, the soil was covered with the monuments of Roman art.

Many of these were destroyed, but there still remained, in the 6th century, a great number of public and private edifices which had been spared.

---

[123] "Les Arts au Moyen Age et la Renaissance."
[124] "Ecclesiastical Antiquities of France," P. 27.
[125] Aurifex partissimus atque in omni arte fabricaudi doctissimus. "Spicilegium," t.v ., in Vita S. Eligii.

In fact, there is at Nimes a temple and an aqueduct still remaining, in a state of excellent preservation.

The former is now used as a museum of antiquities, and the latter, known as the pont du gard, is solid and strong, and is admitted by antiquaries to be the noblest Roman monument in France.

The people, during a long period of subjection to the Roman rule, had been traditionally educated in the architectural taste and spirit of Rome, and hence with the revival of the art of construction in the 6th, 7th and 8th centuries, the Christian churches became but the reflection of the Pagan basilica, and the palaces of kings and the castles of nobles were but copies of the Romano-Gallic villas.

Hence French Masonic writers have, with a great claim to plausibility, assumed that the Masons of France were a continuation in regular and uninterrupted descent of the Roman Colleges of Artificers.

This view has been strengthened by another historical fact, that admits of no doubt, that Charlemagne, whose name and that of his grandfather Charles Alartel are frequently referred to as patrons of Masonry in the old English records, was distinguished for his zeal in the erection of churches and palaces and brought many architects from Byzantium into France, founding there, or rather transplanting there, the Byzantine Order of Architecture which, however, afterward gave place to the Gothic, or that Order of which the mediaeval Freemasons were, it is generally conceded, the inventors.

Rebold,[126] who, as an historian, occupies a middle term between the incredulous iconoclasm of the modern school and the facile credulity of the early Masonic annalists, says that after the final evacuation of Gaul by the Romans, about the end of the 5th century, though many of the Colleges of Artificers which had been established under the Roman domination remained in Gaul, yet their organization underwent important modifications.

In the first place the general association of the dim erent artisans who were necessary to the pursuit of architecture, religious, naval, and hydraulic, or the building of temples, of ships, and of bridges and aqueducts, being no longer able to maintain itself in a country which had been abandoned by the Romans, and having lost its center of action and its principal school at Rome, no longer practiced architecture as a profession in common and under one head, but was divided into various associations, each of which occupied itself thereafter with only the study and practice of a single art or trade.

---

[126] "Histoire des Trois Grandes Loges," p. 24.

It is in this way that he accounts for the rise of the corporations which flourished subsequently in the Middle Ages, and which were in the transition period between the ancient colleges and the modern lodges.

Of these different sodalities, which sprang out of the general association of artisans existing under the Roman Empire, the corporation of builders or masons, as being the most important fraction, preserved, says Rebold, their ancient organization and their ancient privileges, because the countries in which they resided after the departure of the Romans, being greatly in need of their services as builders, freely accorded to them the privileges which they had possessed under the Romans.

The Teutonic invaders of Gaul who drove out the Romans, though barbarians, were wise enough not to destroy the old monuments of Roman art and civilization, but to make use of and profit by them.

But in the same century the cathedral erected by Naumatius, Bishop of Auvergne, surpassed that of Perpeticus.

Gregory of Tours, who was a native of Auvergne, describes the edifice with much eloquence of phrase in his Historia Francorum, and states the fact, interesting as showing the collection of high ecclesiastics with operative Masonry, that he built it according to his own designs-ecclesiam suo studio fabricavat.

The invasion of the Franks into Gaul in the 6th century caused at first, amid the tumult of war, while the arts of peace were silent, the destruction of religious edifices.

But the conversion and baptism of Clovis placed Christianity on a firm foundation and caused the preservation of the remaining monuments of the ancient civilization.

The Franks, who were a bold, enterprising and warlike offshoot from the great Teutonic race, and who were the real founders of the kindom which afterward became modern France, were notwithstanding their intestine broils and their conflicts with neighboring people, inclined to cultivate the arts of peace.

They occupied, says Mr. Church, a land of great natural wealth and great geographical advantages, which had been prepared for them by Latin culture; they inherited great cities which they had not built, and fields and vineyards which they had not planted; and they had the wisdom not to destroy but to use their conquest.[127] The Franks were indeed friendly to Roman culture; preserved many of the Roman laws

---

[127] "The Beginning of the Middle Ages," by R. W. Church, Dean of St. Paul's, p. 85.

and customs, and accepted for their vernacular a modified form of the Latin language.

Hence architecture, which had languished during the stormy period when the Romans were unsuccessfully striving to defend their acquired provinces and the very existence of the empire itself from the barbarous hordes of northern invaders, began, in the 5th and 6th centuries, to revive, The confraternities of builders and the art of architecture to some extent, says Rebold,[128] resumed activity.

The fact, already adverted to elsewhere, that the art of building, especially of religious edifices, had passed into the hands of the monks, is found to prevail also in the history of the art in France at this early period.

The remarks of Mr. Whittington on this subject in his Historical Survey are well worthy of quotation.

"The ancient writers often mention instances of an abbot giving a plan which his convent assisted in carrying into execution.

The edifices of religion owed their first existence to the zeal of the clergy.

The more enlightened prelates invented or procured the plans and carried them into execution.

But although from record as well as from probability we may conclude that the arts in this age were principally cultivated by the clergy, it is no less certain that there were persons who practiced them as a profession.

What that powerful Order found necessary to promote by their own exertions, they did not fail to patronize in others, and to the common masons and carpenters who might be found in the different cities of France persons of superior skill and intelligence were added who were invited from distant quarters by the enterprising liberality of the bishops. The superstition of the times and the authority of the Church secured them employment and protection; they gradually increased in numbers and improved in science, till at length they produced the most able artificers from among themselves. France, in fact, at this time was not without professional artists, but they seem to have been neither numerous nor eminent, and the clergy were frequently left to their own exertions and resources.

Gregory of Tours (who flourished in the 6th century) speaks of several of his predecessors as if they had superintended the building of their churches, particularly Ommatius, who rebuilt the Church of Sts.

---

[128] "Histoire des Trois Grandes Loges," p. 25.

Gervase and Protasius and began that of St. Mary; and he expressly affirms that Leo Bishop of Tours was an artist of great skill, particularly in works of carpentry, and that he built towers which be covered with gilt bronze, some of which had lasted till his time.

One general spirit indeed seems to have prevailed among the French Bishops of the 6th century to establish new churches and to improve the towns of their dioceses."[129] The progress of architecture in the 7th century under St. Eloi, or Eligius, and during the reign of Clothaire II., has already been referred to.

In the 7th and 8th centuries the mode of building and the artistic taste of the builders remained about the same as in the 6th, but the features were somewhat enlarged and enriched, and towers and belfries became common.

In the 9th century, architecture and operative Masonry received a new impetus under the fostering care of Charlemagne.

The buildings erected in his reign exceeded in taste and extent the works of preceding monarchs.

There was an increased intercourse with the East and with Byzantine artists.

Italian architects were brought from Lombardy, and the monuments of ancient Rome were imitated.[130] The anonymous Monk of the Monastery of St. Gall, who wrote the Gestes de Charlemagne, in describing the cathedral of Aix-la Chapelle, which was erected by Charlemagne, says that it surpassed in splendor the works of the ancient Romans, and that for its construction he called together masters and workmen from all parts of the continent.[131] Rebold thinks that the fact that Charlemagne had sought for builders in other counties an evidence of their diminution in France. This is scarcely a legitimate conclusion.

The monarch might very properly avail himself of the skill and experience of foreign artists, without necessarily indicating by their importation that there were none in his own country.

The wrecks of the ancient Roman colleges were still remaining in Lombardy, and it has already been shown that there was a flourishing school of architecture at Como.

---

[129] "Historical Survey of the Ecclesiastical Antiquities of France," P. 22.
[130] Ibid., p. 30.
[131] "Basilica, antiquis Romanorum operibus praestantiore, brevi ab eo fabricate, ex omnibus cismarinis regionibus, magistris et opificibus advocatis." Legend, lib, i., cap. xxxii

Indeed it cannot be doubted that the intercourse established by Charlemagne, between France and other countries of Europe, was very favorable to the progress and improvement of the arts.

The number of artists was greatly increased, and they were supplied with better models for imitation.

"Charlemagne," says Sismondi, "was one of the greatest characters of the Middle Ages.

Contrasted with his contemporaries, he possessed all the advantages of a man who was a stranger to his age. As we have seen before his time, extraordinary men who have subjugated a civilized people by the energy of a character hall savage, so in him we see a man who, being in advance of the civilization of his times, has subdued barbarians by the force of his intellect and by his knowledge.

He combined the qualities of a legislator with those of a warrior, and united the genius which creates with the vigilant prudence which preserves and maintains an empire. lie drew together in one chain barbarians and Romans, the con querors and the conquered, and united them in a new empire.

He laid the foundations of a new order for Europe, an order which essentially reposed on the virtues of a hero, and on the respect and admiration which he inspired."[132] Such has been at all times the concurrent opinion of all historians with the exception of Voltaire, and perhaps a few others.

And even they, while charging him with unproved faults and even crimes, admit the magnificence of his enterprises and the splendor of his reign.

It is therefore singular that in the traditions of the early Masons his name has not been permitted to occupy a place.

In the Legend of the Craft, found in the Old Records of the English Masons, the introduction of Masonry into France is attributed to a certain Greek: artist who had been at the building of the Temple of Solomon, and came into France in the time of Charles Martel, who patronized the Craft made Masons, and gave them charges.[133] The gross

---

[132] Sismondi, "Histoire des Republique Italiennes," tome i., chap. i., p. 19.

[133] It may be well to note here an error as to the signification of the name of this celebrated Mayor of the Palace, who, without assuming the title, exercised all the functions of a king. It has been the universal custom to derive the word Martel from the French Marteau, which signifies a hammer, and it has been supposed that he obtained the cognomen from the fact that he crushed the barbarians with whom he fought, as with a hammer as potent as that of Thor. And so it has been very usual with English writers to Anglicize his name as Charles the

anachronism of making a workman at Solomon's temple a visitor at the court of Charles Martel at once, exposes the great ignorance and the liability to error of the original composer of the "legend.

It is not, therefore, at all improbable that he confounded Charles Martel with his grandson Charlemagne.

It is very evident that the spirit of the Legend does not apply to Martel, who, during his administration under two feeble kings, was fully occupied in wars with rebellious subjects, with the Saxons on the north and the Saracens from Spain in the south, and who had neither time nor inclination to devote to the arts of peace.

The monks, who were then the principal builders, were not his favorites, and St. Boniface has not hesitated to call him "the destroyer of monasteries." It is hardly to be doubted that he destroyed more than he built.

Charlemagne, on the contrary, was, as we have seen, the patron of the arts of civilization, and might, with but a little stretch of imagination, be called the founder of ope rative Masonry in France.

His intercourse with Byzantium and the East gives color also to the legend that he was visited by a Greek architect, which is simply a symbolic expression of the idea that Byzantine architecture and Greek art and culture were beginning to be introduced into France and the West during the period in which Charlemagne reigned.

We may, therefore, I think very safely correct the English Legend of the Craft by substituting the name of Charlemagne for that of Charles Martel.

Louis the Feeble, the son and successor of Charlemagne, though, as the sobriquet which was bestowed upon him imports, a prince of no force of character, yet patronized architecture, and in his reign many religious structures were built, under the superintendence of his architect.

"Hammer." But M. de Feller (Biographie Universelle), a very competent authority on French etymology, has shown that Martel is only a synonym of Martin; that Martin was a familiar name in the family of Pepin, of which Charles Martel was a member, and that it was adopted in the spirit of devotion to St. Martin, who was then the favorite saint of the Franks. This note is not exactly germane to the history we are pursuing, but the subject is interesting enough to claim a passing notice. It must, however, in fairness be admitted that M. Michelet (Histoire de France, lib. ii., p. 112), an authority as good, at least, as M. de Feller, recognizes the current derivation from Marteau, which he thinks referred to the hammer of the Scandinavian god Thor, and he thence concludes that Charles was not a Christian.

The name of this artist was Rumalde.

We know scarcely more of him than the fact that he was the architect of Louis.

Whittington thinks it probable that he was not an ecclesiastic, since it is clear that he practiced his art as a profession, and professional architects were at that time becoming common.

The universal belief that prevailed in the 10th century, in the approaching destruction of the world and the advent of the millennium, had naturally the effect of paralyzing all industrial arts, and architecture made little or no progress.

But in the 11th century there was a revival, and the records of that period contain the names of many distinguished architects, who were not monks but professional architects, for Masonry had for some time been passing away out of the hands of the ecclesiastics in those of the laity and the guilds.

The guilds or trade corporations, in France began about this time to take an active existence and to exert a powerful interest on the progress of the arts. The consideration of their history is well worthy of a distinct chapter.

But our attention must now be turned to the early history of Masonry in other countries.

CHAPTER VI

EARLY MASONRY IN BRITAIN

From the time of the conquest of Britain by Claudius to the final evacuation of the island by the Romans in the beginning of the 5th century, a period of about three hundred and fifty years had elapsed.

During this long occupation the Romans had held, if not undisputed, at least dominant sway over the greater part of the island.

Roman legions had been permanently stationed in different towns; Roman colonies had been established; Roman citizens had immigrated and settled in greater numbers; Roman arts and civilization had been introduced; and, as we have already shown in a preceding chapter, the native inhabitants had become almost Romanized in their manners and customs.

It is not to be supposed that the domination for so long a continuity of years of a powerful empire, distinguished for its cultivation of the arts, should not have been productive of the effects that must always result from the protracted mixture of a refined with an uncivilized people.

Among the arts introduced by the Romans, there is none that could have so much attracted the attention of the natives as that of architecture.

Of all the methods of human industry that are intended to supply the wants or promote the comforts of life, the art of building is placed in the most prominent position.

All the arts says Cicero, which relate to humanity have a certain bond of union and a kind of kinship to each other.

But it must be acknowledged that the art which proposes to secure to man a protection from the elements and a shelter from the inclemencies of the seasons must hold the highest place in the family scale.

It is the first art that man cultivates in his progress from utter barbarism to civilization.

It is the most salient mark of that progress.

No sooner did the primitive Troglodytes emerge from their cave dwellings than they began to erect, however rudely, huts for their habitation.

And so when a nation or a tribe begins to make an advancement in civilization, its first step is to improve its mode of dwelling.

When conquest brings a superior race to ail ignorant and uncultured people, the industrial arts of the former are speedily diffused among the latter, and architecture, as the most striking and the most useful, more speedily attracts the attention and is more readily imitated than any other.

When the Romans first invaded Britain they found the country inhabited by various tribes deriving their origin from different nomadic stocks, and therefore somewhat heterogeneous in their condition and their habits.

The Belgians, for instance, who had passed over from Gaul and occupied, by the right of conquest, the coast bordering on the British Channel, were an agricultural people, and are described by Camar as being more advanced in the arts of civilized life than the tribes in the interior who were pastoral, who lived on milk and flesh and were clothed in skins.

Mela Pomponius, the Roman geographer, who wrote about the same time, describes the Britons as being in general uncivilized and much behind the continental nations in their social culture.

Fields and cattle constituted their only wealth.

Mr. Wright, in an Essay of the Ethnology of South Britain at the Extinction of the.Roman Government, says that "we may form a notion best and most correctly of the mode of life and of the degree of civilization of the ancient Britons, by comparing them with what we know of those of the wild Irish and of the Celtic highlanders of Scotland in the Middle Ages.

Living in sects or clans, each collected round a petty chieftain, who had his residence or place of refuge in the least accessible part of his little territory, they had no towns, properly so called, and no tie of union except the temporary one of war or a nominal dependence on some powerful chieftain who had induced by some means, a certain number of the smaller clans to acknowledge his sovereignty."[134] Their houses, says Turner, were chiefly formed of reeds or wood, and were usually seated in the midst of woods, a space being cleared on which they built their huts and folded their cattle.[135] The improved condition of Britain, in consequence of their intercourse with their more civilized conquerors, is thus described by Mr. Wright:[136] "Under the Romans, on the contrary, Britain consisted politically of a number of cities or towns, each possessing its own independent municipal government, republican in form and principle within themselves, but united under the empire through the fiscal government of the province to which they were tributary.

Each of these cities inhabited by foreigners to the island, was expected to defend itself if attacked, while three legions and numerous bodies of auxiliaries protected the province from hostilities from without and held it internally in obedience to the imperial government.

The country was unimportant and the towns were everything." The numerous inscriptions found in England in recent times prove another fact, namely, that the legionary troops which were sent from Rome to Britain did not pay merely ephemeral or transitory visits, from which no important influence could have been derived, but that they remained in the same locality during the whole occupation of the country by the Romans, and actually constituted military colonies, making homes in the towns in which they lived, and insensibly imparting the use of the Latin language and the adoption of Roman manners to the people.

So much, in fact, did they become identified with the native inhabitants, that they often made common cause with them in tumults or insurrections against the imperial government.

The result of this constant intercommunication must have been just that which might anywhere, under such circumstances, have been expected.

The architects who accompanied the legions in their visits to Britain and who remained with them during its occupation did not confine their labors to the construction of military works, such as the erection of defensive walls and fortresses.

They engaged during the period tranquillity which had been secured by the presence of strong bodies of troops in the peaceful avocations of their art.

---

[134] Thomas Wright, "Essays on Archaeological Subjects," vol. i., p. 68.
[135] "History of the Anglo-Saxons," vol. i., p. 64.
[136] "Essays on Archaeological Subjects," vol. i., p. 69.

They organized their Colleges of Artificers, which, considering the works in which they were engaged, might correctly be designated as Colleges of Masons; they began the building of temples and other public edifices; they took to their assistance the more intelligent natives, and introduced their Roman architecture by methods which imitated those of the Colleges at home. The rude huts of the native Britons were replaced by more comfortable houses, and the art of building, under the guidance of the Roman Masons, assumed a new form and was prosecuted by new methods, which thus introduced the character and customs of the Roman Colleges into the island, and thus by the example of associated workmen continued the chain of connection which was to be more fully extended in Anglo-Saxon times by the establishment of building guilds.

Tacitus has shown us, in his Life of Agricola, how and at what an early period this system of Romanizing Britain began.

In the last quarter of the 1st Christian century, Agricola arrived in Britain, having been appointed governor of the province.

The island, which had hardly yet recovered from the recent insurrection of Queen Boadicea, was still in an insurgent condition.

The first efforts of Agricola were of course directed to the restoration of peace and order, and to the correction of civil and political abuses.

His next business was to introduce a system of regulations whose tendency should be to civilize the natives.

He encouraged them, therefore, says Tacitus,[137] by his exhortations and aided them by public assistance to build temples, courts of justice, and commodious dwellings.

He praised those who were cheerful in their obedience; he reproached those who were slow and uncomplying, and thus excited a spirit of emulation.

He established a plan of education and caused the sons of the chiefs to be instructed in learning and to cultivate the Latin language.

The Roman dress was adopted by many, and the Britons, allured by the luxurious example of their conquerors, began to erect baths and porticoes and to indulge in sumptuous banquets.

To do all this was not within the narrow scope of native skill.

In the erection of these improved edifices the Britons, being only partly reclaimed from their pristine barbarity, must have invoked and received the advice and assistance of the Roman architects.

---

[137] "Vita Agricolze," cap. xxi.

The cooperative and guild-like methods of building practiced by these, as well as their skill in architecture, was thus imparted to the Britons.

What had been wisely begun by Agricola was as wisely imitated by his successors in the provincial government, and the Roman Collegiate system was completely established in the island long before the extinction of the Roman domination and the fall of the Roman empire.

That the builders or Masons introduced into Rome, or educated there by their Roman Masters, had increased to a very great number is evident from a remark of the panegyrist Eumenius in his Panegyric of the Emperor Maximian.

He describes the ancient Gallic city of Bibracte, afterward Augustodunum, but now the modern Autun, which abounds in the remains of Roman architecture, many of them in a good state of preservation.

The re-edification of private houses and the construction of temples and other buildings with which Maximian had embellished the city, he attributes to the concourse of architects whom the emperor had brought from Britain, which province, he says, abounded with them.

The number of these Roman architects in Britain was so great and their skill so preeminent, that, as we shoal hereafter see they were exported into many of the continental cities to construct buildings in the Roman method.

The remains of Roman buildings found at different times in England and a multitude of ancient inscriptions testify to the fact that the conquerors had brought their architectural art with them into Britain.

But the mere existence of pieces of architecture would not alone serve to establish the connection of these Roman architects and their British disciples with the mediaeval guilds.

In this way we might, as Anderson has done, write a history of architecture, but would hardly be authorized to call it a history of Freemasonry.

It is necessary to show that the Roman architects not only brought with them their skill in the art of building but also introduced the associated methods of organization which had been practiced by the ancient Roman Colleges.

Of this we have ample evidence.

The Reverend James Dallaway, in his Collections for an Historical Account of Masters and Free Masons, appended to his

Discourses upon Architecture in England, says that the first notice that occurs of an associated body of Roman artificers who had established themselves in Britain is a votive inscription in which the College of Masons dedicate a temple to Neptune and Minerva, and to the safety of the family of Claudius Caesar.

It was discovered at Chichester in the year 1725. It is a slab of gray Sussex marble and was found by the workmen who were digging a cellar and who ignorantly or carelessly fractured it.

Having been pieced together the slab is now preserved at Goodwood, the seat of the Duke of Richmond, near Chichester.

In his History of West Sussex, Mr. Dallaway gives a facsimile of the slab and the inscription, which is in the following words: EPTVMO ET MINERVAE TEMPLVM B. SALVTE. DO. DIVINAE AVCTORITA. CLAVD. GIDVBNI. R. IC. . . . . . CAI. BRIT. . . . . GIVM. FABROR. E. QVI. IN. FO. C.D.S.D. DONANTE. AREAM.. .. ENTE. PVDENTINI. FIL.

The original is here given, to furnish to the unlearned reader an idea of the character of the inscriptions, which are the palpable monuments of the labors of these Colleges of Artificers, which have been found in all countries into which the Romans extended their power.

The literal, but in some places conjectural, translation of this inscription is as follows: "The College of Artificers and they who there fireside over the sacred rites by authority of King Cogidubnus, the Legate of Tiberius Claudius Augustus in Britain, dedicated this Temple to Neptune and Minerva, for the welfare of the imperial family. Pudens, the son of Pudentinus, having given the site." In an article on the Origin and Progress of Gothic Architecture, by Governor Pownall, inserted in the 9th volume of the Archaeologia of the London Society of Antiquaries, this subject of the influence of the Roman artists on the native Britons is exhibited in an interesting point of view.

When the Romans conquered and held possession of our isle, says Governor Pownall, they erected every sort of building and edifice of stone or of a mixture of stone and brick, and universally built with the circular arch.

The British learned their arts from these Masters.

But the Continent being more subject to the ravages of invading barbarians than the isolated province of Britain, many of the Gaulish cities and the fortresses on the Rhine were destroyed.

And when Constantius Chlorus resolved, at the close of the 3rd century, to rebuild them, he sent to Britain for architects to execute the work of re-edification.

By this withdrawal of the builders from the island of Britain and by transferring them to the Continent, Britain itself soon lost the knowledge which it had formerly acquired of the Roman architecture.

But after the establishment of the Christian religion in the empire, missionaries being sent to the provinces to convert the inhabitants, they brought with them from Rome not only the new religion but a revived knowledge of the arts, and especially of architecture, which was necessary for the building of churches.

As to the influence produced upon the Britons by their conversion to Christianity, Camden tells us that no sooner was the name of Christ preached in the English nation, than with a most fervent zeal they consecrated themselves to it and laid out their utmost endeavors to promote it by discharging all the duties of Christian piety, by erecting churches and endowing them; so that no part of the Christian world could show either more or richer monasteries.[138] Thus the skill, which for a time had been suspended if not lost, was again revived by the architects and builders who were again brought from Rome to Britain by the Christian missionaries, who, says Pownall, were the restorers of the Roman architecture in stone.

The huge buildings of stone erected by the monks in England, ought perhaps to be attributed to a later period when the Saxons had gained possesion of the island But as Christianity had been introduced into England before that period and under the Roman domination, we may accede to the hypothesis that some of that kind of work was done at that early period.

We may, therefore, grant a large amount of plausibility to that part of the Legend of the Craft which reports the tradition that under the usurped reign of Carausius, St. Alban had organized the fraternity of Masons and bestowed upon them his patronage.

Whether the Legend is correct or not in attributing this important work to the protomartyr, it may at least be accepted as traditionally preserving the historical fact that Freemasonry was reorganized after the Roman method by the Christian missionaries.

There is abundant evidence in the old chronicles that the method of building in stone and with circular arches was always designated as opus Romanum or the Roman work, and an edifice so

---

[138] Camden, "Britannia," p. cxxxii.

constructed was said to be built more Romanum, or according to the Roman method.

The error of the legendists, however, is that they attributed personally to Carausius, the usurper of the imperial power, the patronage of Masonry and the appointment of St. Alban as his chief architect or Master Mason; an error in which they have been followed by Anderson and all other Masonic writers.

Of this statement there is no competent historical evidence.

Bede, Matthew of Westminster, and all the other old chroniclers, describe Carausius as a man of very mean extraction, treacherous to the government which employed him, unfaithful to the people whom he was sent to protect, sacrificing their interests to his own greed for spoil, and distinguished only for his ability as a soldier.

Of the piety and Christian constancy of Alban the same writers are lavish in their praises, but they make no reference to his skill as an architect or to his labors under Carausius as a builder.

Even of his martyrdom there are said to be great chronological difficulties.

Matthew of Westminster places its date eleven years after the death of Carausius.

This would not militate against his previous employment by Carausius as the steward of his household, to use the words of Anderson, and the Master of his works, if there were any historical evidence of the fact.

If we appeal to the testimony of Camden, whose laborious researches have left no authority uncollected and no statement unexamined which refer to the early history of Britain under the Romans, we shall find no support for the traditions of the legendists or for their expansion by Anderson and the writers who have servilely followed him.

Of Carausius we only learn from Camden that after his reconciliation with Maximian, he governed Britain in perfect peace, and that he repaired the wall at the mouth of the Clud and fortified it with seven castles.[139] The only reference made by Camden to St. Alban is in a passage where he says that toward the end of Diocletian s and Maximian s reign a long and bloody persecution broke out in the Western Church and many Christians suffered martyrdom, among the chief of whom he names Albanus Verolamiensis or St.t Alban. But he makes no allusion to

---

[139] Camden, "Britarinia," p. lxxiv.

him as an architect, nor does he mention the name of the apocryphal Amphibalus.

Further on he attributes to the town of Verulam the honor of having given birth to St. Alban, whom he calls a man justly eminent for his piety and steadiness in the Christian faith; who with an invincible constancy of mind suffered martyrdom the first man in Britain.[140] He relates the legends which were extant in connection with his passion, but while he dwells on his piety and his constancy to the faith which gave him all his fame, he says nothing of his labors as an architect nor does he in any way connect him with Carausius.

We must, therefore, reject the whole story of Carausius and St. Alban as apocryphal; so far as it implies that the Emperor was a great patron of Masonry and the Saint his Master Workman, we find no historical foundation for it; but we may accept it as a mythical statement, the true interpretation of which is that there was a revival of Masonry in England toward the time of the extinction of the Roman doaana6on, through the influence of the Christian missionaries, a fact for the truth of which we have, as has already been seen, sufficient authority.

Anderson says that the true old Masonry departed from Britain with the Roman legions; for though many Roman families had settled in the south and were blended with the Britons, who had been well educated in the science and the art, yet the subsequent wars, confusions, and revolutions in this island, ruined ancient learning, till all the fine artists were dead without exception.[141] Mr. Fergusson, a more learned and more accurate writer than Anderson, has arrived at almost the same conclusion.

He says: When Rome withdrew her protecting care, France, Spain, and Britain relapsed into, and for centuries remained sunk in, a state of anarchy and barbarism as bat if not wove than that in which Rome had found them three or four centuries before.

It was in vain to expect that the hapless natives could maintain either the arts or the institutions with which Rome had endowed them.[142] But Fergusson subsequently makes a very important admission which greatly modifies the opinion he had just expressed when, in continuing the paragraph, he says: But it is natural to suppose that they would remember the evidences of her greatness and her power, and would hardly go back for their sepulchers to the unchambered mole-hill barrows of their fore fathers, but attempt something in stone, though

---

[140] Camden, "Britannia," p. 296.
[141] "Constitutions," second edition, p. 59.
[142] Fergusson, "Rude Stone Monuments," p. 394.

only in such rude fashion as the state of the arts among them enabled them to execute. This is all that the theory advanced in this work contends for.

The assertion of Anderson is altogether too sweeping and general.

That of Fergusson admits that the influences of Roman domination had not been entirely obliterated by the departure of the legions.

Rome, which had administered the government for centuries, could hardly fail, to use his own language, to leave some impress of her magnificence in lands which she had so long occupied.

The concurrent testimony of all historians will not permit us to deny or to doubt that after the extinction of the Roman dominion in Britain, there was a decadence of architecture as well as of the other arts.

But this did not amount to a total destruction, but only to a suspension.

Nations who have emerged from barbarism to civilization, and who for centuries have enjoyed the refinements of culture, do not at once relapse into their primitive savage state.

There was certainly not sufficient time for the exhibition of this ethnological curiosity in the period embraced between the departure of the Romans and the firm establishment of the Anglo-Saxons.

Nor was there that isolation which was necessary to hasten this fall from national light to national darkness.

The southern parts of Britain, at least, were in too close a propinquity to more civilized and more Romanized Gaul to lose at once all traces of Roman refinement.

And above all, the presence and the influence of the Christian missionaries who, coming from Rome, were uninterruptedly engaged in the task of converting the natives to the new faith, must have been a powerful stay to any downward progress to utter barbarism.

The links of the chain that united the builders of Britain with those of Rome had only rusted; they were not rudely snapped asunder.

The influence of the methods of building pursued by the Roman Colleges of Artificers, who had done so much work and left so many memorials in Britain, were still to be felt and to be renewed when these links were strengthened and brightened by the Anglo-Saxons.

But this is anew and an important subject that demands consideration in another chapter for it brings us to an interesting phase in the history of Freemasonry.

CHAPTER VII

MASONRY AMONG THE ANGLO-SAXONS

After the departure of the Roman legions and the withdrawal of the Roman protection, Britain, left to its own resources, was soon harassed by the invasions of Scots and Picts, by predatory excursions of barbarians from the opposite shores of the North Sea, and by civil distractions which were the natural result of the division of power among many rival petty principalities.

Among the Britons there was one leader, Gwotheyrn, or, as he is more generally called, Votghern, who seems to have assumed, if he did not legally possess it, a predominating position over the other British princes.

Feeling, after various unsuccessful attempts, that he could not, by his unaided forces, repulse the invaders, he sought the assistance of the Saxons.

The Saxons were a tribe of warlike sea-kings who occupied the western shore of what has since been known as the Duchy of Holstein, with the neighboring islands on the coast.

Brought across the sea by the invitation of the Britons, they soon expelled the Picts and Scots.

But, attracted by the delights of the climate and the fertility of the soil, so superior to the morasses of their own restricted and half-submerged territory, they remained to contest the possession of the island with its native inhabitants.

Hence there followed a series of conflicts which led at last to the expulsion of the native Britons, who were forced to retire to the southwestern parts of the island, and the establishment of tlie Saxon domination in England.

During the period of intestine wars which led to this change, not only of a government, but of a whole people, it is not to be supposed that much attention could have been paid to the cultivation of architecture or Masonry.

Amid the clash of arms the laws are silent, and learning and the arts lie prostrate.

Yet we are not to believe that all the influences of the preceding four or five centuries were wholly paralyzed.

Gildas, it is true, complains in querulous language and an involved style,[143] in the Epistle which is annexed to his History, of the wickedness both of the clergy and the laity, but the greatest licentiousness is not altogether incompatible with the preservation of some remains of the architectural skill and taste which had been originally imparted by the Roman artificers.

The Saxons themselves were not a thoroughly barbarous people.

The attempts to subdue the tribes of Germany as they had those of Spain, of Gaul, and of Britain were not very successful.

The ferocious bravery of the Germans under the leadership of the great Hermann, into Herminius by Tacitus, was able to stem the progress of the Roman legions in the interior of the country and to confine them eventually to the possession of a few fortresses on the Rhine.

The German tribes, among whom we are, of course, to count the Saxons, were thus enabled to retain their own manners, customs, and language, while their communication with the legions, both in war and in peace, must have imbued them with some portion of Roman civilization.

Many new ideas, feelings, reasoning and habits, says Mr. Turner, must have resulted from this mixture, and the peculiar minds and views of the Germans must have been both excited and enlarged.

The result of this union of German and Roman improvement was the gradual formation of that new species of the human character and society which has descended, with increasing melioration, to all the modern states of Europe.[144] Dr. Anderson, when describing the Saxon

---

[143] Of all the post-classical writers in Latin none is so difficult to comprehend or to mandate as Gildas. Beddes, the fact that there are in existence only two codices of the original manuscript, and that subsequent editions have indulged in many, various, and sometimes contradictory readings, add to the difficulty of a correct interpretation of his writings.

[144] "History of the Anglo-Saxons," i., p. 96.

invasion of Britain, says that the Anglo-Saxons came over all rough, ignorant heathens, despising everything but war; nay, in hatred to the Britons and Romans, they demolished all accurate structures and all the remains of ancient learning, affecting only their own barbarous manner of life, till they became Christians.[145]

Entick and Northouck, in their subsequent editions of the Book of Constitutions, have repeated this slander, which, even if it were a truth, could not have forever obliterated the connection which we are seeking to trace between the Masonry of the Roman Colleges and that of mediaeval England; because, although it might have been suspended by Saxon barbabsn, it is easy to prove that it could have been renewed by subsequent intercourse with the architects of France.

But against this careless misrepresentation of Anderson and his subsequent editors, let us trace the more accurate and better digested views of the historian of the Anglo-Saxons.

Mr. Turner, when writing of the arrival of Hengist with his Saxon followers in England, says: The Anglo-Saxon invasion of Britain must therefore not be contemplated as a barbarization of the country.

Our Saxon ancestors brought with. them a superior domestic and moral character, and the rudiments of new political, juridical, and intellectual blessings.

An interval of Aaughor and desolation unavoidably occurred before they established themselves and their new systems in the island.

But when they had completed their conquest, they laid the foundations of that national constitution, of that internal polity, of those peculiar customs, of that female modesty, and of that vigor and direction of mind, to which Great Britain owes the social progress which it has so eniinently acquired.[146] The fact is that, though the Saxons introduced a style of their own, to which writers on architecture have given their name, they borrowed in their practice of the art the suggestions left by the Romans in their buildings, and used the materials of which they were composed.

Thus a writer on this subject says that the Saxons appear to bave formed for themselves a tolerably regular and rude style, something midway between the indigenous and the Roman in its details, and he attributes this to the buildings left by the Romans in the country, which, though rare, must have been sufficiently abundant long after their departure from the island.

---

[145] "Constitutions," 2d edition, p. 60.
[146] "History of the Anglo-Saxons," i., p. 179.

Abundant evidence will be shown in the course of the present chapter that there was not a total disruption of Saxon architecture and Masonic methods of associated labor from that which was first introduced into Britain by the architects of the Roman Colleges.[147]

There were, of course, some modifications to be attributed partly to a want of experienced skill, partly to the suggestions of new ideas, and partly to the influence of novel religious relations.

The temple, for instance, of the Romans had to be converted into the church of the Christians, but the Roman basilica was the model of the Saxon church, and the Roman architect was closely imitated, as well as could be, by his Saxon successor.

The spirit and the influence and the custom of the Roman College was not lost or abandoned.

Scarcely more than a century elapsed between the arrival of the Saxons and the entire subjugation of the country, and that space of time is to be divided among the briefer periods required for the continued successes of different chieftains.

Thus it took Hengist only eight years after his first coming to firmly establish himself in the kingdom of Kent.

Only forty years after the establishment of the Saxon octarchy, Pope Gregory sent St. Augustine from Rome with missionaries to convert the Saxons to the faith of Christianity.

During all this interval many Roman buildings had existed in England, which, from their size and magnificence of construction, must have become models familiar to the Saxons.

The temples of the Saxon idols had been constructed of wood, and as Gregory permitted them to be converted into Christian places of worship, the Saxon churches at first were almost all of that material.

There was a deficiency of better materials. But we find an effort to use them whenever they could be obtained, so that a kind of construction called stone carpentry prevailed, in which we find a wood design contending with stone materials.[148] But in not much later times, and long before the Norman Conquest or the introduction of Gothic architecture, the Saxons built their churches, monasteries, and other public edifices entirely of stone.

Although it may be admitted that the pagan Saxons on their first arrival did indeed destroy many of the churches which had been erected by the British Christians and expelled the priests, yet it must be remembered that by the subsequent advent of Augustine from Rome a

---

[147] Paley, "Manual of Gothic Architecture," p, 14,
[148] Paley, "Manual of Gothic Architecture," p. 12.

new life was restored to architecture and the arts, and that as Mr. Paley says, the frequent missions and pilgrimages to Rome, together with the importation of Italian churchmen, which took place as early as the end of the 7th century, must have exercised great influence upon ecclesiastical architecture in England."[149] It will be seen hereafter that the Saxons repeatedly resorted to the aid of foreign workmen from Rome or from Gaul in the construction of their churches, so that the influences of the Roman system which was derived in former times from the Roman Colleges continued at frequent intervals to be renewed, and the link of connection was thus kept unbroken.

The principal difference between the works of the Roman and the Saxon architects has been supposed to be that the former built in shine and the latter in wood.

And if this were true, it is evident that all inquiry into the nature of Saxon architecture must be at an end; for as the wooden edifices must have long since perished, all the remens of stone structures which have been excavated in England will have to be attributed to the age of the Roman domination before the invasion of the Saxons, or to that which succeeded the conquest by the Normans.

The perishable fabrics of timber erected by the Saxons would have left no traces behind.

The erroneous opinion that the Saxons built all their churches of timber was first advanced by Stow, in his Survey of London, and afterward by Mr. Somner in his Antiquities of Canterbury, who says that before the Norman advent most of our monasteries and church buildings were of wood, and he asserts that upon the Norman Conquest these fabrics of timber grew out of use and gave place to stone buildings raised upon arches.

But the Rev. J. Bentham, in his History of the Cathedral Church of Ely, has refuted the correctness of this view with unanswerable arguments.

He has shown that although there were some instances of wooden edifices, yet that the Saxon churches were generally built of stone, with pillars, arches, and sometimes vaultings of the same material.

And he adds the following remarks, which are important in the present connection as showing that the Roman influence continued to be felt in the Saxon times, and thus that the chain which we are tracing remained unbroken.

---

[149] Paley, "Manual of Gothic Architecture," p. 13.

"There is great probability that at the time the Saxons were converted the art of constructing arches and vaultings and supporting stone edifices by columns was well known among them; they had many instances of such kind of buildings before them in the churches and other public edifices erected in the times of the Romans.

For notwithstanding the havoc that had been made of the Christian churches by the Picts and Scots, and by the Saxons themselves, some of them were then in being.

Bede mentions two in the city of Canterbury. Besides these two ancient Roman churches it is likely there were others of the same age in different parts of the kingdom, which were then repaired and restored to their former use."[150] Of the two Roman churches for whose existence Bentham refers to the authority of Bede, that venerable historian says, There was on the east side of the city a church dedicated to the honor of St. Martin, built while the Romans were still in the island, wherein the queen, who, as has been said before, was a Christian, used to pray,[151] and of the other that Augustine recovered in the royal city a church which he was informed had been built by the ancient Roman Christians, and consecrated it to our Saviour.[152] In an article on Anglo-Saxon architecture, published in the Archaeological Journal for March, 1844, Mr. Thomas Wright (no mean authority on antiquarian science) has, like Mr. Bentham, successfully combated the doctrine that all the Saxon churches were wooden.

I think, he says, the notion Anglo-Saxon churches were all built of wood will now hardly find supporters.

He admits, which none will deny, that there were structures of this kind.

A few wooden churches are mentioned in Domesday Book, and we learn from other authorities that there were some others.

But he contends that a careful perusal of the early chroniclers would afford abundant proof that churches were not only abundant among the Anglo-Saxons but that they were far from being always mean structures.

Speaking of the Saxon churches, which Odericus Vitalis tells us were repaired by the Normans immediately after the conquest, he remarks that if they had been mean structures and in need of repairs, it is more probable that the Normans would have built new ones.

---

[150] "History of the Cathedral Church of Ely," sec. v., P. 17.
[151] Bede, "Histoire Ecclesiasticle," lib. i., cap. 26.
[152] Ibid,, lib. i., cap. 33-35

The conclusions which are to be drawn from Mr. Wright s article are that while there were undoubtedly some wooden structures, just as there are in this day, the Anglo-Saxons built many churches, and built them sumptuously of stone, and in the Roman manner.

The Rev. Richard Hart is therefore right when he says, on the authority of the architect Mr. Rukman, that in the construction of their churches, the Anglo-Saxons imitated Roman models; as might naturally be expected, considering that Rome was the source from which their Christianity had been derived, the birthplace of many of their prelates and clergy, and at that period the very focus of learning and civilization.[153] It has been conceded that during the comparatively brief period that was occupied by the Saxons after their arrival in Britain until they obtained complete possession of the country, the intestine wars between them and the natives must have had the effect of suspending the pursuit of architecture.

But it has been shown that this suspension did not altogether obliterate the influence of the Roman builders. who had established their methods of building when the island was a province of the empire.

And it has also been seen that the destruction by the Saxons of the Christian churches which had been built by Roman architects was not so thorough or so universal as has been supposed by some writers, and that they did not, as Northouck, amplifying the language of Anderson, says, root out all the sands of learning and the arts that the Romans had planted in Britain.[154] On the contrary, we have the evidence of the Venerable Bede and the repeated testimony of modern excavations that there were at the time of the Saxon conversion to Christianity at least two Roman churches standing which might serve as models for the Saxon Masons, and numerous remains of Roman buildings which afford materials for new structures.

And now, after the conversion, we find the chain connecting Roman Masonry with that pursued by the Saxons renewed and strengthened not only by these models, but by the direct influence of the prelates who were sent from Rome, and who brought with them or sent for workmen to Rome and Gaul, who might carry out More Romano (in the Roman manner) their designs in the building of churches and monasteries.

Butler, in his Lives of the Saints, a work, however, in which we must not place implicit confidence, says that on the permanent settlement of Augustine in Britain, at the close of the 6th century, when

---

[153] "Ecclesiastical Records," ch. v., note 2, p. 217.
[154] Northouck, "Constitutions," Part II., ch. ii., p. 90.

Ethelbert, the King, had been converted, and the people generally were accepting the new, religion, the princes and nobles were very zealous in building and endowing churches and religious houses, and many of them travelled to Rome and other foreign parts to improve themselves in the sacred sciences.[155] That there was at that time a constant and uninterrupted communication between Rome and Britain is evident from the frequent epistles from Gregory, the Pontiff, to Augustine and to the King, Ethelbert.

Missionaries were also sent to Britain to assist Augustine in his pious work, and it is not at all improbable that Masons came with them from Rome, or from Gaul, to be employed in the construction of churches and monasteries, with which the land was being rapidly filled.

But we have more to rely on than mere supposition.

There are abundant records showing that workmen were imported from abroad for the purpose of building, and that thus the Roman method was renewed in the island.

Anderson is not, therefore, strictly correct when he says that the Anglo-Saxons, affecting to build churches and monasteries, palaces and fine mansions, too late lamented the ignorant and destructive conduct of their fathers, but knew not how to repair the public loss of old architecture.[156] It has been shown that there were some models of Roman buildings still remaining, and there was no ignorance of the need of obtaining workmen from Rome or Gaul, and no want of opportunity to obtain them.

He is, therefore, more historically right when he adds, though it contradicts his former assertion, that these works required many Masons, who soon formed themselves into societies or lodges by direction of foreigners who came over to help them.[157]

He is altogether wrong in saying that the Saxons adopted the Gothic style in building. That style of architecture was not invented until long afterward.

In the year 627, Edwin, King of Northumbria, who had been converted by Paulinus, one of the missionaries of Augustine, was baptized in the city of York, the capital of his kingdom.

While receiving the necessary religious instructions he built a temporary church of timber, in which the sacrament of baptism might be administered.

---

[155] Lives of the Saints," vol. v., pp. 418, 419.
[156] "Constitutions," 2d edition, p. 61.
[157] Ibid.

But immediately afterward, under the direction of Bishop Paulinus, he caused the foundation to be laid of a larger and nobler church, of stone, which, although immediately begun, was not finished until after his death, by his successor, Oswald.[158] Although Bede, in narrating the event, says nothing of any foreign aid that had been asked or received in its construction, yet it is evident from the facts that the church was built of stone and in a square form, like a Roman basilica,[159] and would imply the necessity of Roman Masons, or other foreigners imbued with the Roman method, to superintend the work.

In the assembling of foreign Masons at York to erect St. Peter s Church, under the auspices of King Edwin, is supposed by modern Masonic writers to be the assembly incorrectly referred to in the Legend of the Craft as an assembly held at York, under the patronage of Prince Edwin, the son of Athelstan, three hundred years afterward.

But this subject has been so thoroughly discussed in the preceding part of this work, under the head of the York Legend, that it is unnecessary to renew the controversy.

Besides St. Peter s, at York, Paulinus built many other churches.

Some of them we know were of stone, and the others might have been of the same material, as Bentham says, for aught that appears to the contrary.

He was certainly a great patron of ecclesiastical architecture, but Anderson makes no mention of him, although, according to his fashion, he should have styled him, as he does Charles Martel, a Right Worshipful Grand Master.

Another distinguished architect, of a not much later period, was Benedict Biscop, Abbot of Weremouth, whom the Roman Church has canonized.

In the year 675 he built a church at Weremouth, and two monasteries, one at Weremouth and one six miles distant from Jarrow.

Of these Bede has given a particular account in his history of them.

He tells us that the abbot went over into France to engage workmen to build his church after the Roman manner, and brought

---

[158] Bede, " History," lib. ii., cap. 14.

[159] This is the very word used by Bede. "Majorem et augustiorem de lapida fabricare curavit basilicam." The Roman basilica, or Hall of Justice, was the model of all the early churches built by Roman architects, and the old basilica, were often converted with but little change into churches by the Christian emperors.

many back for that purpose The monk was prosecuted with such vigor that within a year the church was completed and divine service performed in it.

But a very important fact stated by Bede is that when the church was nearly finished Benedict sent over to France for artificers skilled in the mystery of making glass (an art hitherto unknown in Britain), who glazed the windows and taught the art to the Saxons.

We learn from this statement that it was customary with the Saxons to seek assistance from the skill of the continental artists and handicraftsmen.

This will explain the true meaning of the passage in the Legend of the Craft, which refers to the introduction of French and other Masons into England in the 7th century, in the time of Charles Martel, and afterward at the supposed Assembly at York, in the 10th century.

And it affords a confirmation of what has been frequently said in the previous part of this work, that the Legend of the Craft, though often chronologically absurd and incorrect in many of its details, yet has throughout in its most important particulars a really historical foundation.

The historians of that period supply us with many proofs that churches and monasteries were erected by the Saxons of stone after the Roman manner, or that they sent abroad for architects to superintend the construction of their buildings.

Eddius Stephanus, who flourished at the beginning of the 8th century, and whose name has been transmitted to posterity by his Life of Saint Wilfrid, informs us that that saint, who was also Bishop of York about the middle of the 7th century, erected many sumptuous buildings in his diocese and thoroughly repaired the church of St. Peter at York, which had been much injured in the war between the Mercians and the Northumbrians.

But Eddius especially refers to two churches built by Wilfrid, the one at Ripon in Yorkshire and the other at Hexham in Northumberland.

Of the former he says that Wilfrid built a church at Ripon from the foundations to the top of polished stone,[160] and supported it with various columns and porticos. This polished stone as a material and these columns and porticos, where arches would probably be required, indicate the presence and the instruction of Roman architects, whether they came from Rome or Gaul.

---

[160] Polito lapide is the language used by Eddius. "Vita S. Wilfridi," cap. xvii., p. 59. He uses the same words in describing the materials of the church at Hexham.

But of all his works, the church of St. Andrew at Hexham seems to have been the most magnificent.

Hexham was a part of the crown- lands of the Kings of Northumbria, and, having been settled in dower on Queen Ethelrida by King Egfrid, a grant of it was made to Wilfrid for the purpose of erecting it into an episcopal see.

Wilfrid began to lay the foundations of the cathedral church in the year 674.

Eddius speaks of it in terms of great admiation, and says that there was no other building like it on this side of the Alps.

He describes its deep foundations and the subterranean rooms, all of wonderfully polished stones, and of the building consisting of many parts above ground, supported by various columns and many porticos, ornamented with a surprising length and height of walls, and surrounded by mouldings, and having turnings of passages sometimes ascending or descending by winding stairs, so that he asserts that he had not words to explain what this priest, taught by the spirit of God, had contemplated doing.

Five centuries after, in 1180, the remains of this famous church were still standing, though in a condition of decay.

Richard, Prior of Hexham, who lived at that time, describes the church with still more minuteness.

He says that the foundations were laid deep in the earth for crypts and subterranean oratories, and the passages underground which led to them were contrived with great exactness.

The walls were of great length and height, and divided into three separate stories, which were supported by square and other kinds of well-polished columns.

The walls, the capitals of the columns which supported them, and the arch of the sanctuary were decorated with historical representations, images, and various figures in relief, carved in stone and painted in an agreeable variety.

The body of the church was encompassed with penthouses and porticos which, above and below, were divided with wonderful art by partition walls and winding stairs.

Within the staircases and upon them were flights of stone steps and passages leading from them, both ascending and descending, which were disposed with so much art that multitudes of people might be there and go all around the church without being perceived by any one who was in the nave.

Many beautiful private oratories were erected with great care and workmanship in the several divisions of the porticos, in which were altars in honor of the Blessed Virgin, of St. Michael, Archangel, of St. John the Baptist and of the holy Apostles, martyrs, confessors, and virgins, with the proper furniture for each.

Some of these, Prior Richard says, were remaining; at his day, and appeared like so many turrets and fortified places.[161] Of a church of such grand proportions, such massive strength, and such artistic construction, it cannot, for a single moment, be supposed that it was built by the uncultivated skill of Saxon Masons.

The stone material, the supporting arches, the intricate passage, the winding stairs, all proclaim the presence of foreign architects and a continuation or a resumption in England of the methods of Roman Masonry.

Nor is this at all improbable.

Wilfrid, although a Saxon, had from an early age received his ecclesiastical education in Rome, and after his return to Northumberland had not only maintained a constant correspondence with, but had made several visits to, the imperial city, and was personally well acquainted with France.

When, therefore, he commenced the construction of important religious houses of such magnitude, he had every facility for the importation of foreign workmen, and there can be no reason for denying that he availed himself of the opportunities which were afforded to him.

Indeed the Venerable Bede conceeds this when he says that the most reverend Wilfrid was the first of the English bishops who taught the churches of the English nation the Catholic, that is the Roman, mode of life.[162] During the long period of forty-five years, in which he occupied the Episcopal See of York, Bishop Wilfrid caused a very great number of churches and monasteries to be built, and must in that way have greatly enlarged and improved the architectural skill of his people by the introduction of foreign artists.

Singularly enough, neither Anderson nor his successors, Entick and Northouck, in the various editions of the Rook of Conctitutions have thought him to be worthy of the slightest mention, though undoubtedly we have historical evidence that he was far better entitled than that less important and less useful man, St. Alban, to have it said of him that he loved Masons well and cherished them much.

---

[161] Richardi, Prior Hagustal," lib. i., chap. iii
[162] Bede, "Histroy" lib. iv, cap. ii.

Indeed all that is said in the Legend of the Craft of the protomartyr might with more plausibility be ascribed to Wilfrid, Bishop of York.

Bentham, in his History of the Cathedral Church of Ely, [163] has said of Wilfrid, relying on the almost contemporaneous authority of Bede, of Eddius Stephanus and of Richard, the Prior of Hexham, that in consequence of the favor and the liberal gifts bestowed upon him by the kings and the nobility of Northumberland, he rose to a degree of opulence so as to vie with princes in state and magnificence and was thus enabled to found several rich monasteries and to build many stately edifices.

In the prosecution of these great undertakings he gave due encouragement to the most skillful builders and artificers of every kind who were eminent in their several trades.

He kept them in his service by proper rewards, or, as the Legend of the Craft says of St. Alban, he made their pay right good. Some of these he obtained at Canterbury, whither they had been introduced by Augustine to aid him in the construction of the churches in Kent.

Eddius is distinct on this point, for he says, in his Life of Wilfrid, that when he returned home from his visit to Canterbury, he brought back not only skillful singers, who might instruct his choirs in the Roman method of singing, but also Masons and artists of almost every kind.[164] Richard, Prior of Hexham, says that he secured from Rome, Italy, France, and other countries where he could find them, Masons and skillful artificers of other kinds, whom he brought to England for the purpose of carrying on his works.[165] William of Malmesbury also says that to construct the buildings that Wilfrid had designed Masons had been attracted from Rome by the hope of liberal rewards,[166] and both Eddius, his biographer, and William of Malmesbury

---

[163] "History of the Cathedral Church of Ely," P- 23

[164] Eddius, "Vita S. Wilfridi,"cap.xiv. Camentariis is the word employed by Eddius. Now, caementarius was the word used in mediaeval Latin to designate an Operative Mason. Ducange cites Magister caementariorum, the "Master of the Masons," as used by mediaeval writers to denote one who presided over the building, him whom he calls the Master of the Works.

[165] De Roma quoque, et Italia, et Francia, et de aliis terris ubicumque invenire poterat, camentarios et quoslibet alios industrios artifices secum retinuerat, et ad opera sua facienda secum in Angliam adduxerat. "Richardi, Prior Hagustal," lib. i., cap. V.

[166] "Caementarios, quos ex Roma spes munificentioe attraxerat. Gulilm. Malsmb. de Gestis Pontif." Angl., P. 272. The "spes munificentiae" was the expectation of

concur in declaring that he was eminent for his knowledge and skill in the science of architecture.

The spirit of improvement and the skill in architecture which had been introduced into Northumberland by its Bishop were not confined to his own country, but through his influence were extended to the other kingdoms of the Heptarchy.

They made their way even into the more northern parts of the island, for Bede informs us[167] that in the beginning of the 8th century, Naitan, King of the Picts, sent messengers to Ceolfrid, Abbot of the Monastery of Weremouth, praying to have architects sent him to build a church in his nation after the Roman manner.

Hence, says Bentham, it should seem that the style of architecture generally used in that age in England was called the Roman manner, and was the same that was then used at Rome in Italy and in other parts of the empire.[168] Mr. John M. Kemble, when commenting on circumstances like these in the learned Introduction to his Diplomatic Codex of the Saxon Era, has very justly said that the great advance in civilization made especially in Northumberland before the close of the 7th century proves that even the rough denizens of that inhospitable portion of our land were apt and earnest scholars.[169] The next eminent Saxon patron of Masonry of whom we have any record is Albert, who in 767 became the successor of Egbert as Archbishop of York.

The church which had been built by Paulinus in the 7th century, having been much dilapidated by a conflagration and not having been sufficiently repaired, was wholly taken down by Albert, who determined to rebuild it.

This he did with the assistance of two eminent architects, his disciples, Eanbald, who succeeded him in the see of York, and the

---

higher wages, just what the "Legend of the Craft" says that St. Alban established. It is curious to remark how everything that that Legend ascribes to St. Alban may with equal propriety be attributed on historic authority to St. Wilfrid. It is strange that the later Masonic writers as well as the legendists should have completely ignored St. Wilfrid, who was the real reformer, if not actual founder, of the English Masonry in connection with the Roman.

[167] In Book V., chapter xxi. of his "Ecclesiastical History."
[168] "History of the Cathedral Church of Ely," p. 25.
[169] "Codex Diplomaticus Aevi Saxonici." This learned and laborious work, edited by Mr. Kemble and published in 1839, in six large octave volumes, by the English Historical Society, contains copies either in Saxon or in Latin of nearly all the royal and other charters issued during the Saxon domination which have been preserved in various collections.

celebrated Alcuin, who afterward introduced learning into the court of Charlemagne, of whom he became the preceptor.

Alcuin, in a poem On the Pontiffs and Saints of the Church of York,[170] has given a full description of the rebuilding of the church, from which we may learn the degree of perfection to which architecture had then arrived.

We find in that description the account of a complete and exquisitely finished piece of architecture, the new construction of a wonderful church, as Alcuin expresses it, consisting of a tall building supported by solid columns, with arches, vaulted roofs, splendid doors and windows, porticos, galleries, and thirty altars variously ornamented.

This templum, says the poem of Alcuin,[171] was built under the orders of the Master Albert by his two disciples, Eanbald and Alcuin, working harmoniously and devotedly.

The predatory aggressions of the Danish pirates, and their more permanent invasion in the latter part of the 9th century, though marked by all the atrocities of a barbarous enemy, and with the destruction of innumerable churches and monasteries and the burning of many towns and villages, must of course have suspended for a time all progress in architecture.

But it could have been only a temporary suspension.

Their occupancy lasted but twelve years, and the knowledge of the Roman method which had been acquired by the Saxons could not have been lost in that brief period, nor were all the monuments of their skill destroyed.

Enough remained for models, and many of the old Masons must have been still living when civilization was renewed in England by the restoration of Alfred to the throne.

Asser, the contemporary and the biographer of Alfred or whoever assumed his name,[172] admits that during the Danish

---

[170] "Pontificibus et Sanctis Ecclesise Eboracensis." It was published in 1691 by Dr. Thomas Gale in his "Historian Britanicm," Saxonioe et Anglo-Danicoe Scriptores quindecim, usually cited as " Gale's XV Scriptores."

[171] "Hoc duo discipali templum doctore jubente, Ædificarunt Eanbaldus et Alcuinus, ambo Concordes operi devota mente studentes." Alcuin De Pontifet Sanct. Eccl. Ebor.

[172] Doubt has been entertained by Mr. Wright, and plausible reasons assigned for the doubt, of the authenticity of Asser's "Life of Alfred," which work he is disposed to believe was written as late as the latter part of the 12th century ("Essays on Archaeology," i., 183). But even if this were correct, it would not affect the truth of the statement in the text.

domination the arts and sciences had begun to be neglected, but the wise and vigorous measures pursued by Alfred on his accession soon restored them to more than their former condition of prosperity.

Matthew of Westminster, a Benedictine monk who lived in the 14th century and whose narrative of events is valuable because it is that of a careful observer, tells us that with a genius of his own, not hitherto displayed by others, Alfred occupied himself in building edifices which were venerable and noble beyond anything that had been attempted by his predecessors, and that many Frenchmen and natives of other countries came to England, being attracted by his amiable and affable character and by the protection and gifts which he bestowed on all strangers of worth, whether noble or low-born.

Among these foreigners we must naturally suppose that there were many architects and builders from France and Italy, who came to find employment in the various works on which the king was engaged.[173] Matthew also tells us that Alfred bestowed one-sixth of his revenues on the numerous artisans whom he employed and who were skillful in every kind of work on land.[174] Florence of Worcester, a monk who wrote in the 12th century, says that among the other accomplishments of Wilfrid he was skilled in architecture and excelled his predecessors in building and adorning his palaces, in constructing large ships for the security of his coasts, and in erecting castles in convenient parts of the country.[175] Indeed all the chroniclers of his own and following ages concur in attributing to the great Alfred, the best and wisest monarch who ever sat on the English throne, the resuscitation of Saxon architecture and the introduction anew into the kingdom of foreign architects from Italy and France, so that the connection between the Roman and the Saxon was continued without material interruption.

In the last year of the 9th century, Alfred was succeeded by his eldest son, Edward, a prince who has been described as inferior to his father in learning and the love of literature, but who by his martial prowess greatly extended the boundaries of his dominions.

---

[173] "Matthew of Westminster," c. xvi., ad annum 871.
[174] Ibid., ad annum 888.
[175] Flor. Wegorn, ad annum 871, 887. He calls him "in arte architectonica sumonus " (preeminent in the art of architecture). Though not so great a patron of architecture as his predecessor, the science was not deteriorated during his reign.

He founded or repaired some churches and monasteries, and built. several cities and towns, which he encompassed with massive walls as a protection against the sudden incursions of the Danes.

In 924 Edward was succeeded by his illegitimate son, Athelstan.

Although the records of the old chroniclers of England speak only of a few monasteries that were founded by Athelstan, the legendary history of the Craft assigns to him an important character as having granted a charter for the calling of an Assembly of Masons at the city of York.

And to this Assembly the legendist as well as all modern writers up to a very recent period have sought to trace the origin of Freemasonry in England.

This subject has already been very fully discussed in the chapter on the York Legend, in the first part of the present work, and it will be unnecessary to renew the discussion here.

I will only add that since writing that chapter I have diligently examined all the charters granted by King Athelstan, copies of the originals of which are contained in the Codex Diplomaticus, published by the English Historical Society, and have failed to find in them any one in which there is the slightest allusion to the calling of an Assembly of Masons at York.

If such a charter ever existed (of which I have no idea), it has been irretrievably lost.

The non-appearance of the charter certainly does not prove that it never was granted, but its absence deprives the advocates of the York theory of what would be the best and most unanswerable evidence of the truth of the Legend. In fact Edgar, his nephew, who ascended the throne in 959, after the brief reigns of his father, Edmund, his uncle, Edred, and his brother, Edwy, was a greater encourager of architecture, or, as the old historians of Masonry would have called him, a better patron of the Craft, than Athelstan.

During his reign the land was so seldom embroiled in strife that the early chroniclers have styled him Edgar the Pacific.

Thus was he enabled to devote himself to the improvement of his kingdom and the condition of his subjects.

He founded more than forty monasteries, and among them the magnificent abbey of Ramsay, in Huntingdonshire.

From a description of this abbey, given in its history, which has been preserved by Gale, we are led to believe that in the reign of Edgar the old style of building churches in the square form of a basilica or

Roman Hall of justice was beginning to be abandoned for the cruciform shape, as more symbolically suited to a Christian temple.

He built also the old abbey church of Westminster, which Sir Christopher Wren says, in the Parentalia, was probably a good, strong building after the manner of the age, not much altered from the Roman way.

This way, Wren says, was with piers or round pillars (stronger than Tuscan or Doric), round-headed arches and windows.

And he refers, as instances of this method borrowed from the Roman, to various buildings erected before the Conquest.

Whatever may be said of the private and personal character of Edgar and he can not be acquitted of the charge of licentiousness, as a monarch he certainly sought to improve the condition of his kingdom, to secure the comfort of his subjects, and to encourage the cultivation of the arts and sciences, among which architecture was not the least prominent.

It is hardly necessary to pursue the details of the condition of the art of building in the few remaining years of the Anglo-Saxon dynasty.

Such a plan would be appropriate to a professional history of English architecture.

But enough has been said to maintain the hypothesis of the origin and rise of Masonry, which is the special object of the present work.

It has already been shown that the system of associated workmen in the craft of building arose in the Roman Colleges of Artificers, of Builders, or of Masons, call them by either name; that this system, with the skill that accompanied it, was introduced from Rome into Britain at the time of the real conquest of that island by Claudius, by the artisans who followed the legions and became colonists of the province; that on the accession of the Saxons to the government of the country, though the Britains were driven to the remoter parts of the island in the West, monuments of the Roman workmen remained to perpetuate the method; that the Saxons themselves were not a wholly barbarous people, and that by their rapid conversion to Christianity the communication with Rome was renewed through the missionaries who came to them from that city; that when the monks began the construction of religious houses they sent to Italy or to Gaul for workmen who were educated in the Roman method; and that thus, by the architectural works which were accomplished under ecclesiastical auspices, the continuous chain which connected the Masons of the Roman Colleges with the Saxon builders remained unbroken.

From the death of Edgar to the final extinction of the Saxon dynasty and the establishment of the Norman race upon the throne of England, though history records few great architectural achievements, nothing was absolutely lost of the skill and the methods of Masonry which had been acquired in the lapse of centuries and from continual communications with foreign artists.

Even the interpolation of the reigns of three Danish kings, of which two were very brief, produced no disastrous effects.

So when Harold, the last Saxon monarch, was slain at the battle of Hastings, in the year 1066, and the crown passed into the possession of the Norman William, many specimens of Saxon architecture were still remaining.

There is one episode in the history of the Anglo-Saxons which is of too much importance to be passed over without an extended notice.

I allude to the establishment of Guilds.

These were confraternities which, as will hereafter be shown, gave form and feature to the organization of the modern Masonic Lodges.

But this is a subject of so much interest in the present inquiry that it can not be dismissed at the close of the investigation of a different though cognate topic.

Its consideration must therefore be deferred to the succeeding chapter.

CHAPTER VIII

THE ANGLO-SAXON GUILDS

A guild signified among the Saxons a fraternity or sodality united together for the accomplishment by the cooperative exertions of the members of some predetermined purpose.

The word is derived from the Anglo-Saxon verb gildan, "to pay," and refers to the fact that every member of the Guild was required to contribute something to its support. Hence Cowel defines Guilds to be " fraternities originally contributing sums towards a common stock." Assuming that the characteristic of a Guild organization is that it is a society of men united together for mutual assistance in the accomplishment of an object, or for the cultivation of friendship, or for the observance of religious duties, we may say that the Guild has under some of these aspects existed in all civilized countries from the earliest ages.

The priesthood of Egypt was a fraternity containing in its organization much that resembles the more modern Guild, the priests possessing peculiar privileges and constituting a body isolated from the rest of the nation, by the right of making their own laws and electing their own members, who were received into what may be appropriately called the sacerdotal Guild, by certain ceremonies of initiation.

The trades and handicrafts were divided into their various professions.

Thus the artificers and the boatmen of the Nile were each a separate class,[176] and as the practice of a trade was made hereditary and was restricted to certain families, we may well suppose that each of these classes constituted a Guild.

---

[176] Kenreck, "Ancient Egypt," vol. ii-, p. 36.

And it may be remarked, in passing, that while the handicraftsmen and traders were generally held by the higher orders among the Egyptians in low repute, the art of building seems to have occupied a higher place in the national estimation, for while we find no record on the funeral monuments of any of the other working-classes, the names of architects alone appear in the inscriptions with those of priests, warriors, judges, and chiefs of provinces, the only ranks to which the honor of a funeral record was permitted.[177] The Eranos among the Greeks was in every minute respect the analogue of the Guild. Donnegal defines it to be " a society under certain rules and regulations having a fund, contributed by the members, formed for various purposes, such as succoring indigent members."[178] Clubs or societies of this kind established for charitable or convivial purposes, and sometimes for both, were very common at Athens, and were also found in other cities of Greece.

These Grecian Guilds were founded on the principle of mutual relief.

If a member was reduced to poverty, or was in temporary distress for money, he applied to the Eranos, or Guild, and the relief required was contributed by the members.

Sometimes it was considered as a loan, to be repaid when the borrower was in better circumstances.

The Eranos met at stated periods, generally once a month, had its peculiar regulations, was presided over by an officer styled the Eranarches, and the Eranistai, or members, paid each a monthly contribution.

There does not really appear to have been any material difference between the organization of these sodalities and the Saxon and mediaeval social Guilds.

It is scarcely necessary, after the description that has already been given of the Roman Colleges of Artificers, to say that they were analogous to the Craft Guilds.

Indeed, it is a part of the hypothesis maintained in the present work, that the latter derived, directly or indirectly, the suggestion of their peculiar form as associated craftsmen from the former.

The Agape or Love Feasts of the early Christians, though at first established for the commemoration of a religious rite, subsequently, became guild-like in their character, as they were sustained by the

---

[177] Kenreck, "Ancient Egypt," vol. ii., p. 37.
[178] "Lexicon," in voce.

contributions of the members, and funds were distributed for the relief of widows, orphans, and the poorer brethren.

Indeed, they are supposed by ecclesiastical writers to have imitated the Grecian Eranos.

The Government looked upon them as secret societies, and they were consequently denounced by imperial edicts.

Brentano, who has written a learned introduction to Toulmin Smith's English Guilds, published by the Early English Text Society, is disposed to trace the origin of Guilds to the feasts of the old German tribes from Scandinavia, which were also called Guilds.

Among the German tribes, all events that especially related to the family, such as births, marriages, and deaths, were celebrated by sacrificial feasts in a family reunion.

Similar feasts took place on certain public occasions and anniversaries, which often afforded an opportunity for the conclusion of alliances for piracy and plunder by one tribe or another.

I am not inclined to trace the origin of the Saxon and English Guilds to so degenerate a source, and I subscribe to the opinions expressed by Wilda,[179] one of the ablest of the German writers on this subject, who cannot find anything of the true nature of the Guild in these Scandinavian feasts of the family.

Hartwig,[180] who has also investigated this point, agrees with Wilda.

Yet it is very evident that the sentiment of the Guild-that is, the desire to establish fraternal relations for mutual aid and protection-was not peculiar to the Saxons.

It may rather be contemplated as a human sentiment, arising from the innate knowledge of his own condition, which makes man aware of his infirmity and weakness in isolation, and causes him to seek for strength in association with his fellow-man.

The similitude, therefore, if not the exact form of the Guild, has appeared in almost all civilized nations, even at the remotest periods of their own history.

Wherever men accustom themselves to meet on stated occasions, to celebrate some appointed anniversary or festival and to partake of a common meal, that by this regular communion a spirit of fraternity may be established, and every member may feel that upon the association with which he is thus united he may depend for relief of his necessities or protection of his interests, such an association, sodality, or

---

[179] "Das Gildwesen in Mittelalter."
[180] "Untersuchungen uber die ersten Anfange des Gildveerens."

confraternity, call it by whatever name you may, will be in substantial nature a Guild.

Wilda thinks that the peculiar character of the Guilds was derived from the Christian principle of love, and that they actually originated in the monastic unions, where every member shared the benefits of the whole community in good works and prayers, into the advantages of which union laymen were afterward admitted.

But the untenableness of this theory is evident from the fact that the same characteristic of mutual aid existed in the pagan nations long before the advent of Christianity, and was presented in those sodalities which represent the form of the modern Guild.

Besides the admission of Wilda and Hartwig that the early Saxon Guilds were so tinctured with the superstitious customs of the pagan sacrificial feasts, and that the Church had to labor strenuously and for a long time for their suppression, would prove that we must look beyond the monasteries for the true origin of the Guild.

I am inclined, therefore, to attribute them to that spirit of associated labor and union of refreshment which had existed in the Roman Colleges of Artificers, where, as has been already shown, there exited that organized union of interests which continued to be displayed in the Guilds.

I will not aver that the Guilds were the legitimate and uninterrupted successors of the Roman Colleges, but I will say that the suggestion of the advantages to be derived from an association in work, regulated by ordinances that had been agreed on, governed by officers who might judiciously direct the exercise of skill and the employment of labor, the result of all of which was a combination of interests and the growth of a fraternal feeling, was suggested by these Roman institutions, and more especially adopted by the Craft Guilds, which, at a later period in the Middle Ages, directed all the architectural labors in every country of Europe.

Of these Craft Guilds many authors have traced the origin to the Roman Colleges.

Brentano does not absolutely deny this hypothesis, but he thinks it needs to be proved historically by its defenders.

He thinks it more probable that they descended from " the companies into which, in episcopal and royal towns, the bond handicraftsmen of the same trade were ranged under the superintendence of an official, or that they took their origin from a common subjection to police control or from common obligations to pay certain imposts."[181]

It was in Germany that these episcopal communities existed.

Arnold, in his Constitutional History of the German Free Cities,[182] describes one at Worms in the 11th century.

To the Manor of the Bishop were attached, among other dependants, a class of villeins or bondsmen called dagewardi.

These were divided into colossi, or workmen on the country manor, and operaiii, or handicraftsmen, who were ranged, according to their trades, into different unions or societies.

And it is from these that the continental Guilds of the Middle Ages have been erroneously supposed to have been derived.

Still, when their bondage ceased, these societies may have developed themselves into Free Guilds; but the Free Guilds existed before, and the bond unions enforced by episcopal authority must have been organized simply for the convenience of the employer.

There could not have been in them any of the peculiar characteristics of the free and independent Guild.

But even if this speculative notion of Brentano, that the Guilds were derived from the enforced association of the episcopal and royal bond handicraftsmen, were admitted to be correct, it would be only lengthening the chain which connects them with the Roman Colleges by the insertion of another link, for we should have to look to these Roman sodalities for the idea of union and concerted action, which in either of those instances must have influenced the combination of handicraftsmen.

However, Brentano immediately repudiates the views which he had just advanced, and admits that they deserve no further consideration, because Wilda has shown that the Craft Guilds did not spring from subjection, but arose from the freedom of the handicraft class.

Now, it is precisely in this point that the Craft Guilds most resemble the Roman Colleges.

Founded originally in the earliest days of Rome for the express purpose of giving to the workingclasses a separate and independent place in the public polity, they preserved this independence to the latest times and cultivated the spirt of freedom which sprang naturally from it.

Their spirit of freedom and independence indeed often bordered upon excess.

---

[181] "English Guilds," in Early English Text Society Publications, p. 114.
[182] "Verfasserungs geschichte der Deutschen Freistadte."

Thus they were watched and feared in the latter days of the republic and during the empire because their love of freedom sometimes led them to inaugurate conspiracies against the Government, which they supposed had the design of subverting or diminishing their privileges.

To protect these privileges and to preserve this freedom they instituted the office of Patrons, men of distinction and influence, not of their trade, but selected from the order of patricians who were to be the conservators of their franchises.

There is abundant historical evidence that the system of Guilds was well known to the Anglo-Saxons.

Mr. Toulmin Smith, to whom we are indebted for the collection of Guild charters of a later date, says that "English Guilds, as a system of widespread practical institutions, are older than any kings of England.

They are told of in the books that contain the oldest relics of English laws.

The old laws of King Alfred, of King Ina, of King Athelstan, of King Henry I., reproduce still older laws in which the universal existence of Guilds is treated as a well-known fact, and in which it is taken to be a matter of course that everyone belonged to some Guild.

As population increased Guilds multiplied; and thus, while the beginnings of the older Guilds are lost in the dimness of time and remain quite unknown, the beginnings of the later ones took place in methods and with accompanying forms that have been recorded."[183] But it is not upon those laws alone that we have to depend for proof of the antiquity of the Saxon Guilds.

The records of a few of the old Guilds still remain and show that the idea of association for mutual assistance, which is the very spirit of the Guild organization, was prevalent at least twelve centuries ago among our Saxon ancestors.

Among the laws of Ina, who reigned from 688 to 725, are two which relate to the liability of the brethren of a Guild in the case of slaying a thief.[184] King Alfred also refers to the duties of the Guild when he decrees that in the case of a crime the Brothers of the Guild (gegyldan) shall pay a portion of the fine.[185] The Judicia Civitatis Lundonia or Statutes of the City of London, contain several ordinances

---

[183] Traditions of the Old Crown House," p. 28.
[184] Thorpe's "Anglo Laws," Ina 16, 21.
[185] "Leges 'Elf," 27. and the realme (for service by them done), which requested to have a certaine portion of land on the east part of the city, left desolate and forsaken by the inhabitants by reason of too much servitude."

for the regulation of the various Guilds, and prescribing the duties of the members.

The " Cnyhten Gyld," or Young Men's Guild, is mentioned by Stow as existing in the time of King Edgar, who granted the liberty of a Guild for, ever to "thirteene knights or soldiers well beloved of the king[186] Thirteen was a favorite number in the religious guilds. Ducange explains the reason in a quotation which he makes from an Epistle to the Church of Utrecht, wherein it is said that a fraternity, commonly called a Guild, was formed, consisting of twelve men to represent the twelve apostles, and one woman to represent the Virgin Mary."[187] The text of the " writing," or charter, by which Orky instituted a Guild at Abbotsbury has been preserved.

Orky was the " huscarl," of one of the household troops, [188] of Edward the Confessor, and there is a charter of that monarch extant in which he gives permission to Tole, the widow of Orky, or Urk, to bequeath her lands to the monastery at the same place in which the Guild was established.

The original charter of Orky's Guild, as written in the AngloSaxon language, with a generally correct translation into English, has been inserted by Thorpe in his Diplomatarium.[189] As it is one of the earliest of the Saxon charters that is extant, and as it will be interesting in enabling the reader to collate its provisions with those of the later Guilds on the pattern of which the Masonic Guilds, or Fraternities, were formulated, it is here presented entire.

It must, however, be observed that it was not a Craft, but a religious Guild, and hence we find no allusion to the privileges and obligations of the former, which always composed a part of their ordinances.

"Here is made known in this writing that Orky has given the Guildhall and the place at Abbotsbury to the praise of God and St. Peter, and for the guildship to possess now and henceforth of him and his consort for long remembrance.

Who so shall avert this, let him account with God at the great day of judgment. I have ventured to make a few alterations in Thorpe's translation, to conform more strictly to the Anglo-Saxon original.

---

[186] "Survaye of London," p. 85.
[187] Ducange, " Glossarium " in voce, Gilda.
[188] The "huscarlas," says Kemble, were among the Saxons, and, until after the Norman Conquest, the household troops or immediate body-guard of the King. "The Saxons in England," vol. ii., p. 118.
[189] "Diplomatarium Ang.," pp. 605-608.

"Now these are the covenants which Orky and the guild brothers at Abbotsbury have chosen to the praise of God and the honor of St. Peter and their souls' need.

"This is first: Three nights before St. Peter's Mass, from every guild brother one penny, or one penny worth of wax, whichever be most needed in the monastery, and on the mass' eve one broad loaf, well raised and well sifted, for our common aims; and five weeks before Peter's Mass day let every guild brother contribute one guildsester full of clean wheat, and let that be rendered within two days, on pain of forfeiting the entrance fee (ingang), which is three sesters of wheat.

And let the wood be rendered within three days after the corn contribution, from every full guild brother (riht gegyldan)[190] one burthern (byrthene) of wood, and two from those who are not full brothers, or let him pay one guild sester of corn.

And he who undertakes a charge, and does it not satisfactorily, let him be liable in his entrance fee, and let there be no remission.

And let the guild brother who abuses another within the guild, with serious intent, make atonement to all the society to the amount of his entrance, and afterward to the man whom he abused, as he may settle it, and if he will not submit to compensation, let him forfeit the fellows lip and every other privilege of the Guild.

And let him who introduces more men than he ought, without leave of the steward and the purveyors (feomera), pay his entrance. And if death befall anyone in our society, let each guild brother contribute one penny at the corpse for the soul, or pay according to three guild brothers (gylde be pry gegildum). [191]And if any one of us be sick within sixty miles, then we shall find fifteen men who shall fetch him; and if he be dead thirty; and they shall bring him to the place which he desired in his life.

---

[190] There is some difficulty here. The words "riht gegyldan" in the original mean literally "lawful members of the Guild;" and the word "ungyldan" signifies "those who are not members," for the particle un has the privative power in Anglo-Saxon as in English. Thorpe translates as "regular and non-regular guild brothers." I have adopted with hesitation Kemble's translation ("Saxons in England," i-, 511). But what are "nonregular " or "not full brethren?" As " gegyldan " also means " to pay a contribution," we might suppose that the " riht gegyldan " were those who had paid their dues to the guild, and the " ungegyldan " were those who were in arrears. This would be a reasonable explanation of the passage; but there are grammatical difficulties in the way.

[191] Literally translated, but unintelligible. Kemble does not attempt a translation, but gives the passage the benefit of a blank.

And if he die in the vicinity, let the steward have warning to what place the corpse is to go, and let the steward then warn the guild brothers, as many as ever he can ride to or send to, that they come thereto and worthily attend the corpse and convey it to the monastery and earnestly pray for the soul.

That will rightly be called a guildlaw which we thus do and it will beseem it well both before God and before the world; for we know not which of us shall soonest depart hence.

Now we believe through God's support that this aforesaid agreement will benefit us all if we rightly hold it.

"Let us fervently pray to God Almighty that he have mercy on us; and also to his holy Apostle St. Peter, that he intercede for us and make our way clear to everlasting rest; because for love of him we have gathered this guild (gegaderodon).

He has the power in heaven that he may let into heaven whom he will, and refuse, whom he will not; as Christ himself said to him in his Gospel: 'Peter, I deliver to thee the key of heaven's kingdom; and whatsoever thou wilt have bound on earth, that shall be bound in heaven, and whatsoever thou wilt have unbound on earth, that shall be un- bound in heaven.' Let us have trust and hope in him that he will ever have care of us here in the world, and after our departure hence, be a help to our souls; May he bring us to everlasting rest." These covenants, which in later Guild charters are called ordinances, and by the Mason Guilds constitutions, very clearly define the objects of the association.

These were not connected with the pursuit of any handicraft, but were altogether of a religious and charitable nature.

Infirm brethren were to be supported, the dead were to be buried, prayers were to be said for the repose of their souls, and religious services were to be performed.

There was an annual meeting on the feast of St. Peter, and regulations were made for the collection of alms on that day for the benefit of the poor.

Especial attention was paid to the preservation of fraternal relations of mutual kindness between the members.

In all this we see the germ of those similar regulations which are met with in the " Constitutions of the Freemasons," compiled in the 15th, 16th, and 17th centuries, and which were, mutatis mutandis, finally developed in the regulations of the Speculative Masons in the 18th century.

The essence of the regulations of this as well as of two other Guilds established about the same time, one at Exeter and the third at

Cambridge, was the binding together in close fraternal union of man to man, which was sometimes fortified by oaths for the faithful performance of mutual help.

The charter of the "Thanes' Guild at Cambridge " has been published by both Thorpe and Kemble from a Cottonian manuscript. As it contains some points not embraced in the charter of the Orky Guild, it is here presented, as a further means of collation with the charters of the later Craft Guilds. The original is of course in Anglo Saxon, and I have adopted the translation of Thorpe, with the exception of a few emendations.

Here in this writing is the declaration of the agreement which this society has resolved in the Thanes' Guild at Cambridge.

That then is first that each should take an oath to the others on the halidom of true fidelity before God and the world.

And all the society should support him who had most right If any guild brother die let all the guildship bring him to where he desired; and let him who should come thereto pay a sester (about eight quarts) of honey; and let the guildship inherit of the deceased half a farm.

And let each contribute two pence to the alms and thereof bring what is fitting to St. Aetheldryth.

And if any guild brother be in need of his fellows' aid and it be made known to the fellow nearest to the guild brother and, unless the guild brother himself be nigh, the fellow neglect it, let him pay one pound.

If the lord neglect it, let him pay one pound unless he be on the lord's need or confined to his bed.

And if any one slay a guild brother let there be nothing for compensation but eight pounds.

But if the slayer scorns the compensation let all the guildship avenge the guild brother and all bear tile feud.

But if a guild brother do it let all bear alike.

And if any guild brother slay any man and he be an avenger by compulsion and compensate for his violence and the slain be a nobleman let each guild brother contribute half a mark for his aid; if the slain be a churl (ceorl) two oras (100 pence) if he be Welch one ora.

But if the guild brother slay any one through wantonness and with guile, let himself bear what he has wrought.

And if a guild brother slay his guild brother through his own folly let him suffer on the part of the kindred for that which he has violated, and buy back his guildship with eight pounds, or forever forfeit our society and friendship. And if a guild brother eat or drink with him who slew his guild brother unless it be before the king or the bishop of the diocese or the aldermen, let him pay one pound unless with his two bench comrades (gesetlung) he can deny that he knew him.

If any guild brother abuse another let him pay a sester of honey unless he can clear himself with his two bench comrades. If a servant (cniht) draw a weapon let the lord pay one pound and let the lord get what he can and let all the guildship aid him in getting his money. And if a servant wound another let the lord avenge it and all the guildship together, so that seek he whatever he may (sece whet he sece) he have not life (feorh).

And if a servant sit within the storeroom let him pay a sester of honey; and if any one have a footstool let him do the same.

And if any guild brother die out of the land or be taken sick let his guild brethren fetch him and convey him, dead or alive, to where he may desire, under the same penalty that has been said, if he die at home and the guild brother attend not the corpse And let the guild brother who does not attend his morning discourse (morjen space) pay his sester of honey." In this agreement of an early Guild, we will again notice that, though the regulations are few, they all partake of that spirit of mutual kindness which has characterized the Guild organizations of all ages, and of which the Masonic Lodge is but a fuller development The principal points worthy of notice are as follows: 1.There was an oath of fidelity. 2.The sick were to be nursed and the dead buried. 3.A brother was bound to give aid to another brother if he were called upon. 4. If a member got into trouble or difficulty the Guild was to come to his assistance. 5. The injuries or wrongs of a member were to be espoused by the Guild. 6. To associate knowingly with one who had done injury to a member was a penal offense. 7. The severest punishment that could be inflicted on a member was expulsion from the body.

These seven points embrace the true spirit of the Masonic institution, and may be advantageously collated with the mediaeval Constitutions, and with the regulations and obligations of the modern Lodges.

That this collation of the older and the newer Constitutions may be more conveniently made, it will be necessary to anticipate the chronological sequence, and to present the reader the ordinances of two Craft Guilds, both of the 14th century.

The first of these Constitutions, though the date affixed to it makes it apparently sixty years later than the second, was really much older. Foulmin Smith says that "the internal evidence shows that the substance of the ordinances is older than the date given." As, in the beginning, they are said to be ordinances "made and of ancient time assigned and ordained by the founders of the Guild," he conjectures that they were first written in Latin, and that what we have " are the early translation of a lost original with some later additions and alterations." The document now presented to the reader, and which has been taken from Toulmin Smith's collection of English Guilds, which was published by the Early English Text Society, is the Guild of the Smiths of Chesterfield.

The Guild united with that of the Holy Cross of Merchants in 1387. But as has already been said, the date of its institution must have been much earlier.

(The paragraphs are numbered for the convenience of future reference. There is no numbering in the original.) 1. "This is the agreement of the Masters and brethren of the Guild of Smiths of Chesterfield, worshipping before the greater cross in the nave of the church of All Saints there. The head men are an Elder Father, Dean, Steward and four Burgesses by whose oversight the guild is managed. Lights are to be found and be burnt before the cross on days named. 2. " If any brother is sick and needs help, he shall have a half- penny daily from the common fund of the guild until he has got well. If any of them fall into want they shall go, singly, on given days, to the houses of the brethren where each shall be courteously received, and there shall be given to him, as if he were the Master of the house, whatever he wants of meat, drink and clothing, and he shall have a halfpenny like those that are sick and then he shill go home in the name of the Lord. 3. " On the death of a brother twelve lights shall be kept burning round the body, until buried, and offerings shall be made. Round the body of a stranger or of the son of a brother, dying in the house of a brother four lights shall be kept burning. 4. " If it befall that any of the brethren, by some hapless chance, and not through his own folly, is cast into prison, all his brethren are bound to do what they can to get him freed and to defend him. 5. "If any sick brother makes a will, having first bequeathed his soul to God, his body to burial and the altar gifts to the priests, he shall then not forget to bequeath something to the guild according to his means. 6. " Whenever any one has borrowed any money from the guild, either to traffic with or for his own use, under promise to repay it on a given day, and he does not repay it, though three times warned, he shall be put under suspension, denunciation and excommunication - all contradiction, cavil and appeal aside-until he shall have wholly paid it. If he has been sick, the claim of the guild must be first to be satisfied. And if he dies intestate, his goods shall be held bound to the guild, to pay what is owing to it, and shall not be touched or sequestrated until full payment has been made to the guild. 7. " Should it happen, [which God forbid] that any brother is con- tumacious; or sets himself against the brethren; or gainsays any of these ordinances; or being summoned to a feast will not come; or does not obey the Elder Father when he ought nor show him due respect; or does not abide by what has been ordained by the Elder Father and greater part of the guild: he shall pay a pound of wax and half a mark.

Moreover he shall be put under suspension, denunciation and excommunication, without any contradiction, cavil or appeal. 8. "Any one proved to be in debt, or a wrong-doer, shall be deemed excommunicate, and shall presume to come to the meetings of the brethren, his company shall be shunned by all, so that no brother shall dare to talk with him, unless to chide him, until he has fully satisfied the Elder Father and the brethren, as well touching any penalty as touching the debt or wrong doing. 9. " To keep and faithfully perform these constitutions, all the brethren have bound themselves by touch of relics." Although, as its name imports, this is the sodality of a body of handicraftsmen, yet there is no reference to any regulations for work.

In this respect it more resembles a Social than a Craft Guild.

This deficiency is, however, supplied in the ordinances of the Tailors' Guild at Lincoln, which is next to be given.

This circumstance is ,one of the internal evidences that the Smiths' Guild was much older than its charter purports.

The Tailors' was a Craft Guild, and its provisions for the regulation of labor, though few, are striking and may be profitable compared with the more developed system subsequently adopted by the Masonic Craft Guilds.

The date of the institution of the Tailors' Guild is the year 1328. The paragraphs are here numbered for reference, as in the case of the former Guild.

1.."All the brethren and sisters shall go in procession in the feast of Corpus Christi. 2. "None shall enter the Guild as whole brother until he has paid his entry, a quarter of barley, which must be paid between Michaelmas and Christmas. And if it is not then paid, he shall pay the price of the best malt as sold in Lincoln Market on Midsummer day. And each shall pay 12 pence to the ale. 3. If any one of the Guild falls into poverty (which God forbid) and has not the means of support he shall have every week 7 pence out of the goods of the Guild; out of which he must discharge such payments as become due to the Guild. 4. "If any one dies within the city, without leaving the means for burial, the

Guild shall find the means according to the rank of him who is dead. 5. " If any one wishes to make pilgramage to the Holy Land each brother and sister shall give him a penny; and if to St. James or to Rome a halfpenny; and they shall go with him outside the gates of the city of Lincoln, and on his return they shall meet him and go with him to his mother church. 6. "If a brother or sister dies outside the city on pilgrimage or elsewhere, and the brethren are assured of his death they shall do for his soul what would have been done if he had died in his own parish. 7. "When one of the Guild dies, he shall, according to his means, bequeath 5 shillings or 40 pence or what he will to the Guild. 8. "Every brother and sister coming into the Guild, shall pay to the chaplain as the others do. 9. "There shall be four mornspeeches held in every year, to take order for the welfare of the Guild; and whoever heeds not his summons shall pay two pounds of wax. 10. "If any Master of the Guild takes any one to live with him as an apprentice in order to learn the work of the tailors' craft, the apprentice shall pay 2 Shillings to the Guild or his Master for him, or else the Master shall lose his Guildship. 11. "If any quarrel or strife arises between any brethren or sisters of the Guild, (which God forbid) the brethren and sisters shall with the advice of the Graceman and Wardens do their best to make peace between the parties, provided the case is such as can be thus settled without a breach of the law. And whoever will not obey the judgment of the brethren shall lose his Guildship, unless he thinks better of it within three days, and then he shall pay a stone of wax, unless he have grace. 12. "On feast days, the brethren and the sisters shall have three flagons and six tankards with prayers and the ale in the flagons shall be given to the poor who most need it. After the feast, a Mass shall be said and offerings made for the souls of those who are dead. 13. "Four lights shall be put round the body of any dead brother or sister until burial and the usual services and offerings shall follow. 14. "If any Master of the Craft keeps any lad or sewer of another Master for one day after he has well known that the lad wrongly left his Master, and that they had not parted in a friendly and reasonable manner he shall pay a stone of wax. 15. "If any Master of the Craft employs any lad as a sewer, that sewer shall pay 5 pence or his Master for him. 16. "Each brother and sister shall every year give 1 penny for charity when the Dean of the Guild demands it, and it shall be given in the place where the giver thinks it most needed together with a bottle of ale from the store of the Guild. 17. "Officers who are elected and will not serve are to pay fines." It will be seen, on an inspection of these seventeen ordinances, that the Guild of Tailors of Lincoln combined the character of a Religious and a Craft Guild, The 15th and the 16th statutes regulate the conduct of the Masters in the prosecution of their trade, but all the others are appropriate to the regulation of religious services, to the practice of charity, and the inculcation of friendly and fraternal relations among the members.

In process of time the Craft Guilds, without losing altogether their religious features, which have been preserved to this day in the institution of Speculative Masonry, which is descended from them, began to enlarge the number of their ordinances for the regulation of work and workmen.

As it will be necessary to give directly a specimen of the old Constitutions of the English Mediaeval Masons, which were nothing more nor less than ordinances of Masonic Craft Guilds, it will be proper, at the expense of a little recapitulation, to glance at the progress of these Craft Guilds.

Some of the facts will refer equally to the Craft Guilds of the Continent, but only incidentally, as that topic will be treated hereafter as an independent topic. For the present our attention must be directed exclusively to the rise and growth of the English Guilds of Craftsmen It has been already seen that in the 11th century, and even before, the inhabitants of a town were divided by the officers who governed the municipality, into freemen and bondsmen.

To this last class belonged the handicraftsmen who were subjected to the payment of certain taxes and the performance of certain feudal services.

But there was also a class of free handicraftsmen who were not, as respects the carrying on of their business, subjected to the same servile indignities as the bondsmen.

As the law made the distinction between the bond and free craftsmen, there was no necessity for the latter to enter into any association for the protection of their rights and privileges.

They already formed a part of the governing and law-making power of the municipality, and were thus able to protect themselves.

But by a course of revolutions, which it is unnecessary to detail, the free handicraftsmen lost their place in the general Guild of the citizens.

The burghers then began to feel a desire to subject them to the same imposts as were paid by the bond craftsmen.[192] These burghers, anxious for the prosperity of their towns, allowed foreigners. on the

---

[192] Brentano, "Development of Guilds," p. 115

payment of a fee, to carry on their trade, which of course greatly affected the interests of the free craftsmen, by introducing competition.

Hence arose the necessity of association for that mutual protection of interests, which could not have been effected if the craftsmen continued in an isolated state, and from this arose the formation of Craft Guilds, which took the suggestion of their form from the older Guilds which had preceded them, most of which were, however, of a social or religious character.

The Craft Guilds thus established to suppress the encroachments of the burghers on their rights consisted at first, both in England and on the Continent, in France and in Germany especially, of the most eminent of the Craftsmen who were free, freedom being an indispensable qualification for admission into the fraternity.

But after the bond craftsmen were, by the liberal and humanizing progress of the age, emancipated from their bondage, many of them, leaving the companies into which they had been distributed during their bondage by there masters, became members of the Guilds of free craftsmen.

So now the handicrafts were divided into those who had always been free and those who had originally been bondsmen.

And the only way in which the ci-devant bond craftsman could mingle on equal terms with the free craftsmen was by obtaining admission into and becoming, as it is called, "free of the Guild." This was a high privilege and not easily conceded or obtained.

The free craftsman always held aloof from the craftsman who was not free, the word free not being used as the opposite of bondsman, but only to indicate one who was not a freeman of the Guild and who worked outside of its regulations.

We find that this allusion to freemen of the Guild is constantly used in the old charters.

Such expressions as Free Carpenters, Free Weavers, Free Tailors, are not, it is true, to be found on record, though it is not unlikely that they were in colloquial use.

But in the charter of the Guild of Tailors of Exeter, granted by Edward IV., and the original of which is in the archives of the Corporation of Exeter, whence it was copied by Toulmin Smith,[193] is the following heading of one of the sections of the Ordinances: "The Othe of the Free Brotherys "-i.e., The Oath of the Free Brothers.

---

[193] "English Guilds," in Early English Text Society Publications, p. 318.

" Free Brothers " was a recognized expression in the early period of the organization of Craft Guilds, to indicate one who was a freeman of the Guild.

The Masons appear to have preserved the use of the epithet with great pertinacity and used the term "Freemason" to distinguish those who were free of the Guild from those "rough layers" or "cowans" who had not been admitted to the privileges of the fraternity and with whom they were forbidden to work.

In every Masonic Constitution that has been preserved is the ordinance that "no Mason shall make any mould, square, or rules to any rough layer." The Free Mason could not, by the laws of the Guild, engage in labor with one who was not free.

It is thus that I trace the derivation of the word "Freemason," used now exclusively to indicate the member of a Lodge of Speculative Masons, but originally to denote a Mason who was free of his Guild.

I think this derivation much better than that which was the origin of the term to the French Frere Macon, or Brother Mason.

Such a derivation would necessarily assign the birth of the English Masonic Guilds to a French parentage, a theory not only wholly unsupported by historical authority, but actually in contradiction to it. Indeed the French themselves have repudiated the idea, for they call a Freemason not a "Frere Macon," or brother Mason, but a "Franc Macon," Franc being the old French for free.

At first the Craft Guilds were voluntary associations, and could enforce their regulations only by the common consent of the members, but as in time some of these, unwilling to submit to the restrictions laid upon them, would withdraw and carry on their trade independently, it was found necessary to obtain the authority from the law, of the land to punish such contumacy and to protect the interests of the Guilds.

This was effected by a confirmation of the Guild ordinances by the lord, the citizens, or afterward by the King, and in this way arose the charters under which, after the time of Henry I., all the Craft Guilds acted and continued to act to the present day.

This process did not, however, entirely cure the evil, and in the 12th century artisans of different trades and mysteries in London, being unwilling to unite with the incorporated Guilds or being un, able to obtain admission into them, erected themselves into fraternities without the necessary powers of incorporation. These were not recognized by the companies of freemen and were condemned by the king for their contumacious proceedings. [194]They were opprobriously denominated "Adulterine Guilds," and they remind us of the Collegia illicita, or unlawful Colleges, among the Romans, as well as of the "clandestine Lodges " among the modern Speculative Masons.

The number of these Adulterine Guilds in the year 1180 was, according to Madox in his History of the Exchequer, fourteen, but no Guild of Masons is enumerated in the list.

Before proceeding to a comparison of the statutes, ordinances, or regulations of these early Guilds with the Masonic constitutions contained in the Old Records of the Order, it will be proper, at the expense of some recapitulation, to survey briefly the condition and character of these Saxon and Norman Craft Guilds.

I have said on a former occasion, and here repeat the assertion, that an investigation of the usages of these Mediaeval Guilds and a comparison of their regulations with the old Masonic Constitutions will furnish a fertile source of interest to the Masonic archaeologist and will throw much light on the early history of Freemasonry.

The custom of meeting on certain stated occasions was one of the most important of the Guild regulations.

These meetings of the whole body of the Guild were sometimes monthly, but more generally quarterly. At these meetings all matters concerning the common interests of the Guild were discussed, and the meetings were held with certain ceremonies, so as to give solemnity to the occasion.

The Guild chest, which was secured by several locks, was opened, and the charter, ordinances, and other valuable articles contained in it were exposed to view, on which occasion all the members uncovered their heads in token of reverence.

The Guild elected its own officers.

This was a prerogative peculiar to the English Guilds.

On the Continent the presiding officer was frequently appointed by the municipal or other exterior authorities.

In the early Saxon Guilds, and for some time after the Conquest, the presiding officer was called the " Alderman." At a later period we find him designated sometimes as the "Graceman," sometimes as the "Early Father," and sometimes by other titles.

But eventually it became the uniform usage to call the chief officers of the Guild the " Master and Wardens," a usage which has

---

[194] Allen, "New History of London," vol. i., p. 61.

continued ever since to prevail and which was adopted by the Speculative Masons.

The Craft Guilds not only directed themselves to the welfare of their temporal concerns, such as the regulation of their trade, which was called a " Mystery," but also took charge of spiritual matters, and for that purpose employed a priest or chaplain, who conducted their religious services and offered up masses or prayers for the dead.

In this connection each Guild appears to have had a patron saint, and they were often connected with a particular church, where, on appointed occasions, they performed special services, and received in return a participation in the advantages of all the prayers of the church.

In these respects they resembled the Roman Colleges of Artificers, which, it will be remembered, were often connected with a particular temple, and the College was dedicated to the God worshipped therein.

Almsgiving was also practiced by the Guild, and while there was a general distribution of food and money to the poor indiscriminately, special attention was paid to the wants of their own indigent members, their widows and orphans.

To support the current expenses of the Guild an entrance-fee was demanded from every one on his admission, and all the members contributed monthly or quarterly a certain sum to the general fund.

The Guild administered justice among its members, and inflicted punishments for offenses committed against the statutes of the Guild. These punishments consisted of pecuniary fines, or of suspension, or even expulsion, commonly called excommunication.

They discouraged suits at law between the members, and endeavored to settle all disputes, if possible, by arbitration.

Finally, there was an annual festival on the day of the patron saint of the Guild, when the members assembled for religious worship, almsgiving, and feasting.

It was deemed an offense for any one to be absent from this general assembly without sufficient excuse.

There was also a ceremony of admission and an oath administered to the candidate on his reception.

As these will be of great importance in a comparison of the usages of the Saxon Guilds with the Masonic sodalities, I copy the following form of admission and oath from the charter of St. Catherine's Guild at Stamford.

The date of this charter is 1494, but Smith observes that there is internal evidence showing that the Guild was established at a much earlier period.

Then it is ordained that when the said first even-song is done, the Alderman and his brethren shall assemble in their hall and drink; and there have a courteous communication for the weal of the said Guild.

And then shall be called forth all those that shall be admitted brethren or sisters of the Guild; and the Alderman shall examine them in this wise: 'Sir or Syse be ye willing to be brethren among us in this Guild and will desire and ask it in the worship of Almighty God, our Blessed Saint Mary and of the Holy Virgin and Martyr Saint Catherine in whose name this Guild is founded and in the way of charity? And by their own will they shall answer, 'Yea' or Nay. Then the Alderman shall command the Clerk to give this oath to them in form and manner following: "'This hear you, Alderman: I shall true man be to God Almighty, to our Lady Saint Mary, and to that Holy Virgin and Martyr Saint Catherine in whose honor and worship this Guild is founded; and shall be obedient to the Alderman of this Guild and to his successors and come to him and his brethren when I have warning and not absent myself without cause reasonable.

I shall be ready at scot and lot and all my duties truly pay and do; the ordinances, constitutions and rules what with the council of the same Guild, keep, obey and perform and to my power maintain to my life's end; so help me God and halidome and by this book.' And then kiss the book and be lovingly received with all the brethren; and then they drink about; and after that depart for that right" Such is a brief sketch of the principal characteristics of the early Guilds.

The main object of presenting it has been to enable the reader to compare these regulations with those of the Old Masonic Constitutions of the 15th, 16th, and 17th centuries, so as to show the growth and development of the Masonic law from them.

It will, for the sake of convenient reference, be therefore necessary to select from these Old Masonic Constitutions one at least, and one of the earliest, that the reader may in making his comparison have the regulations of the Guild and the charges of the Masons side by side before him.

But this investigation will perhaps be better continued in a separate chapter.

www.ingramcontent.com/pod-product-compliance
Lightning Source LLC
Chambersburg PA
CBHW071518160426
43196CB00010B/1568